英语
说课与评课的
理论和实践

傅瑞屏 / 编著

民主与建设出版社
·北京·

图书在版编目（CIP）数据

英语说课与评课的理论和实践 / 傅瑞屏编著. —北京：民主与建设出版社，2019.12

ISBN 978-7-5139-2788-8

Ⅰ.①英… Ⅱ.①傅… Ⅲ.①英语课—教学研究—中小学 Ⅳ.①G633.412

中国版本图书馆CIP数据核字（2019）第239209号

英语说课与评课的理论和实践
YINGYU SHUOKE YU PINGKE DE LILUN HE SHIJIAN

出 版 人	李声笑	
编 著	傅瑞屏	
责任编辑	程 旭	周 艺
封面设计	姜 龙	
出版发行	民主与建设出版社有限责任公司	
电 话	（010）59417747 59419778	
社 址	北京市海淀区西三环中路10号望海楼E座7层	
邮 编	100142	
印 刷	北京虎彩文化传播有限公司	
版 次	2022年6月第1版	
印 次	2022年6月第1次印刷	
开 本	710毫米×1000毫米 1/16	
印 张	18.25	
字 数	329千字	
书 号	ISBN 978-7-5139-2788-8	
定 价	45.00元	

注：如有印、装质量问题，请与出版社联系。

前 言

FOREWORD

  说课与评课或议课是外语师范生必须掌握的两个专业技能。在职前，师范生参加教师招聘考试会碰到说课的考核形式。在职后的教研工作中，常常会面对说课的任务。可以说，说课是每个英语师范生和每位一线教师必备的技能。对于师范生来说，通过学习评课能够了解什么样的课是好课，以评促学，为入职后上好英语课做好充分的准备。对于中小学英语教师来说，评课、议课是最常见的教研方式。通过评课、议课，教师能够更新教学理念、提升教学能力，从而促进自身的专业发展。因此，评课、议课是师范生和一线教师必备的专业素养和能力。

  目前，在高校的外语师范教材中，缺少一本把说课和评课的内容结合在一起的教材。本书作者长期以来致力于中小学英语教师教育和发展工作，深知说课和评课对教师专业发展的重要性。在开展教师教育和教师发展工作过程中对说课和评课的资料有了一定的积累，已出版了《英语优质课例分析与评价》和《小学英语优质课例分析与评价》，并发表多篇评课文章。笔者开设英语说课与评课课程多年，苦于没有一本能够系统整合说课和评课两方面内容的教材或者编著，于是笔者觉得有必要编写这样的教材或著作。

  本书共有六章，即第一章英语说课的理论、第二章英语说课的实践、第三章英语课堂观察和反思、第四章英语评课的理论、第五章英语评课的内容、第六章英语评课的实践。书中的说课和评课的案例大多是笔者根据视频转写而成，这些视频多数是正规出版社的出版物，少数视频由笔者的学生苏美婷等慷慨提供。

  本书是广东第二师范学院2015年精品教材立项项目"英语说课与评课"的成果。感谢笔者所在单位广东第二师范学院为本书的编写提供的资助。感谢广东第二师范学院外语系2011、2012、2013、2014、2015、2016六个年级的师范学生，本书的部分内容已经在他们的英语说课与评课和英语教学综合技能训练等课程中使用，感谢他们提供的意见和反馈。

本书的使用者主要是高等院校英语师范专业的学生。书中以实录方式出现的中小学英语课例可供一线教师、在校学生以及参加教师资格证考试的学习者模仿和借鉴。

特别感谢允许我使用他们说课视频、上课视频及相关教学资料的老师，特别是东莞松山湖学校的韩松锦老师、广州外国语学校的叶静老师、中山纪念中学的蔡球老师、南沙金业小学的李奕婷老师、广州沙面小学的陈凤霞老师、福田教科院附小英语科组的老师们。此外，还要感谢深圳福田区小英教研员孙艳老师、东莞小英教研员张凝老师，她们指导的课例为本书的编写提供了优质的资源。书中不少课堂实录根据金太阳出版的《课堂教学案例集录像》转写而成，感谢这些课例的执教者。感谢我的家人对我编写工作的支持。感谢对本书的出版付出辛勤劳动的编辑。

由于笔者水平有限及时间仓促，书中难免有错误，敬请同行和读者指正。

傅瑞屏

2019年6月于帝景华苑

目 录
CONTENTS

第三章　英语课堂观察和反思

第四章　英语评课的理论

第五章　英语评课的内容

第六章　英语评课的实践

第 一 章

英语说课的理论

第一节　说课的概念和说课的类型

什么是说课？说课是教师就某一次课关于教材、教法、学法、授课程序等方面的思路、教学设计及其理论依据等，面对面地对同行做全面讲述。简单来说，说课就是说你准备教什么、怎样教、为什么要这样教。

什么是英语说课？英语说课，就是以英语教育科学理论和英语教材为依据，针对每课或每单元的具体特点，由讲课教师向其他英语教学或教研人员口头表达该课的具体教学设想及其理论依据。说课是讲课教师对教学课题的设计与分析。

需要特别指出的是，英语说课主要指的是英语课程，它并不特别指用英语作为语言媒介来说课。英语说课可以用汉语，也可用英语。

从不同的角度来分，说课有如下的类型：

（1）课前说课：指教师在授课前说课。

（2）课后说课：指教师在授课后说课。

（3）示范说课：指给同行学习的说课。

（4）竞赛说课：指为了比较说课技能的说课。

（5）考核说课：指教师为晋升或评职称以及学生为了获得教师职位或者教师资格证而进行的说课。

（6）主题说课：指围绕某一主题而进行的说课，以工作中遇到的重点、难点问题或热点问题为主题。例如，如何上好一节读写课、如何在小学阅读教学中培养学生的学科核心素养、如何在初中英语教学中整合信息技术等，都可以作为说课的主题。

（7）有辅助说课：有辅助说课也叫计算机辅助说课，即说课时说课者可以借助预先做好的PPT进行说课活动（详见高中英语说课案例2）。由于可以借助课件进行说课，说课者能够说得比较流畅、直观以及较有逻辑性，因而使聆听者听得更轻松、更好地抓住说课者的设计思路。

在上述的不同说课类型中，说课的详略程度有所不同。比如，说课后说课，教师会说到教学反思。但是，对于课前说课的教师来说，反思是一个可以省略的内容，因为课还没有上，其教学结果不得而知。如果真的反思的话，可能会落在教学设计的亮点和不足上面，但这毕竟是纸上谈兵，没有实效。而在学生参加的教师招聘考试中，学生的说课可能会在步骤和内容上力求做到面面俱到，紧扣教科书中的要求。

目前，说课既有无辅助说课，也有有辅助说课。无辅助说课要求说课者非常熟悉说课的流程和说课内容。因为没有使用辅助手段，说课者无须操作说课工具，能够把一些注意力分配到声音和手势的运用上去，从而使说课更加具有感染力。有辅助说课能够减轻教师的记忆负担，说课的条理会更加清晰。两种说课方式各有其优点，如何选择视说课的情境而定。

第二节　英语说课的意义和作用

英语说课是英语教师必备的职业技能。英语说课有助于促进教师的专业发展。具体来说，说课有以下作用：

一、英语说课有助于提升教师的教学理念

教学理念是人们对教学活动的看法和持有的基本态度和观念，是人们从事教学活动的信念。教学理念有理论层面、操作层面和学科层面之分。教学理念对教学活动有着极其重要的指导意义。说英语课时教师要说教学理念，说这些教学理念如何落实，特别是在英语课上如何落实。以"以学习者为中心"的理念为例，在操作层面上，有的教师会说"把时间还给学生，让学生做课堂的主人"。在学科层面上，"以学习者为中心"体现在课堂上要让学生有更多的练习语言和运用语言的机会。为了说好教学思想和教学理念，说课教师必须学习

和更新自己的教学理念并在教学设计中加以运用。

二、英语说课有助于提升教师的教学能力

说课虽然不同于上课，但它们的共同之处是需要备课和教学设计。在备课的过程中，教师要分析教材和学情，要设计教学目标，选择教学方法，确定教学辅助手段，设计教学过程及师生活动。在这个过程中教师逐步发展了自己的教学能力。说课不但有助于提高说课者的教学能力，通过探讨教学中存在的问题以及热点问题，也能提高听者的教学能力。

三、说课有助于提高教师的反思能力

说课的内容之一是反思，因此，通过说课，教师可以培养自己的反思能力，从而提高教学的效果。说课中的反思通常是反思说课者的教学设计的合理性、科学性、优缺点等。

四、说课是一种简便易行的教研方式

说课不需要某个班级的学生的配合，说课的听众往往是同行或领导。从这个角度来看，说课组织比较简单，在说课后能直截了当地就要探讨的问题展开直接的讨论。

第三节　说课的依据、内容和话语结构

一、英语说课的依据

英语说课的依据来自英语学科教学理论、《英语课程标准》、教育学理论、心理学理论以及学习理论等。

英语学科教学理论是说课的主要依据。一方面，英语教学理论指导我们怎

样教。另一方面，英语教学理论也为我们这样教而不那样教提供支持和依据。以阅读教学为例。首先，在学生阅读前我们要激活学生的背景知识以及激发他们的阅读动机。在阅读中，我们通常在学生进行某一次阅读活动前给学生布置阅读任务，让学生带着阅读目的和阅读任务去阅读，以便达到好的阅读效果。在阅读后要基于话题和所学文本开展复述、讨论、辩论等活动。文本中的生词怎么处理？可以在读前集中处理，也可在读中需要时处理，顺便培养学生在语境中猜词的能力。以上是关于阅读课怎么教，而我们为什么可以这样教呢？依据在哪里呢？依据在这些英语教学理论和二语习得理论上：

1. 信息的加工模式

（1）自上而下的信息加工模式。它告诉我们阅读教学前需要激活学生的背景知识。

（2）由下而上的信息加工模式。它告诉我们阅读是个解码的过程。读者先读懂较小的语言单位，如词语；然后再读懂较大的语言单位，如句子；最后读懂整个语篇的意思。

2. 阅读的理论

（1）阅读的本质。阅读是读者从印刷文字中建构文本的意义。

（2）阅读两个层次行为的理论。阅读涉及两个层次的行为，首先，是用眼睛摄入视觉信号的识别行为；其次，是认知行为，包括阐释视觉信息、把接收到的信息跟读者的世界性知识联系起来，重构作者要表达的意义。

（3）阅读的心理过程。古德曼认为，阅读是一个涉及心理和语言的猜测游戏。在阅读过程中，读者不断地进行预测和假设，不断在文本中寻找证据支持或反驳自己的预测和假设，以建构文本的意义。

（4）阅读和阅读教学的目标。阅读有多元目标，阅读教学也有多元的目标。阅读课是我们培养学生英语学科核心素养的主阵地。阅读课的活动要对应这些教学目标，在我们着重培养学生阅读技能的同时，我们也要培养他们的学习能力、文化品格和思维品质。

3. 输入、互动、输出理论

阅读是输入，如何把阅读中获得的信息、知识、观点、语言等内化成学习者自己的知识和能力，需要学习者跟文本互动、跟作者互动、跟教师互动、跟同伴互动。输出是学习者习得语言能力的手段和结果。通过输出，我们给学生提供运用语言的机会，同时通过输出的质量，我们也检测学生阅读的效果及教学的效果。一节阅读课，如果只停留在对信息的理解和处理上而没有对信息进行运用，那么，这样的阅读课就太低效了。

《英语课程标准》是英语教学的依据，也是我们说课的重要依据。《英语课程标准》中的课程目标、课程内容以及其倡导的教学理念都是英语说课的依据。目前，英语课程的目标被定位为培养学生的学科核心素养，即英语课程要培养学生的语言能力、学习能力、文化意识和思维品质。课程内容包括六个要素：主题语境、语篇类型、语言知识、文化意识、语言技能和学习策略。

教育学中的教育思想、原则、原理也可以作为英语说课的依据。以近体原则为例，近体原则是指在教学过程中，尽可能缩小教与学之间在时间和空间上的距离及心理和情感等方面的差异，在有限的时间内达到满意的教学效果。也就是说，教师应在充分了解所教学生的心理状况、年龄层次和知识水平的基础上，认真分析教材，并对教材进行创造性的处理，缩小存在于教学内容与学生之间的时空、心理及情感面的差距，使教学内容与学生的实际之间更加相关，因而更加具有个人意义，从而充分激发学生学习的积极性、主动性和创造性，提高教学效果。近体原则可分为时间近体原则、空间近体原则、心理近体原则等。

近体原则在课文教学中的运用是：如何对教材内容进行增删处理，如何设计跟学生相关的话题，如何激发学生的兴趣、引起学生的共鸣或共情等。

二、说课的内容

要了解说课的内容首先要了解课的构成要素。一节课包含哪些要素呢？课的要素包括：教师、学生、教材、教学目标、教学方法、教学辅助手段、教学过程以及教学评价等。课的成分或者要素就是我们说课的内容。

从大的方面来讲，说课要说清楚教什么、怎样教和为什么这样教，简称 what，how，why。其中，说教的依据是说课稿和教案不同的地方之一。一般来说，说课包括说教材、说学情、说教学目标、说重难点、说教学辅助手段、说教法和学法、说教学过程以及说教学反思等内容。说课时可以直接按照这些内容一一说出来，也可以对这些内容进行有机的整合，例如，把教学目标和重难点的陈述放到教材分析部分。不管用哪种方式，目的都是把该说的内容有效地说出来。

1. 说教材

说教材包含下面这几个方面：①在认真阅读教材的基础上，说明教材的地位、作用；②明确提出本课时的具体教学目标。课时目标是备课时所规划的课时结束时要实现的教学结果。课时目标越明确、越具体，说明教者的备课认识越充分，教法的设计安排越合理；③分析教材的编写思路、结构特点、教材的重难点及其确定依据。

2. 说教法和学法

说教法主要说明教学方法及教学手段的选择和运用。教法是根据教材的特点和学生的情况而选择的，是达到教学目标的手段。英语教学方法多种多样，每一种教学方法都有其特点和适用范围，不存在任何情况下对任何年龄学生都有效的教学方法。以直接法为例，直接法运用实物、图片、手势语等直观的教学手段进行教学，它比较适合幼儿园和小学英语教学。但直接法对于高中英语教学来说就没有那么有效了，因为高中英语课程内容更多的是比较抽象的人文、社科知识，需要运用那些能够发展学生理性思维的教学方法。因此，说课者要从实际出发，选择恰当的教学方法。教法的选择，很大程度上取决于对学情的分析。

随着教学改革的不断深入，要创造性地运用新的教学方法。新的教学方法反映学科教学的新发展，对新的教学方法的运用能够给教学带来新的理念、举措和更好的教学效果。

任何一节英语课都不只是运用一种教学方法，而是对多种教学方法的综合运用。因此，说课者要注意说明这节课的教学内容应以哪种教学方法为主，采用哪些教学手段。无论以哪种教法为主，都是基于教学情境特别是学校现有的设备条件的基础上的选择。要注意教学方法的实效，不要生搬硬套某一种教学方法。

说课不但要说教师是如何教的，也要说学生是如何学习的，特别要说明教师是如何指导学生学习的。说课活动中虽然没有学生，看不到师生之间和学生之间的多边活动，但教师必须说明如何根据教学内容和围绕教学目标指导学生学习，教给学生什么样的学习方法、培养学生哪些能力、如何调动学生积极思维、怎样激发学困生的学习兴趣等。教师的说课过程中要体现以学生为主体，充分发挥学生在学习活动中的作用。

3. 说教学过程

说教学过程是说课的重点部分，因为通过这一过程的分析才能看到说课者独具匠心的教学安排，它反映了教师的教学思想、教学个性与风格。只有通过对教学过程设计的阐述，才能看到其教学安排是否合理、科学，是否具有艺术性。

（1）说明教学思路与教学环节安排。

（2）说明教与学的双边活动安排。

（3）说明重点与难点的处理。要说明在教学过程中，怎样突出重点和解决难点，解决难点运用什么方法。

（4）说明采用哪些教学手段辅助教学、什么时候、什么地方用，这样做的道理是什么。

（5）说明板书设计。

（6）说明布置作业。要说明布置什么作业，为什么要布置这样的作业。

总的来说，当我们在说课时，教学设想是我们说课的明线，而理论依据是暗线。

三、说课的话语结构

说课一般包括六个话段，即介绍、分析、陈述、描述、反思以及致谢。

介绍：包括简单的问候、说课者的自我介绍和对说课内容和说课程序的简单介绍。

分析：分析教材和学情，说明教材内容和对教材的理解，确定教材的地位和作用，说明学生的知识和技能基础、学习兴趣和认知风格等。

陈述：陈述重难点、教学目标、教材处理、教学方法和教具、学法指导等。

描述：描述教学设计思路、教学过程的组织与调控、师生活动及其效果、作业布置与板书设计等。

反思：反思总体教学效果、教学设计亮点。反思总体教学效果在课后说课中比较常见，而课前说课比较侧重说教学设计的亮点。

致谢：在说课快要结束时，说课者出于礼貌常常对听众致谢，感谢他们的聆听。

在上述的这六个话段中，陈述和描述部分是说课的重点。说课时要突出重点，呈现亮点，在把自己的意图有效传递给听众的同时，尽量给他们留下深刻的印象。

值得注意的是，上述的说课话语结构只是比较常用的一种。实际上说课的模式还有其他一些变体。但万变不离其宗，只要牢固地掌握具有典型意义的一种，就可根据说课的类型进行适当的发挥。

第四节　说课的标准和评价

说课没有绝对的标准，但好的说课有下面几个特征：①诠释先进的教学思想；②突出新的教学理念；③体现教学能力；④展现教学境界。

好的说课能够诠释先进的教学思想，突出新的教学理念。说课时说why涉及教学思想和教学理念。一节好课是建立在先进的、新颖的教学思想和教学理念的基础上。全人教育、人本主义教育、生本教育、社会文化理论、建构主义学习观，交际教学法、任务型教学、合作学习、自主学习、翻转课堂、先学后教、课堂互动、启智、发现式学习、活动观、学生中心、项目式教学、学科核心素养等都是教师在说依据时提及的教育思想、教学理论或者理念，它们是指导教学设计和教学行为的原理和准则。它们在某种程度上是比较先进的、新颖的教育教学思想和理念。

在说what和how时，教师展示了自己在学情分析、教材处理、教学目标设立、教学方法、教学策略和教学手段的选择以及活动的设置和安排方面的能力和风格。虽然好的教学理念和好的教学设计并不一定会产生一节好课，但至少它们是一节好课的前提。

教学是有境界之分的。有的教学只是保本经营，即仅仅能够完成教学任务或者达成教学目标，有的教学却能高效完成教学任务并实现教学目标；有的教学只在传授学科知识和培养学科能力，但有的教学却能培养学生英语语言能力，同时也启迪学生思维，开启他们的心智，带给其美的享受，甚至震撼或塑造他们的灵魂。

我们说课的标准是从好的说课特征建构而成的。说课应该是说者有较新的教育、教学观念，能很好地理解教材、了解学生，准确地把握重点难点，并有效地进行处理；能合理地灵活运用教育学、心理学的一般原理，采用的教学策略手段符合学生认知规律和学科教学特点。说课应该逻辑性强，条理清晰，层次分明，语言准确、形象、生动，富有启发性和感染力；还能够体现说者较强的取舍、处理、组织能力，知识面广，对所述问题有独特的见解等。

因为听众是通过听来接收信息的，所以说课对作为媒介的语言质量要求较高，对信息合理安排的逻辑性也有要求。说课者通常使用第一人称"我"来叙述事件和陈述过程。

此外，说课一般为3～15分钟。以每分钟220个字的速度说课，3分钟能说上大约600个字。说一个以lesson为单位的课，最好掌握在3～5分钟之间，而专门的说课比赛可能会稍长一点。单元说课，尽量控制在10～15分钟。说得太长听者会觉得疲劳，从而不能聚精会神地聆听，说课效果会因聆听者听觉疲劳而降低。

第五节　教材分析

说课涉及说教材，说教材就是对教材进行分析。对没有教学实践经历的师范生来说，说教材常常会出现说得不到位的情况。因此，有必要学习根据不同的说课场合或简单或详细地进行教材分析的技能。如果是上课前或上课后的说课，说教材可以简单些，即把教材的背景（包括教材版本、教学年级、课型等）、主题、内容、教材地位、编写理念简要说出来即可。但如果是专门的说课比赛，则可以在教材内容方面多说一点，说得深入一点，除了说教材本身，还可说自己对教材的处理，包括如何挖掘教材留白、如何把教材留白处作为一个生成点来为学生创造语言运用或者情感体悟的场景。良好的教材解读能力还包括创造性地使用教材，即不拘泥于原有教材，而是对教材做科学的加减法。从说教材中可以看出说课者的语言素养、文体素养、文化品格和思维品质。

编写理念。教材的编写理念统摄了教学的各个方面，决定了教学方法和教学策略的选择和教学过程的设置。要真正地设计好一节课，需要透彻了解教材的编写理念。以牛津上海版三年级（上）的教材为例，其编写理念有下面四个：

（1）以学习者为中心的指导思想。

（2）采用模块建筑式编写体系。

（3）以话题·功能·结构·任务为编写框架。

（4）以先进的中外语言教学理论为理论依据。

文本分析。教材分析可以借助文本分析的方法，然后把文本分析的结果应用到说课中的说教材。那么，从哪些方面入手分析文本呢？概括起来，文本分析有三个维度，即what，why和how（见图1-1）。

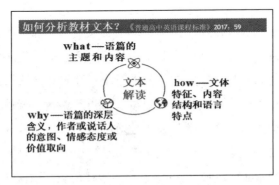

图1-1 文本解读

文本分析的三个维度：what，why，how

What is in the text?

Why does he write this text?

How is the text organized? How are the feelings/meanings expressed by means of linguistic resources?

上面的这三个维度可以细化为五个维度。其中what包含主题意义和主要内容；why包含作者意图；how则包含语言修辞及文体结构。为了说明具体如何进行文本分析以及分析后有什么样的结果，下面将提供三个国内外的文本分析范本。

文本分析范例1：To the South Pole

1. 背景介绍

授课年级：九年级

教材：北师大版义务教育阶段九年级英语（全一册），2017年7月第3版；第82页

单元名称：Unit 7 Journeys

单元构成：Lesson 19是一篇游记，介绍了游历丝绸之路的过程；Lesson 20是一首诗，把人生比喻成旅行；Lesson 21描述了南极探险的艰难过程。三篇文章涉及不同的旅行。

主题探索：三篇文章涉及不同的旅行，从不同角度把学生带入或远或近、或实际或想象的旅途，将旅游这一主题进行了多角度的阐释。

本课课型：阅读课。

2. 文本分析

What is in the text? 这是南极探险考察离目的地几英里时主人公即作者的随笔或日记。主要讲述作者和他的团队南极探险45天的艰难经历以及探险过程中他们遇到的重重困难：每天超过12小时的行走；冰雪和暴风雪的袭击；食物的准备以及脚的保护等。他们用榜样的力量、恰当的路线、合适的食物和医生的护卫等克服了各种困难。作者还描述了他对即将到达目的地的美好憧憬和对探险旅程的感悟。

Why does the writer write this text? 通过叙述南极探险所遇到的各种困难及解决办法的经历，作者使读者明白要克服重重困难取得成功，不仅要具备优秀的个人品质，如坚强的毅力、坚定的信念和永不放弃的精神等，还必须要做充分的准备。

How is the text organized? 本文按照典型的日记写作风格展开，明线是讲述作者一行在探险中遇到的各种苦难和克服困难的办法，以及他对到达目的地的憧憬和感悟。暗线是体现探索者挑战南极之旅成功的根本原因，即优秀的个人品质和各种充分的准备。

在描述各种困难时，各段分别用总—分结构和表示顺序的词或短语，如first, another challenge of the journey, the hardest part等，随后，用表示转折的词如however, luckily, even so等来阐述他们如何克服困难。这些词或短语使文章结构清晰，意义明确。同时，也便于读者推断总结出上面的信息，即克服困难取得成功的主、客观因素。

How are the feelings expressed by means of linguistic resources? 文本用大量一般现在时态和现在完成时态描述作者一行遇到并已克服的困难，突出了探险是常态；用了三个一般过去时的句子表明作者曾经有过的一时的想法和感受；用一般将来时表达作者对到达南极的憧憬；用现在完成时表示自己已经产生的感慨和感悟，进而说明自己对此行的满足及欣慰感，同时也反映出正是作者期盼到达南极的强烈愿望，使他坚持克服困难，取得胜利。作者还用直接引语形象、真实、生动地表达出了在艰难探险路上的感受。文章还用了虚拟语气表达如果因脚受伤而不能继续前行，不能到达目的地将非常遗憾。

文本分析范例2：Oliver Button Is a Sissy!

Background Introduction

Oliver Button is a Sissy is a picture book written by DePaola，T and published by HMH，New York in 1979.

Text analysis

Oliver Button is a Sissy is a good example that represents a variety of universal themes，as it depicts the story of a boy who stands up to bullies not by fighting but by staying true to himself. The story features the theme of accepting and remaining true to oneself even against expectations of the mainstream. Readers can explore discrimination and bullying，as Oliver is constantly teased and called "sissy" by his classmates. The ability to cope with stressful situations is also addressed in Oliver's behavior. Another frequent theme of overcoming fears is also described in the story as Oliver increases his practice time of dance lessons in hopes of winning the big talent show. In the end of the story，T reveals that the bullies' prejudices diminish when they get to know Oliver，as he discovered that someone has crossed out the word "sissy" on the school wall and added a new word that reads "Oliver Button is a star！"

In terms of the level of difficulty of Oliver Button is a Sissy，the learners need 260 words to read the text. Since Japanese junior high school students have learned 900 English words，junior high school graduates can understand the overall meanings of the text using the thirty percent of the knowledge of English vocabulary. In terms of the grammatical features，the text includes the majority of grammatical items that are suggested for junior high school students to learn，which are suggested by the Ministry of Education. The tenses used in the text include present tense，present progressive，past tense，past progressive，and simple future tense. Sentence structures used in the text include affirmative sentences，negative sentences，interrogative sentences，imperative sentences，and comparison. To-infinitives，

passive voices, past participles, auxiliary verbs and gerund are used as well.

文本分析范例3：人教版教材高一Book 2，Unit 2 The Olympic Games，Reading: An Interview

本单元的阅读文本类型是一个访谈，题目叫An Interview。访谈实际上是一则对话。文本中有两个人物：古希腊的作家Pausanias和北京奥运会志愿者Li Yan。文本主要通过采访者的提问和被采访者的回答来推进语篇的发展。其主要内容是通过采访者和被采访者之间的问及答来表现古代奥运会与现代奥运会的特征和异同。

对话所涉及的词语主要是跟奥运会有关的各种名词，语言结构是过去将来时的被动语态。本文阅读的难点在于生词和文本的信息分布特征。

原文内容较为过时，且大都是学生已知信息，如果只是就文本进行阅读，学生的兴趣难以被调动起来。对本课的阅读设计不应只满足于对文本的表层信息的提取和一些简单的练习，而应该充分挖掘学生的已有经验，将奥运会与自己的生活联系起来，形成情感共鸣。文本涉及的信息比较繁杂，需要用非常规的阅读教学方式来帮助学生提取信息、处理信息和运用信息。

第六节　学情分析

说课包括说学情，因此，对学情还没把握的师范生有必要从理论的角度并基于别人的案例来学习如何进行学情分析。如前所述，学情分析要分析学生已有的知识和能力、学习风格和心理特征等。简单说还是详细说取决于说课的场合和活动类型。下面是深圳市一位小学英语教师在教材培训讲座所做的关于三年级学生的比较详细的学情分析，可以让我们窥见学情分析能从哪些方面入手。

学情分析案例1

以学习者为中心的指导思想要考虑学生的心理特点、知识结构以及已有经验。要激发他们的学习兴趣，调动其学习积极性，鼓励分享个人经历和观点，加深自己对他人及周围的认识和了解。我们三年级的学生有什么样的心理特点呢？

1. 三年级学生知觉的发展

三年级学生感知事物比较笼统，往往只注意表面现象和个别特征，时空特性和知觉也不完善。随着教学过程的深入，小学生知觉的有意性和目的性明显发展。他们从知觉对象区分出基本的特征和所需的东西，对于时间单位和空间的辨别能力也逐渐增强。处于这个阶段的学生有发展性也有局限性，因此，我们在安排教学内容、安排教学任务、布置课外作业的时候要充分考虑到这个年龄段学生的心理特征。

2. 想象的发展

这个阶段的儿童有意识的目的性逐渐增强，比起一二年级创造性也显著发展，想象力逐渐丰富，但没有达到非常丰富的程度，想象的现实性有了显著提高。在此前的阶段（一二年级、幼儿园）他们都是天马行空，到三年级逐渐回归现实。

3. 思维的发展

这个时期学生虽然有了抽象的概括能力，并且掌握了一些概念，能初步进行一些判断和理解，但思维水平总的来说是非常低的，教师不能把他们的思维能力想得非常高，要根据学生的特征来调整我们想象中的教学或者想象中的任务。学生仍具有很大的想象性，所以教学手段也应富于想象性。思维过程往往依靠表象，不容易理解抽象或者与他们的经验很少联系的教材。思维还带有很大的依赖性和模仿性，这个阶段的孩子独立而灵活地思考问题的能力还很差（有些孩子很好），不善于使自己的思维活动服务于一定的任务。我们是任务型教学，学生在思考问题时往往被一些不相干的事物所吸引，以致离开原有的事物。

4. 注意力的特点

该时期的儿童注意力范围狭窄，不善于分配自己的注意力。如果要求他们同时做几件事，他们往往做不到，他们的注意力还不稳定，容易被不相干的事物所吸引。注意力集中的时间可达15～20分钟。

5. 情感、意志、个性等方面的发展

在学习情感方面，学习、教师、同伴等社会情感开始占主导地位。出现与学习成绩、班级等有关的理智感、集体荣誉感、责任感等。儿童情感表现外露，不易维持。此时若学业压力过重，容易发生学校恐惧症、社交退缩症和攻击行为。同伴在儿童生活中占据越来越重要的地位，表现出同伴明显的依从性和同伴倾向，开始在兴趣相投的基础上形成内聚力不大的小团体，男女兴趣、活动明显分化。在个性发展方面，儿童的个性更加明显，开始按照成人和同伴的评价来评定自我，在学习过程中逐渐形成与学习相关的个性品质，如勤奋或懒惰、细致或粗心、守纪律或散漫等。在道德判断方面，从只注意行为后果发展到能考虑行为动机，道德行为尚不稳定。

学情分析案例2

对象是广州市××外国语学校三（7）班的学生。总体来说，学生学习基础较差，班级有四位同学由于英语基础较差，参与课堂学习的难度非常大，班级也没有英语书面表达特别优秀的同学，成绩最优秀的同学在书面表达方面也有不少细节错误。在平常的课堂上，有过限时训练写作的经历，但总有十来位同学无法在规定的时间内完成，四位同学根本无法下笔。学生曾写过英文电子邮件，了解书信的大致结构，但没有详细学习过如何用电子邮件真诚规范地表达自己的问题和困惑以及寻求帮助和建议，这方面的词汇和句型知识十分欠缺。因此，在活动设计的过程中，应注重基础：激发学生兴趣、合理安排活动难度、提供更多语言知识的支架，引导学生尽量完成学习任务。

其他情况：虽然7班的同学们英语学习不甚理想，但班上天性活泼开朗、大度的孩子较多，在平时课堂上热情活跃，与英语老师相处融洽愉快。授课前通过简单的问卷调查了解了同学们的困惑和苦恼，为了方便课堂教学把他们的问题和困惑归纳为四类，在课堂分组表达，既学习了书面表达，又为同学们解决了现实生活中的问题。

学情分析案例3

对高一的学生来说，事实性阅读内容的解读很简单，因此，完成浅层练习题的教学方式不能调动学生的深度参与性，也难以真正提升学生的阅读能力。高一是高中阶段的开始，是形成价值观的重要节点，也是学生遇到各种困惑比较集中的时间段。奥运会所代表的意义——人类的健康、性别和种族的平等、世界和平等以及其所宣扬的体育精神——拼搏、超越自我、改变等都能给学生带来正能量，帮助他们正确认识个体的渺小与伟大。

第七节　提升说课效果的策略

对于还处在职前的师范生来说，说课不是件容易的事情，特别是把课说好更是不容易的事情。首先，对于学生来说，他们缺乏课感，他们对自己的说课感到虚或者不踏实。如果先前修的课程中有教学设计和教材分析课程，那么情况会好些。在写说课稿时，他们把握不住学情，因为没有真正的学生。他们所说的学情不是从教育学、心理学的相关书籍中摘过来，就是从其他人的说课中学来的。因此，他们说课中的学情分析往往流于形式，或者都是一些套话，缺少真正的信息价值。其次，他们对教材的分析流于表面。教者要说明自己对教材的理解，因为只有对教材理解透彻，才能制定出较完满的教学方案。最后，其难以说明教学设计里面蕴含的教学理念。

如何才能说好课呢？下面是提升说课效果的几个策略。

1. 认真备课和写好说课稿

说课和上课相同的地方就是要经过备课。一般来说，如果经过自己备课并且说课稿是自己写的，教学设想是自己构思出来的，说课者只要熟悉自己的说课步骤和细节，一般都能自信地说出来。如果不是自己备课和创作所得，就要经过一个把材料内化成自己说课能力的过程。总的来说，备好课、写好说课稿是说好课的前提。

2. 加深对教材的研究

备课的内容之一是对教材的研究和分析。对教材理解越透彻，对教学目标以及重难点的把握和设置越精准。就像庖丁解牛，游刃有余。说教材几乎是说课的第一步，所以，说好教材对说好整个课起着重要的作用。对教材的研究和分析一方面要以《英语课程标准》为依据，另一方面则可借助文本分析方法。说教材不是做详细的文本分析，而是应用文本分析的结果。

3. 熟悉《英语课程标准》的内容和理念

说课者首先要学习《英语课程标准》关于课程内容的描述，了解课程内容的内涵。新的《英语课程标准》（2017年版）强调英语课程内容的六要素，即主题语境、语篇类型、语言知识、文化知识、语言技能和学习策略。

主题语境涵盖人与自我、人与社会和人与自然，涉及人文社会科学和自然科学领域等内容，为学科育人提供话题和语境。语篇类型包括口头和书面语篇以及不同的文体形式，如记叙文、说明文、议论文、应用文、访谈、对话等连续性文本，以及图表、图示、网页、广告、漫画等非连续性文本，为语言学习提供文体素材。

语言知识涵盖语音知识、词汇知识、语法知识、语篇知识和语用知识，是构成语言能力的重要基础。语言技能分理解性技能和表达性技能，具体包括听、说、读、看、写等。学生基于语篇所开展的学习活动即是基于这些语言技能，理解语篇和对语篇做出回应的活动。文化知识是指中外优秀的人文和科学知识，既包含物质文明知识，也包含精神文明知识，是学生形成跨文化意识、涵养人文和科学精神、坚定文化自信的知识源泉。学习策略包括元认知策略、认知策略、交际策略、情感策略等，有效选择和使用策略是帮助理解和表达、提高学习效率的手段，是学生形成自主学习和终身学习能力的必备条件。

了解课程内容的六要素有助于说课者宏观上理解和把握教材的功能和作用，在此基础上可以对其进行文本分析。文本分析的维度一般有：话题、词汇、语法、结构、功能、文化等。

4. 加深对英语教学理论和相关理论的学习

没有理论的说课是平乏的、没有深度的、没有灵魂。说课不但要说教学设计思路，还要说后面的理论依据，而且理论要新颖。在现在的中小学英语课堂教学中，如果教师还说"本课主要应用语法翻译法进行教学"，那么这个理念就落后了，虽然我们并不否定语法翻译法也有一些积极的因素。在当今倡导活动教学、任务教学、交际教学、社会文化理论、建构主义的环境下，这个教学方法的运用无疑会受到质疑，除非有非常特殊的教学情境。在考试型说课中，体现新理念、新理论显得特别重要，说课者需要向考核者展示其接受最新的教育，有最新的教育、教学理论素养。对于一线教师也一样，只有掌握了新的教育、教学理论，才能不断适应新的教学环境和教学要求，使自己在专业发展道路上能够保持发展力和竞争力。

现代外语师范生要了解外语教学的历史，更应该学习先进的教学理论和方法。在世界外语教学史上，几乎每二十多年就有一种新的教学理论或教学方法出现。这些新理论、新方法吸收了前面的优点，摈弃了它们的缺点，能够给外语教学带来活力和成效。因此，外语师范生需要系统学习新的学科教学理论及其他相关理论。

5. 加强自己的口头语言表达能力，特别是讲解的能力

说课稿写得好只是说课成功的第一步，要取得说课的全面胜利，说课者还需要具备良好的口头表达能力。如果说课时条理清楚，语言清晰、流畅、富有感染力，且能辅以适当的手势语，那么说课能够取得好的效果。需要注意的是，说课里的语调和手势语都不能夸张，不能弄得像演讲那样的抑扬顿挫、慷慨激昂。有辅助说课，教师的语言压力相对会减轻一点，但操作设备会分散说课者的激情和注意力。

第二章

英语说课的实践

第一节　小学英语说课案例

说课案例一　人教版PEP小学英语教材六年级
Unit 6 How Do You Feel?

广东第二师范学院15级英语教育C班　苏美婷

Hello，everyone！My name is Su Meiting. I'm so glad to present my teaching ideas here. This lesson is chosen from PEP English of primary school，the first semester of Grade six，Unit 6. The main topic of this unit is about feeling. And this is the third period. So my students have the basic knowledge about this class.

In this lesson，students can learn the new words：sad，worry and the sentence "What should he do？He should..." And they can use these sentences to show their ideas about how to deal with bad feelings.

Here comes to the teaching procedures.（Projecting the PPT，略）

In warming up，I will take out a mysterious box and ask students to guess what's in the box. And then I will quote from *Pandora's* box to lead in the topic-bad feelings. Now here comes to the task. At first，I will show Sam's video and ask students to tell me how does Sam feel and why. And then I will show the WeChat responses from Sam's friends and ask my students to classify the responses. And next，I will teach them fixed mindset and growth mindset and the differences between them. In consolidation，I will show Jane's problem and ask students to tell her some suggestions. This lesson will end with a chant. I will invite my students to sing a chant with me. Is that all？No. I will invite them to create their own chants. At last is the homework.

That's all for my teaching design. Thank you!

Task：This presentation is aided with PPT. It is a presentation given at the Contest of Teaching Skills for Normal University Students. Read and ponder over the following questions：

1. Is this presentation comprehensive？ What aspects of teaching are included in it？ What not？

2. Does the presenter succeed in informing you what she will teach，how she will teach and why she will teach？ Which aspect is not covered in this presentation？

3. It is a presentation given before having the simulation class. How effective do you think it is as a presentation of this kind？

4. If you are the presenter，what difficulties would you expect in preparing and giving such a presentation？

说课案例二　说课《攀登英语》分级阅读第三级
The Food Action绘本课

深圳福田区教科院附小　高欣玮

各位领导，各位来宾，大家好！我是教科院附小的英语老师高欣玮。下面由我来说一说我校方思颖老师The Food Action的设计思路。

绘本The Food Action选自《攀登英语》分级阅读第三级，该绘本属于fiction的文体，故事性强，趣味性强。讲述了食物家族是如何聚在一起想办法赶走到厨房偷吃食物的老鼠，该主题贴近学生的生活，能有效激发学生的阅读兴趣，同时，该故事有明显的事件发展脉络，因此，教师以where，who，why，how，what为大框架设计问题链，一步步引导学生观察、发现、预测和解决问题。

本课的授课对象为三年级学生，该学段的学生在一、二年级的学习中有了一定的语言储备，能够在话题的框架内认读常见的单词，也能够用简单的句子回答问题（这一段说课稿有，但现场说课没有）。

本课的授课老师利用一首与食物相关的歌曲进行热身，让孩子们愉悦并快速地进入到课堂状态。在引入部分，老师给学生创设了厨房的大情境，提出问题，即厨房里会有什么东西（What do we have in the kitchen）？以此激活学生在该话题下已有的词汇并引导学生结合生活经验进行思考和讨论。此后，教师提出问题，这个故事里的厨房有什么呢（What can you see in this kitchen）？在该环节，学生共同观察封面，分享自己在封面看到了什么食物，教师则在学生分享后对绘本封面出现的相关词汇进行进一步激活和巩固，利用问题引导学生关注食物们的表情和情绪，并通过图片上食物从开心到焦虑的情绪变化自然地推动情节往下发展。教师在此设计问题，本来开心的食物为什么会变得如此焦虑呢（Why are they worried）？这个问题启发了学生的思维，鼓励他们结合已有生活经验分析食物情绪变化的原因，并要求学生利用已有的语言知识进行观点的分享。

教师把该绘本的学习过程分为猜、听、讲、演、练五个步骤，在阅读故事文本前，学生首先观察绘本中的图片，对图片的要素进行简单描述并根据老师的问题对情节进行猜测。故事的开始，教师展示绘本中的黑影并提问：这是谁的影子？他在做什么（Who is the shadow? What is he doing）？从而引出故事的主人公老鼠，学生在猜测过程中逐步走进故事里，在此基础上再听故事的文本并进行剖析，同时，教师设计开放式问题：如果你是食物家族的一员，你会怎么做？（If you are the food, what can you do）以此启发学生的思维，学生通过小组讨论的形式学会合作、学会自主思考，提出自己的解决方案。这一环节十分灵活，学生在讨论和分享中互相进行思维的碰撞，提出了许多有创意的想法，这时教师再通过文本中老玉米说"我有一个好办法"（I have a good idea.）自然地从学生的好办法回归到文本中的好办法，引出标题The Food Action，并用关键词how引导学生关注食物们是怎么样一步步赶跑老鼠的。

食物总动员的过程中包含了很多动作、很多角色，涉及复杂的语言。教师通过图片环游的方法鼓励孩子进行观察、发现和预测，在有了初步的想法后再共同听和学习绘本的文本，在学习理解文本过后，通过role-play的形式进行进一步吸收内化，这一环节既能活跃课堂气氛，又能使学生积极参与到课堂活动中。

在呈现之后，学生完整地听、读整个绘本故事，进行理解和知识内化，该环节为下一环节的小组活动进行铺垫。在小组活动中，同组的学生要合作完成一份story map，根据story map上的线索在小组内理清整个故事的主线，并能共同完成故事的回顾与分享，从学习理解到应用实践的层次。

本节课的课后作业要求学生完成文本迁移的任务，需要学生阅读故事A toothless tiger并回答相应的问题，设计的问题以故事发展脉络为主线，主要考察学生在who，where，why，how，why大框架内学习了fiction的阅读方法后，能否把这样的思路和方法运用到别的类似的故事中。

在该绘本中，当食物遇到困难时，一个大家族都共同想办法解决困难，学生在阅读该故事后，除了学习理解和应用实践，更应该掌握解决问题的思路和方法。教师分享该绘本故事时也需加强引导学生进行深刻的思考，如果在生活中遇到困难时应该如何处理，让学生在学习的过程中自己感知团结协作、集思广益的重要性，这样才能真正做到知行合一、学科育人。

（该课的授课教师是方思颖老师，由高欣玮老师说课，她们来自深圳福田教科院附小。说课活动于2018年9月27日上午进行）

任务：

该课说课者并非授课教师，说课稿是科组教师的集体创作，说课是在授课之后进行的。

该课属于主题研讨课，研讨的主题是绘本教学。请阅读说课录音转写稿，回答下列问题：

（1）说课教师在教材分析时说到教材的哪些方面？

（2）说课教师提到哪些外语教学理念？

（3）说课教师在哪一（些）部分说得最好？

说课案例三 《攀登英语》分级阅读四年级Robot

深圳福田下沙小学　邓梦倩

这个故事是《攀登英语》第四级的读物，讲述的是发生于Daddy和Ben之间的故事。一开始，Ben为有个电脑工程师爸爸而骄傲，然而，每当他需要父亲陪伴的时候却求而不得，因此变得失望，Ben已经不期待他父亲的陪伴了，只是要求一个Daddy Robot的陪伴。Daddy看到这一幕非常震惊，最后，放下手头的工作来陪伴Ben。当我们看到这个故事的时候，我们决定把它落实在亲子之爱上，让孩子们通过感受Ben的情绪起伏传达亲子之爱在于陪伴的道理。我们用孩子们很喜欢的一首关于robot的歌曲来作为导入，吸引孩子们的注意力，然后，通过倒叙的方法提出Ben有很多的robots，但为什么他仍然不开心呢？让孩子们对故事产生强烈的兴趣，让他们发挥想象去猜猜为什么。教师通过提问，将Ben被拒绝后产生的强烈情绪对比展现给孩子们，然后，让学生猜测对话、演练对话及感受情绪，成功找出Ben失落的原因以及Daddy的改变。本课的后半段通过展示照片让他们思考自己过去的亲子关系并进行引导，回想与父亲一起欢度国庆的内容，既完成了绘本也实现了与现实的连接，深化了感情。

（授课教师为福田下沙小学邓梦倩老师，说课的是下沙小学的教师代表）

任务：

思考下列问题：

（1）这个说课案例属于授课后说课，它是否帮助听课者更好地了解授课教师的设计思路？

（2）案例中说课者说到了课的哪些方面？

说课案例四　五年级英语诗歌写作主题扩展课
Seasons and Poem

广州沙面小学　陈凤霞

今天，我要进行说课的内容是写关于四季的英语诗歌的教学过程：

一、学情分析

本年级的学生已经完成M1有关季节气候话题的学习，已积累了由此话题引出的表达喜爱的季节、地域时间的划分、气候特点、衣着穿戴和季节性活动的词汇和句型基础，但学生对英语诗歌的创作还是首次接触和尝试，所以，在教学的策略上宜尽可能地利用学生已有的知识基础和相关的认识联系。对于五年级的学生来说，他们在语文学科中对古诗的学习已经达到一定的水平，因此，老师以此为切入点，进行本次的主题拓展的设计。

二、教学目标

（1）学生通过对中外诗歌的欣赏和对比活动，谈论四季特点，通过找共同点，利用学科迁移的方法启发学生掌握写诗的方法，更多地了解诗歌的特点及发展学生的英语写作能力。

（2）学生通过对中文诗歌的赏析，进一步丰富他们对中外诗歌特点和结构的了解，如仿写和修改英语四季之诗。

（3）通过制作季节卡（a season card），表达对四季和自然的喜爱，并用诗歌的形式写下来。

三、教学思路

本课教学设计基于4+x理念，旨在进行有关四季诗歌的写作策略的扩展，即引导学生在主题写作课中掌握基本知识，感悟基本方法，养成基本习惯，训练基本思维（四基），从而提高学生英语学科核心素养（x）。教学过程围绕中外诗歌赏析—概括特点—初步写作—评析作品—再次修改—制作季节诗卡—朗诵分享的活动环节，结合语文教学已有的古诗学习基础和诗歌撰写技巧，引导学生将英语知识学以致用，把对四季的喜爱通过诗歌的创作和朗诵表达出来，同时扩展学生英语诗歌的写作能力，激发学生对诗歌创作的热情。

四、教学过程设计

根据"写关于四季的英语诗歌"这一课的特点，结合这门课和学生的认知能力，让学生们能够轻松地理解教学重点和内容，本节课主要运用的是以下教学方法。

1. 准备阶段

赏析我国经典古诗范例，复习旧知，促进迁移。

赏析我国有关四季的古诗，归纳诗歌特点。

（1）首先，教师介绍我国古代诗人，教师通过问题"Do you know who they are？"导入本课教学任务。教师说：They are all Chinese famous poets. 这时，教师顺便教词汇poet & poem。他们都是我国古代著名的诗人，好的诗人会诵诗、赏诗和作诗。今天，我们来当一回诗人，用英语来Read poems，enjoy poems and compose poems.（揭示本课任务：诵诗，赏诗和作诗）。

（2）然后，学生诵读我国四季古诗经典范例，组内讨论中国诗歌的特点。教师说：Here are some famous poems. They are about seasons. Please read and enjoy them，then discuss questions：①What season are they？②And how do you know?

（3）提问和回答：教师追问和学生汇报。教师播放PPT：好雨知时节，当春乃发生。随风潜入夜，润物细无声。教师问：What season is it? How do you know? It is from《春夜喜雨》杜甫。教师继续播放PPT：毕竟西湖六月中，风光不与四时同。接天莲叶无穷碧，映日荷花别样红。《晓出净慈寺送林子方》杨万里。问：What flowers can you see in summer in this poem? 教师第三次播放PPT：何处秋风至？萧萧送雁群。朝来入庭树，孤客最先闻。《秋风引》刘禹锡。并问：What's the weather like in autumn? Where will the wild geese fly in autumn? Can you feel and read "萧萧"？Let's read. 第四次播放PPT：千山鸟飞绝，万径人踪灭。孤舟蓑笠翁，独钓寒江雪。《江雪》柳宗元。教师问：So in winter，do you like fishing by the river?

（4）教师小结：刚才我们欣赏了我国描写四季的古诗，在平时的诗歌阅读里，能感动你的诗歌有什么特点？教师用英语说：If you are a poet，then how to write a good poem？接着师生一起归纳诗歌的特点。

2. 陈述阶段

赏析英语诗歌典型，感悟写作方法，激发创作愿望。

（1）诵读英语诗歌，以景激情。

T：How beautiful your pictures are！Different people like different seasons. Would you like to compose an English poem for your favorite seasons？Let's enjoy some English poems of seasons.（PPT 呈现诗歌，并播放诗歌的音频）

（2）组内评析诗歌，提升学生思维能力。

Tasks：

① Read the poems with music.（自读）

② Compare the poems，find out what you like best and discuss why.（对比诗歌并找出你最喜爱的诗歌及说出原因）

3. 学生汇报

提炼诗歌的写作方法。

T：What are the features of the seasons in these poems？（找关键词）

T：这些诗歌还用了什么写作手法？来，分享一下你最喜欢的诗句。（找最美诗句）运用修辞手法（比喻，拟人……）。画出例子：If you see a robin（知更鸟），you will know that spring is near.（象征）The wind blows and the snow comes along.（拟人）句子的韵律，运用音素的呼应作句末押韵。例子：It is fun. And run run run.

T：How can we write a good poem？

英语不是学生的母语，经过刚才对本土古诗的赏析，启发学生进行了诗歌特点的迁移。而这一环节则回归到第二语言的写作方法的引导——泛读，为仿写做准备。在这个小组活动里，笔者选取了四首风格各异的描写四季的英语诗歌，布置了个人诵读——概括内容（思维导图）——（组内）评析与总结的学习任务，目的在于让学生通过个人和小组协同合作的方式，赏析英语诗，让学生对不同的英语诗歌的架构和写作手法进行初步了解，利用有效的教学策略促进学生思维能力的培养，使其具有逻辑性、创新性、辐射性，激发学生的想象力和创作的愿望。

4. 实践和评估阶段

诗歌创作，体验修改过程，学会自评互评，提升思维品质。

教师提出学生《我最喜爱的季节》主题英语诗写作的任务。在这一环节，教师为学生提供了两次写作的机会：创作——个案评析——再次修改。在第一次写作的环节，教师放手让学生们尝试独立写作，鼓励他们将想法和感受写出来，表达出来，给学生提供一个敢于试错的机会。通过对两位学生（水平差异大，教师预设选择）两份作品的追踪性集体评析（有声思考think aloud），引导学生发现问题，提出改进方向和方法，推己及人，进行二次修改，从而完善诗歌的写作。

创作——个案评析——再次修改，笔者认为试错、感悟和自我修改，这是一个学生写作习惯养成和能力提高的关键过程。在课堂教学中，教师的角色只是一位引导者，在学生对知识点有充分的认知后，应放手让学生通过在真实的语言活动中操练，通过自我体验和实践来获得知识，形成技能。第一次写作后，通过分层个案的评析，让学生发现自己的问题所在，从内在的要求出发，感受和内化写作策略，训练基本思维，培养学生比较、架构、评价、推介等策略，帮助学生发现、分析和解决实际问题，提高思维品质。

5. 拓展阶段

制作季节卡，创造展示和交流机会，培养学生创作的兴趣。

教师要求每位学生为亲人或朋友制作一张season card，在卡上写上自己创作的《我最喜爱的季节》的诗歌。最后，通过举行赏诗会，给学生一个展示自己作品和欣赏他人的舞台，激发学生用英语写作的热情和学英语的兴趣。

教师给每位学生制作和展示season card的机会，是想让每位学生通过学以致用、互为赏析的方式，在真实的任务中真切地感受本次诗歌写作的学习策略的重要性，培养他们的策略使用能力。同时，通过赏诗会这个舞台，给学生一个展示作品的机会，从而提高学生的创作热情和兴趣。

五、教学反思

本课教学设计基本课是五年级英语学科的主题拓展写作课，需要两课时完成教学任务。本课教学设计基于4+x理念，从学生的已有经验出发，打破语文和英语学科的界限，进行知识的迁移，创设了多个让学生体验和自我发现的学习任务，从中外诗歌中学习诗歌知识、吸取写作经验、挖掘写作素材、点拨写作思路、引发写作灵感、培养写作习惯，从而提高学生英语学科核心素养。教师需要注意的是，除了课堂拓展外，在日后的学习过程中，教师应不断创造机会让学生运用这些策略完成任务，把学习策略迁移拓展到其他英语学习任务方面，真正地发展其自主学习能力，培养英语核心素养。

（此说课稿系陈凤霞老师提供，略有修改）

任务：

（1）这个说课稿哪部分给你留下深刻印象？

（2）从这个说课稿中找出说课者的教学理念。

说课案例五　科教版四年级下册
Module 4 Activities单元说课

广州南沙金业小学　李奕婷

大家好！（打开PPT）现在我就四年级下册Module 4 Activities进行整体说课。下面跟大家分享我们的整体设计思路。

一、教材整合，主题确定

此部分包括教材分析、学情分析、单元主题确定（打出PPT，如图2-1）。

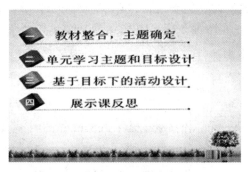

图2-1　PPT展示

1. 教材分析

Module 4 Activities主要围绕日常活动来展开，它包括Unit 7 What do you do when you have free time? 和Unit 8 What are you doing? 其中Unit 7包括 Fun with Language，Sing Along and Sound Family。Let's Talk是Jiaming和Janet谈论空闲时候经常做什么事情的一个小对话，学生需要掌握一些日常活动短语，而且能够互相询问、谈论空闲的生活习惯、做的事情。接下来是Unit 8，包括Let's Talk，Fun with Language，Story Time和Did you know? Let's Talk是Ben向爸爸介绍自己拍的照片的小对话，这节课学生需要掌握现在进行时的用法并且能够正确运用现在进行时来描述人们正在做的事情。

2. 学情分析

首先，语言知识和语言技能。学生能够简单谈论在家里和学校经常做的一些事情，而且能够用简单的交际用语进行交流。他们能够借助图片和提示模仿例子完成语句和完成我们的小短文，有一定的拼读、阅读和观察能力，但是学生搜集信息和小组分工的能力还有待加强。

其次，学生的年龄特点和学习特点。四年级的学生好奇心重，喜欢在唱歌、游戏中学习英语。虽然他们的思维方式逐渐从具体的形象思维转到抽象的逻辑思维，但仍需以具体的形象作为支柱，而且学生的注意力持续时间比较短，因此，教师要利用图片、视频等资源来整合我们的新旧知识，让学生能够在情境中学习，并且教师要设计多样的游戏活动来提高学生对英语的学习兴趣，积极投入课堂的学习。另外，学生的动手能力强，有较高的表现欲，给他们提供机会来展示自己的学习成果能够提高他们学习英语的自信心，也让学生体会到分享和成功的喜悦。

因此，我们本模块的主题确定为：We Love Our Life。这个主题与我们本模块的内容紧密联系，让学生能够运用新旧知识来进行表达，而且它与《课标》要求一致，具有趣味性、挑战性并富有教育意义。我们这个模块总共设计了六个小学习主题，在每个学习主题下也设置了相应的学习目标。我们一起来看一下。

目标1：What do you do when you have free time? 学生需要掌握一些日常活动的短语并能够互相询问、谈论空闲时间喜欢做什么。目标2：What do your friends do at their spare time? 学生能够询问、谈论自己的朋友空闲时间喜欢做什么。目标3：What do your family like doing at the weekend? 学生要学会描述、介绍自己和家人周末时候喜欢做的事情。目标4：What a busy weekend! 学生要能够正确地使用现在进行时来描述图片中自己和家人正在做什么。目标5： I love my life. 学生能够通过口头和笔头来分享他们在学校和周末喜欢进行的活动以及原因。目标6：We love our life. 学生能够分享和展示We love our life 的海报。

为了达到这六个课时的目标，我们在每个课时都设计了相应的输出活动。第一课时，同桌就空闲时能够做的事情进行对话并提出建议。第二课时询问和谈论朋友空闲时候做什么。第三课时谈论自己和家人周末时喜欢做的事情。第四课时，学生用现在进行时谈论照片中自己和家人正在做什么。第五课时是拓展课，学生制作卡片，分享自己在学校和周末喜欢做的活动及原因。第六课时是成果展示课，学生分享和展示We love our life的海报。

那么，接下来我跟大家分享六个课时的教学思路。

Period 1：What do you do when you have free time？（教师播放PPT）

在这个课时我们创设情境，利用Unit 7 Fun with Language里面的Read and Number部分两个人物Wolf和Piggy来复习我们的日常短语，并以此引出新的短语和句型的学习。此外，我们还通过图片进行猜测游戏活动让学生加强对新知识的理解和运用，最终达到学生之间能够互相对话、互相询问、谈论空闲时候做什么事情这样的目的。

Period 2：What do your friends do when they have free time？在这个课时我们围绕朋友空闲时候做的活动来展开教学，通过图片、听听力学习对话的互动，让学生能够理解和掌握如何询问朋友空闲时间喜欢做什么，以及谈论朋友空闲时候喜欢做什么。最后，我们利用图片对课文进行重构。

Period 3：What do your family like doing at the weekend？本课时主要是围绕学生及家人在周末的活动展开教学。我们利用了学生及其家人周末活动的一些照片激发其学习兴趣，而且易于理解新单词、新句型。此外，我们还让学生通过观察和听来总结动词-ing的变化规律和发音规律。我们改变Unit 7 Fun with Language的 Look and Write部分，让学生知道如何谈论自己和家人周末时候喜欢做什么并且进行分享，也为下节课的教学作铺垫。

Period 4：What a busy weekend! 这一课时我们通过老师、学生和学生家人的照片，围绕照片上的人物的活动来展开教学，让学生理解和掌握现在进行时的用法。同时，我们还用图片猜测听力对话，让学生进一步练习和巩固如何谈论照片中自己和家人正在做什么，并进行笔头的输出。

Period 5：I love my life！这是一节拓展课。这节课我们对《新起点英语》四年级上册Unit 2 On the Weekend的Story Time进行改变并创设情境，围绕Bill's Life来开展教学，让学生通过猜测、描述图片、朗读故事、听听力和文本重构来发现Bill没有电脑之后生活发生的改变，并以此了解我们经常玩电脑游戏的危害以及体会学习和举行有意义活动的乐趣。最后，学生能够思考自己的行为方式，制作卡片，分享在自己学校和周末喜欢进行的活动的原因，增加对生活的热爱。

Period 6：We love our life！这是一节成果展示课。（播放PPT，PPT略）上节课我们布置的作业是让学生小组合作把小组成员的卡片进行完善和整理，最后用海报的形式进行呈现。那么，这节课我们就可以给学生提供平台让他们在小组里面分享自己的生活方式，接下来，再让小组成员上台一起分享We love our life的海报。他们在分享的时候，其他小组必须要根据评价的标准来对他们进行评价。最后，学生和老师一起选出三幅最佳的作品在学校里展示。

二、展示课反思

展示课Period 5 I love my life。我们设计的目标是学生能够善于利用图片和关键词来了解故事的内容，能够综合运用新旧知识来描述自己在学校和周末喜欢做的活动以及原因，了解玩太多电脑游戏的危害以及知道如何正确地利用空闲时间增加对生活的热爱。为了达到这些目标，我们创设了这些情境，让这节课紧紧围绕Bill's Life来展开教学。从Bill有电脑时无心学习以及跟家人关系疏远，到最后Bill没有电脑时认真学习取得不错的成绩而且跟家人一起玩、一起聊天的一些转变，让学生知道玩电脑游戏的危害以及如何用有益的活动来充实自己的生活。那么，在本节课，为了让学生更加投入学习，我们利用了图片、视频、音乐资源制作了动作歌曲、绘本故事、故事朗读音频、猜测游戏等。其中，Action Song是由视频片段、图片和自编的chant组成。它与模块内容相关，又能复习到相关的内容和日常活动，同时激发学生的学习兴趣，为下节课做准备。这是我们Action Song里面的内容。下一个是绘本故事。我们改编《新起点》四年级下册英语Unit 2中Weekend，通过对故事的删减、改动并增配了一些照片，形成了新的故事，让这个故事富有趣味性和教育意义。我们的故事朗读音频是选取Bill在没有电脑之后生活方式改变这一部分，朗读并加上背景音乐，以此激发学生的学习兴趣，在听中理解故事的内容并写下自己需要的信息。最后，我们为学生设计的活动是做卡片，分享自己在学校和周末喜欢做的活动及其原因。学生需要先把卡片剪成自己喜欢的形状，贴上自己的照片，接着再写上自己在周末喜欢做的活动及原因，最后进行展示，这也为学生提供一个运用新旧知识表达自己的平台。

这节课就是给学生一些范例。学生和老师如何评价这些作品呢？我们是通过这些标准让学生和老师一起进行评价，教师评价、生生互评。那么，接下来是我们一些作品的展示。

本节拓展课不足的地方就是我们在这一部分给学生准备的时间太短，时间不够。这个班的学生的表现力比较强，而且喜欢上台来展示自己的成果。笔者发现了他们在设计他们的卡片以及贴照片、给照片画画的这一环节花的时间比较多，因此导致展示的时间少了。这是我们在设计的时候就预测到的问题，因此，在第六课时的拓展课，我们在布置作业的时候先让学生互相分享，再制作海报。同样地，Period 6的拓展课我们也用充分的时间先小组内分享自己在学校和周末的生活，再小组上台展示We love our life的海报。这节拓展课也弥补了Period 5学生时间不够展示的遗憾。这就是我们本模块的设计思路。谢谢！

（该说课稿根据说课视频撰写而成，说课者李奕婷老师来自广州南沙区金业小学。编者注）

任务：

这个说课稿属于单元说课，从说课类型看，属于主题说课，也是有辅助说课。这个说课活动是"深度学习"课题的内容之一。请阅读说课稿，讨论并回答下列问题：

（1）该课的主题是什么？授课教师根据什么来确定该单元的主题？

（2）说课者用了哪些方面的理论作为活动设计的理论依据？请在文本相应的地方画上下划线。

（3）说课谈到教师对教材做了整合。请把这部分内容用下划线画出来。

（4）说课教师在衔接过渡方面做了哪些努力？哪些地方还需要改进？

（5）从哪些地方可以看出这个说课稿是集体创作的说课稿？

（6）该说课活动的主题是"深度学习"。你认为教师的教学设计哪些地方体现了学生的深度学习？

第二节　初中英语说课案例

说课案例一　牛津上海版8 A Module 2
Unit 4 Numbers复习课

上海中学东校　周云琴

大家好！我叫×××，来自上海中学东校。本次参赛的教学资源主要来自牛津教材8A Module 2，Unit 4 Numbers的教学内容。本单元主要教授有关数字的知识，例如，数字产生的历史、计算工具的介绍、电脑和人脑的对比，以及在语法部分出现的诸如小数、分数、基数词等数词的读法。

因为二期教改要求教师在教授过程中要引导学生关注生活，注意培养学生的生活能力，又鉴于本校学生均为住宿生，对本校的生活比较熟悉，对校外的生活兴趣十足。因此，综合考虑以上内容，并在本次竞赛主题合理、确定竞赛内容的指导思想下，我确定本课的教学指导思想为：创造贴近生活的语境，让学生在情境中学习、巩固和提高，使课堂教学和实际生活紧密结合，从而使知识在情境中能够达到有效应用。因此，本节课设计为在复习课的基础上做相应的拓展，具体目标为：①通过一些活动的设计，使学生能够有效地复习小数、分数、基数词等数字的读法；②学生能够从中获取相关信息；③学生能够使用数字表达自己的看法。通过这些目标的制定，最终使学生了解数字无处不在，和生活是密切相关的。

在教学目标的指引下，我设置了三种与数字相关的情境：一是学生非常熟悉的本校——上海中学东校。通过对本校相关数字的谈论，一方面复习了书本知识，另一方面使学生加深了对本校了解；二是学校附近的旅游景点之一滴水湖。大部分学生都曾经去滴水湖游玩，因此，对于该环节应该比较感兴趣。为此，我也设计了一些对学生参与情况的统计，让学生们能够用语言把信息组合起来。最后一组是有关东海大桥和南浦大桥的数字。东海大桥被上海市政府列为一号工程，也是我国第一座真正意义上的跨海大桥，它对上海人民，尤其对临港居民来说意义巨大。因此，我先出示一个视频，让学生们对东海大桥有一个直观的印象，接着通过阅读材料的分析和总结让学生们得出东海大桥和南浦大桥的数字，从而发现东海大桥的建设是宏伟的。它的宏伟是由这些惊人的数字组成的，而这些数字又是建设者们创造的。在本课的Post-task activity当中，我设置了这样一些环节：让学生作为宣传大使以临港模拟景点进行宣传。一方面可以复习巩固以前所学，另一方面可以使学生进一步掌握数字在生活当中的应用。如果时间允许，我准备了一个包含临港未来数字的相关视频，从而使学生感到数字可以创造更加美好的未来。

（本说课稿根据光盘转写而成，感谢说课者周云琴老师）

任务：

阅读以上的说课稿并结合观看的视频，回答下列问题：

（1）说课者用第几人称进行说课？

（2）在这个说课稿中，说课说到了哪些方面？

（3）在这个说课稿中为什么没有提及反思？

（4）这个说课稿的重点放在哪里？教材分析、教学目标，还是教学活动的设计？

（5）你如何看待这个说课稿？它的说课效果怎么样？

说课案例二 牛津6A Module 2 Unit 6
Going to School阅读课

上海金山区师大实验中学 周亚妮

各位老师，下午好！我是来自金山区师大实验中学的×××老师。我将执教的是牛津英语6A Module 2 Unit 6 Going to School中的Simon's on His Way to School的第一课。下面，我将从学情、教学内容、教学目标、重点难点、教学过程、课外作业设计等六个方面来展开阐述。

1. 学情

开学这一个月来，大部分学生逐渐养成了跟读录音、模仿语音语调的习惯。通过不同形式的表演方式，半数以上的学生能够在课堂上积极表达自己的想法，利用知识的习惯已经逐渐地养成，学习英语的兴趣也越来越浓。同时，他们也学会了多首歌曲，但总的来说，学生的英语学习才刚刚起步，语音水平参差不齐。

2. 教学内容

本课的教学内容是6A第二个Module Activity，第六个Unit Going to School的第三课，Look and Learn和Look and Read两个部分。在第一、二课时，学生对出行方式、路上要花的时间已经有了一定的了解，本课是Reading部分，主要是让学生学会描述出行路上所看到的情况，并能结合自己的实际进行运用。

3. 教学目标

根据《新课程标准》的总体目标，结合本课教学内容和学生已有的知识水平，我将本课的教学目标预设如下：

（1）知识目标：①学会听、说、认读单词和短语advertisement board，hotel和restaurant；②学会when引导的时间状语从句中一般现在时和现在进行时的用法，如：I see a hotel when I am on a bus. when I am walking to school。

（2）能力目标：①掌握用所学的词汇描述自己上学路上所看到的事物的能

力；②学会用所学句型表达何时看到这些事物的能力。

（3）情感目标。通过本课的学习，培养学生的观察能力。

4. 重难点

根据学生已有的知识基础，我确定when引导的时间状语从句为本课的重点。此外，因为学生是第一次接触，所以我把它确定为本课的难点。也希望通过本课的学习和操练，通过参加编写、朗读、吟唱等活动对难点进行突破。

5. 教学过程

本节课主要包括以下几个环节：

（1）主题引入。通过一首儿歌，引入今天的主题，复习巩固并引出when引导时间状语从句。

（2）单词、句型学习。三个新授词汇中，hotel和restaurant已在小学4A中出现过，其中的restaurant一词在6A中也出现过，我们已经作为重点词汇进行学习。所以，本节课上我重点强调了advertisement board，再通过复现这些名词给学生提供多听、多看、多用的机会，同时自然引出状语从句when加介词短语，接着再通过师生一起完成一个chant这一活动来巩固这个句型，然后再通过修改这个chant的方式引出时间状语从句加进行时态。

（3）文本学习。文本学习共分成两个部分，第一部分，听力理解。在单词学习和句型学习的基础上以听力的方式呈现文本，请学生捕捉重要信息，并且用I see something when I'm on the bus / when I'm walking to school表述所听内容，再巩固刚刚学习的基本句型。第二部分，朗读模仿。在朗读中，进一步理解并熟悉巩固今天学习的内容，并注意跟读录音，模仿语音语调。

（4）知识的运用。请学生扮演Alice，并介绍他们在上学路上的情况。在设计这个环节时，我采取的是由易到难、循序渐进的开放式方式，希望学生能够充分利用所学知识进而实现能力迁移。从学生的综合发展出发，促进学生全面发展的设计才是有效的设计，力图在学习知识和发展能力的过程中，激发学生的兴趣、培养学生的想象力。考虑到这一点，在此环节我请学生以小组的形式改写本节课开头时所唱的儿歌，通过chant和角色扮演把所学知识运用到自己的生活实际中。儿歌不仅唱起来朗朗上口，深受本班学生喜欢，更能激发他们的学习兴趣，使他们爱学、乐学。

6. 课外作业设计

（1）跟读模仿、朗读课文五遍。设计这一口头作业是为了培养学生语音语调和跟读模仿的习惯。

（2）为了巩固本节课所学知识，我设计了演唱自己在课堂上改写的英文歌曲这一作业。这也是学生非常喜欢的作业形式，可以进一步激发学生英语学习的兴趣。

（3）为了给学生提供运用本课所学知识的机会，我请学生课外调查自己的父母、朋友或同学中的某一个人出行的情况，并就调查情况写几句话。以上就是我本堂课的设计思路和想法，谢谢大家！

（该说课稿根据光盘转写而成，感谢说课者周亚妮老师）

任务：

阅读上面这个说课稿并结合观看的视频，思考下列问题：

（1）这个说课稿有什么特点？

（2）它反映什么样的教学理念？

（3）它哪个部分说得最好？

说课案例三　外研社版 Module 8
Unit 1 I am from a small village听说课

佛山顺德实验中学　宋娟

Hello! My name is Song Juan, from Shunde Experimental Middle School. My topic is: I am from a small village. It is taken from Unit 1 of Module 8 Student Book 2, by Foreign Language and Research Press. Unit 1 is a listening and speaking lesson. My lecture mainly includes three sections as follow. Firstly, it's about my understanding of the teaching material with three parts.

Part 1 is about status and the function of this period in the teaching material. This is the first period of this module. And the lesson type is listening and speaking. In this period, students can learn something about the past simple with was and were. After this period, students are supposed to talk about the past life and get ready for second period.

Part 2 is about teaching goals. <u>One</u> is knowledge goal. To understand the conversation with past simple "be" and process information about past life in the listening material.<u>One</u> is ability goal, to enhance students' ability of listening and speaking, and how to use the key words and structure to talk about one's past life. <u>Another</u> is a moral goal: Make students learn something from successful people in the book and behave better in future.

Part 3 is teaching important part and difficult part. Important points is to enable students to learn some key vocabulary, such as be born, first, friendly, naughty and well-behave; learn some key structure such as "Where were you born? I was born in a small village and have some listening skills." The difficult points is how to use some words and phrases to talk about some past life.

<u>Secondly</u>, analysis of students' standard. Students of Grade One may know little about past life of some famous people. As a guide, I should not only let them know about some activities in the book, but also get some information about more people in and out of China, take a view of the world and broaden their horizon.

And <u>the third section</u>, maybe the most important section, my teaching procedures—a text. OK, now let me talk about them in details.

Part 1: Warming up. Play a song named *Yesterday Once More* to lead in the key words "was/were" and introduce myself using key structure "be born". OK, let's come to Part 2: Match the photos with the sentences. At first, I will show some famous persons' pictures to students. And ask them to guess where the people were born and match the photos with the sentences in the whole passage studied. Then I lead them to summarize the past simple be. This task can help students get information about some famous people in the world and lead in the phrase "be born". Then, what about Part 3? Learn some new words, show some videos about them and let students know how to use these words. Part 4: Listen and match questions and answers. This task will make students familiar with some structure with past simple, past tense and enhance the ability of listening. Part 5: Listen and answer. I ask students to read through three questions. Then I play the recording for them. This task can make students getting further understanding of past tense and know how to describe past life. Part 6: Read and choose correct answer for each question. I ask students to do this individually and ask pairs of students to ask and answer. This task can let students know question form and positive form and negative form of past simple be. After so much exercise, it's time for us to relax. So Part 7: Play a game. I ask students to guess who he is or she is according to the given information. This task can make students know more about famous people and enhance their ability of speaking. With so much input, students can do some output now. That is the last task: Homework. For homework, I want the students to make a survey about their classmates. Collect some information about the past life and report in the next class. That is the end of my presentation. Thank you for listening!

（注：本说课稿根据宋娟老师说课实录录像转写，文字基本不做改动。感谢宋娟老师）

Tasks for reflection:

1. Why does the presenter of this lesson use "one, one, another"?

2. Why does the presenter use "firstly" "secondly", and "the third section"? How do they contribute to the effectiveness of this presentation?

3. Is the presentation based on some teaching beliefs or conceptions? If yes, what are they?

4. What are the characteristics of this presentation?

说课案例四　外研版七年级下册Module 5
Unit 1 Tony has the longest journey听说课

佛山市汇景中学　李倩

一、教学背景分析

1. 教学内容

本课的教学内容是外研版英语七年级下册Module 5 Unit 1Tony has the longest journey（七年级），这是一节听说课。本单元的中心话题是城市与国家，语言功能是比较两座城市，语法是形容词的比较级。

2. 学生情况

学生是佛山市汇景中学初一（2）班的学生。该班学生对英语学习有一定的兴趣，学习动机较强，英语成绩和智力发展水平在整个年级中属于中上水平。

3. 教学方式和手段

在教学过程中教师主要采用小组合作学习的方式开展课堂活动，小组合作学习具体化为以小组为单位进行PK活动。活动的形式新颖，能够激发学生参与的兴趣和热情。

4. 技术准备

（1）教学中运用计算机多媒体设备，制作了配合教学内容的幻灯片。

（2）在教学过程中使用了OHP（Overhead Projector）。

（3）下载了历史上举办过奥运会的城市的图片。

（4）准备了填空用的handout。

二、教学目标

1. 语言知识目标

学习生词bund（上海滩），kilometer，Victorian Peak（太平山），east,

south；掌握形容词比较级，用来对比两座城市。

2. 语言能力目标

培养学生在以听为主要输入形式的基础上口头对比两座城市不同之处的能力。

3. 学习策略目标

通过小组活动，培养学生合作学习的策略。

4. 文化意识目标

通过对两座城市的比较，了解中国的两座城市与悉尼、巴黎、洛杉矶之间在历史、人口、面积、交通等方面的不同。

5. 情感态度目标

通过比较假设中的申奥城市的不同之处，培养学生的爱国、爱家的积极情感，培养学生的国际视野。

三、指导思想与理论依据

1. 总体设计思路

本课的中心话题是城市与国家，模块任务是比较两个城市。语法重点是形容词比较级，技能重点是学生在听说训练中用所学语言对比两座城市以及其地理和人文特征。将以上四者结合，体现在本课教学目标上，就是让学生观察对比两座城市，并用形容词比较级的句式介绍这两座城市的不同点。为了让学生自然地、带着目的地比较两个城市，教师设计了为2020年奥运会推荐主办城市的课堂任务。四组学生分别负责推荐四座城市。这里为了进行对学生文化意识的培养和文化知识的输入，教师选择了洛杉矶、巴黎、悉尼以及一座待定的中国城市。在课堂里学生将分三部分完成推荐任务：第一，学生将上海和香港进行比较，挑选更有竞争力的那座城市成为中国的申办城市；第二，各小组代表的城市两两比较；第三，各小组推选一名学生做本城市的申奥陈述，阐述自己城市更具实力的优势。学生在完成每一项任务时都是通过使用形容词比较级句式对比两座城市，这样使本课的语言学习有机地融入了话题主线中。这样的设计能使课堂主题鲜明，层次清晰，内容充实，形式生动，并与新标准英语功能——结构——话题——任务有机结合，和以学生为主体的教学理念不谋而合。

2. 本课采用了任务型教学

任务型教学的要义在于用所学的语言来做事。大卫·纽南认为，任务一般包含六个要素，即目标、输入、活动、环境、以及教师角色、学生角色和结果。在英语作为外语的课堂教学中，每个任务都带有一定的目标；教师语言和教材内容充当学生的语言输入，而活动是完成任务的载体，环境则是完成任务的方式，任务可以是学生单独完成，也可以是小组合作完成；任务完成的主体是学生，教师充当为学生提供便利者。此外，埃利斯认为，任务的完成要有一定的结果，可以是语言结果也可以是非语言结果。任务型教学的特点之一是大量的对子和小组活动，学生在完成各种各样任务的时候，运用语言的机会大大地增加了。

3. 本课的主要学习方式是合作性学习

根据维果茨基的社会互动理论和中介学习理论，人的学习和发展发生于与其他人的交往互动之中，课堂教学能否为学生提供大量互动的机会成为掌握语言的关键。采取小组形式的合作性学习，可以最大限度地为学生提供练习和运用语言的机会。

四、教学过程

Step 1：导入话题（Warming-up and lead-in）

教师给出年份和国旗图片的提示，通过提问的方式让学生回忆近几届奥运会举办城市，并导入本课的话题——为2020年奥运会推荐主办城市。在导入阶段，教师运用直观手段充分激发学生对即将讨论的话题的兴趣，为下面的活动做铺垫。

Step 2：呈现任务和词汇教学（Setting up Tasks and Presenting some new words）

（1）教师将学生分为四组，分别代表悉尼、洛杉矶、巴黎和一座待定的中国城市，并提出本课任务：为本组代表的候选城市争取选票。

（2）学生了解自己代表的城市，并明确本课任务：为本组代表的候选城市争取选票。

（3）教师让学生了解候选2020年奥运会主办城市的两个中国城市的情况，利用图片在语境中进行词汇教学（the Bund，kilometer，Victoria Peak，east，south，population）。

（4）学生了解候选2020年奥运会主办城市的两个中国城市的情况，在语境中学习新词汇。

（5）教师让学生通过听力进一步认知新词汇，增加对两个城市在人口、面积和天气方面的了解。

（6）学生听课文录音，做填空练习，逐步加深对新词汇的理解并增加对两个城市在人口、面积和天气方面的了解。

Step 3：呈现目标语法（Presenting the target grammar）

（1）教师播放课文录音，呈现比较级的构成和用法以及读音。

（2）学生听课文录音，填写表格，观察学习形容词比较级的构成和用法，熟悉其读音。

（3）教师提供图片和数据让学生在交通、住房、人文等方面深入对比两个城市，让学生在语境中进一步体验语言和使用语言。

（4）学生对比关于两个城市的图片和数据，学习使用含有比较级的句子来比较两个城市的地理和人文特征。

（5）教师引导学生归纳总结形容词比较级的构成方式。

Step 4：巩固目标语法（Consolidating the target grammar）

（1）进行第一轮PK：要求学生使用含有比较级的句子发表对两个城市的看法。

（2）在此基础上根据大家的意见进行投票，选出上海或香港代表中国参加申奥。

Step 5：交际运用（Communicative use）

（1）进行第二轮PK：小组讨论，为自己代表的城市设计竞选口号。教师将四座城市分为两组，进行两两比较。学生阅读城市资料卡，进行小组讨论，为自己代表的城市设计竞选口号。教师引导学生使用比较级的句式对两座城市进行对比，并约定每条有效口号将为本组赢得一张选票。

（2）进行第三轮PK：小组合作完成申奥陈述稿，由该组代表在全班进行发言，其余组学生代表投票并陈述理由。每组学生选出表达能力出众的同学担任市长，其他组员通过写信或交谈的方式帮助市长完成申奥陈述稿。教师将提供一份北京的申奥陈述稿作为参考，要求在陈述稿中使用含有比较级的句式来介绍自己的城市。当四位"市长"陈述完毕后，每组将由两位代表来投票，并陈述投票理由。

Step 6：评价（Evaluation and comment）

（1）教师总结竞选结果并评价学生的表现。

（2）教师鼓励学生继续努力。

Step 7：家庭作业（Homework）

教师布置学生写一篇小文章，即用形容词的比较级比较自己的中学和小学，并把文章传到博客或QQ空间。

五、学习效果评价

1. 评价方式

（1）通过填空练习，考查学生是否掌握描写地方的形容词及其比较级在语境中的运用。

（2）通过参与PK活动，可以培养学生处理信息的能力和运用语言做事的能力。

2. 评价工具

选票被用来作为评价小组活动结果和成效的手段和工具。教师鼓励学生通过为自己的城市赢得选票的方式来激发他们参与课堂语言活动的热情和动机，符合初一学生喜欢在合作中竞争的心理。

六、教学反思

由于教师对教学任务的精心设计，学生对三个PK活动一直保持高涨的热情。学生在课堂参与度、交往度和思维度上都有较好的表现。教师在教学中也应用了支架教学的理念，在学生用语言来做事前在语言结构方面给学生作了足够的铺垫，因此，学生在两两对比两座城市时基本没有语言上的障碍。教学取得了预期的效果，不同层次的学生在语言知识、语言技能、情感态度、学习策略和文化意识方面都学有所得。

运用Integrated approach，综合训练学生听、说、读、写四项技能，并让学生将课堂上学到的知识和技能进行迁移，解决实际任务，体现在用中学，学用结合的原则。以学生熟悉感兴趣的奥运话题为主线，生成从易到难的任务链，并与语言学习有机结合，体现新课标功能——结构——话题——任务有机结合的教学理念。

尽管学生在本节课的参与程度较高，但也存在小组成员发言的机会不均匀

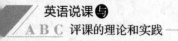

的情况，还有在小组活动时教师很难顾及每个学生。

（本说课稿说课者为李倩老师）

任务：

这个说课稿是在说课者原来说课稿的基础上修改而成的，为了发表的需要做了微修改。认真阅读这个说课稿，讨论、思考下面的问题：

（1）这个说课稿跟前面的说课稿有哪些不同的地方？

（2）这个说课稿在说理论依据方面有什么特点？

（3）如何评价这个说课稿的内容和结构？

（4）这个说课稿是否具有较强的口语特征？

第三节　高中英语说课案例

说课案例一　New Horizons Book 4 The Old Man and Death阅读课

深圳外国语学校　梁洁文

Hello，everyone！The lesson I am teaching is a fable from Unit 9 from New Horizons Book 4，one of our major coursebook for senior students in our school. And the class I am teaching is Class 1，Senior 2，who have great passion and pretty high level of competence in English. And this fable is about an old man who made a wish for death because of the trouble brought by age and hard work，but he regretted and changed his mind when death really appeared.

This passage introduces a very important grammar item. That is the use of if only with the subjunctive mood. Hopefully，this lesson can give the students a touch of what subjunctive is like and prepare them for further comprehensive study of it.

The major teaching tasks and aims of this lesson are: First of all, to provide students with the situation where they naturally to acquire the language, learn and practice the use of if only so as to make sure the learning and use of what they have learned in a very proper way. And secondly, but more importantly, to help the students to understand the moral of this fable and use it to guide their study and life. Since the lesson is a fable, which always teach people some truth to live by. So it's very important for the teacher to guide the students to read between lines and get the message conveyed by this fable. The moral of this fable can be interpreted in more than one way. Humorously, one can say that we should be careful what we wish for because it may come true; or more seriously, one can say people do not treasure their life until they are going to lose it; or it's better to live a hard life than die. However and whatever it may be, the teacher should lead the students to understand and realize how precious life is and treasure it. Besides, the third task and aim is to develop descriptive skill and also to develop students' skill, and also to encourage students to discover language and practice language and also present them methods with learning and using language. As for the teaching approaches, in designing and conducting this lesson, I adopt Situational Approach, Communicative Approach and Task-based Approach. With the help of computer and projector, the class efficiency will be greatly increased.

The teaching procedures are as followed. The first step is leading in. I'll ask the students if they have ever seen shooting stars. By doing so, I can introduce the topic of making wishes and also ask students to prepare for the further understanding this fable. And the second step is anticipating. For this step I'll show them this picture, which is actually an illustration of this fable from our textbook. The purpose is to introduce new words and phrases. And also I'll ask them to invent story of wish based on what they can see and this is to solve the language problem, vocabulary problem and also actually students' necessary vocabulary and also arouse their interest in this lesson. And the third step is listening and note-taking. In this step, students will listen to the recording twice. Meanwhile, they should take notes, which is a very important learning skill that should be emphasized. After the first time of listening, students are supposed to acquire information that they can answer some information questions. After the second time of listening, students are expected to take down some notes for some essential aspect of this fable, such as setting, time, character, event and ending and so on. And at last, students will be instructed to tell the story of the fable in their own words with the help of the notes. The purpose of this step is to give students language input, to develop students' note-taking skill, give them a chance to present the language competence and reproduce language input. The fourth step is reading and practising. Students are now to open their book and read silently in order to fulfil two tasks. One is to complete some sentences with the words and phrases from the passage, and the other is to discover how the old man expressed his wish. Step by step students discover and use language under the teacher's guidance. I design three activities for this purpose. In demonstrating the usage of if only, I provide them with a situation where students can make more than one and quite a few different wishes with if only. And this also taps their creativity. Um This also helps them in the following activity describing situations and making wishes. By describing situations, we can make sure that students use authentic language. And at the same time students can practise their language and present their competence. As for the guessing game, I created a kind of information gap in this game by asking students to suppose that they are one of those celebrities or public figures or people they know well, and then make a wish for this person or the thing they have chosen. But they must keep what they have chosen as a secret. And then I'll pick them up and tell the classmate what their wishes are and let others guess who they are or what they are. I give them examples, for example, I say: If only I have won the electoral vote in Florida! I am sure students can easily guess I am speaking from the point of view of John Carry. By doing so, students can further practice the use of if only in a more funny way and also it arouses students' awareness of what's going on around us or in the world. And the fifth step is reading and understanding. This is kind of brainstorming. Students will work in a group of four, and discuss the moral of this fable. And they will be instructed to collect the moral—all the possible morals that the group members can think of. And they also need to write down the best moral that they agree on on a piece of paper, and then more importantly they need to draw an illustration for the moral that they have chosen. The purpose of this, at last I'll invite some students to the platform and present their group work through the projector to the class and they must explain why these things, the best moral for this fable, why they draw these illustration for this moral. And this is to further understand the fable and also to provide a visual comprehension of the fable, the visual one. And this time I want them to draw a picture. The picture can be very simple like a sketch or even cartoon. And the last step is consolidation and application. And this is actually the assignment. It includes two parts: speaking and writing. The speaking part is to tell the people you know who may most benefit from this fable and the other is to think of examples of our real life to support the moral of this fable. This step is to help students to further understand the fable, relate it to our daily life and apply it to their own advantages. Thank you!

（本课说课稿根据说课录像转写而成，感谢来自深圳外国语学校的梁洁文老师）

Tasks: Read the presentation draft very carefully. Think over the following questions:

（1）This is a more natural presentation. In what way do you think it is natural?

（2）The procedures are presented in a clear way. In some steps the teacher even describe details of an activity. Is it wise to include some details of activity when presenting a lesson? Why?

（3）What teaching beliefs are built in this presentation? Are they new or not?

（4）Why does the presenter mention "The purpose..."?

说课案例二　人教版选修八Unit 2 Cloning：
Where is it leading us? 阅读课

中山纪念中学　蔡 球

课型：阅读课的第二课时之读后活动课。

说课类型：主题式说课。

主题：如何在阅读课中落实指向核心素养的英语学习活动观。

一、说教学背景

主题语境：人与社会—科技发展与信息技术创新，科学精神，信息安全。

语篇类型：说明文

语篇研读：what，why，how

Cloning
1. Definition
2. Major uses
3. The procedures and the impact of Dolly
4. The future of Cloning

重点：

（1）学习理解类活动：语篇填空、个别提问、小组接龙、一站到底等。

（2）应用实践类活动：小组合作，写、画、说、评等。

（3）迁移创新类活动：小组合作，展示、讨论、思考等。

难点：

（1）虚拟语气的运用。

（2）克隆产品的设计以及阐述。

学情分析：

（1）学生较为单纯，学习热情高，具有一定的表现欲。

（2）具备一定的词汇知识，能听懂基本的课堂用语。能用一些词汇、句型进行造句，但不能通顺表达。

（3）学生接触过说明文，对说明文的文本特征有一定的了解。

（4）整体来看，该班学生能用英语提取信息，处理信息，简单表达自己的观点。但是运用英语连贯地描述事物、阐述优缺点和表达自己的观点的能力相对较弱。

二、设计理念

英语学习活动观的定义及解读：

英语学习活动观是指学生在主题意义的引领下，通过学习理解、应用实践、迁移创新等一系列体现综合性、关联性和实践性等特点的英语学习活动，使学生基于已有的知识，依托不同类型的语篇，在分析问题和解决问题的过程中，促进自身语言知识学习、语言技能发展、文化内涵理解、多元思维发展、价值取向判断和学习策略运用。这一过程既是语言知识与语言技能整合发展的过程，也是文化意识不断增强、思维品质不断提升、学习能力不断提高的过程。

解读——新课标提倡的英语学习活动观是：

（1）指向核心素养：语言能力、文化意识、思维品质、学习能力。

（2）六要素整合：文化知识、语言技能、学习策略、主题语境、语篇类型、语言知识。

（3）符合布卢姆的认知六层次理论的活动。

三、说教学目标

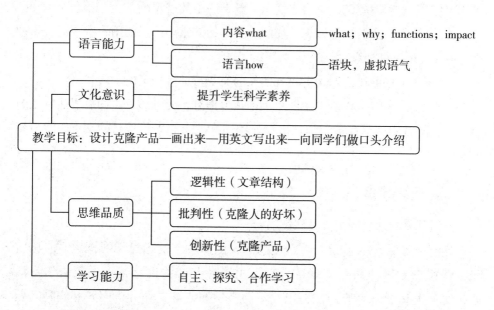

四、说学习活动

表2-1 学习活动内容

教学环节	主要活动内容、活动形式、活动的类型	设计意图	互动时间
活动1 文本 深入解读 （内容+语言）	1. The definition of cloning［语篇填空］——学习理解类活动 2. The structure of the passage［个别提问］——学习理解类活动 3. The procedures of cloning Dolly［看图说话］——应用实践类活动	激活阅读第一课时所学，进入主题语境 进一步深入解读语篇结构，整合语篇重点信息 在分析问题和解决问题中实现语言和知识的内化，为目标活动做铺垫	10ms
活动2 范文解读 （内容+语言）	1. 范文呈现［小组合作接龙游戏］——学习理解类活动 2. 范文学习［朗读+提问］——学习理解类活动 3. 课文和范文语块学习［一站到底游戏］——学习理解类活动	通过游戏训练与主题语境相关的听、说、记、辨的能力，形成学习期待 引导学生赏析范文的结构、内容和语言（语块和虚拟语气） 通过游戏，检查课堂语言学习情况	12ms

续 表

教学环节	主要活动内容、活动形式、活动的类型	设计意图	互动时间
活动3 创新展示	1. 设计你的克隆产品［小组合作、画、写］——应用实践类活动 2. 口头展示［小组合作、说］——迁移创新类活动	小组有序分工、合作，巩固并整合所学语言和内容；应用所学，实现迁移创新 同伴互评，总结在主题语境、语篇类型、语言知识、文化知识、语言技能、策略运用方面的收获	12ms
活动4 自由讨论	讨论克隆人的利弊［思考、讨论］——迁移创新类活动	引导学生多角度进行审辨性思考，训练思维与表达，深化主题，加强德育浸润	3ms
作业	完成个人的克隆产品的短文	巩固、提升	

五、说方法策略

表2-2　方法策略

教学环节	主要活动内容、活动形式、活动的类型	学习策略
活动1 文本深入解读 （内容+语言）	1. The definition of cloning ［语篇填空］——学习理解类活动 2. The structure of the passage ［个别提问］——学习理解类活动 3. The procedures of cloning Dolly ［看图说话］——应用实践类活动	自主学习 自主学习 合作学习
活动2 范文解读 （内容+语言）	1. 范文呈现［小组合作接龙游戏］——学习理解类活动 2. 范文学习［朗读+提问］——学习理解类活动 3. 课文和范文语块学习［一站到底游戏］——学习理解类活动	合作学习 自主学习 合作学习
活动3 创新展示	1. 设计你的克隆产品［小组合作、画、写］——应用实践类活动 2. 口头展示［小组合作、说］——迁移创新类活动	合作、探究学习 合作、探究学习
活动4 自由讨论	讨论克隆人的利弊［思考、讨论］——迁移创新类活动	合作、探究学习
作业	完成个人的克隆产品的短文	

六、说课堂评价

（1）对教学评价的解读

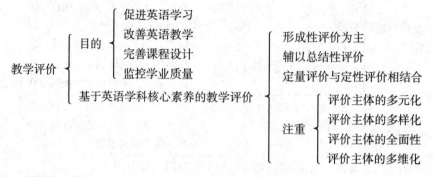

（2）教学评价举例

Content（What）
- The functions of the cloning product
- The reasons why you want to clone it
- The impact of the cloning product

Language（How）
- Subjunctive mood（虚拟语气）
- The phrases & sentence patterns learned

（3）教学评价举例

评价主体的多样化。

七、反思

（1）设计清晰。

（2）以学生的学习为中心，凡是学生能做的，我绝不代替学生去做。

（3）活动丰富、形式多样。

（4）德育浸润和引导。

八、板书

略。

（根据案例集光盘整理，感谢说课者蔡球老师及其团队）

任务：

（1）上面的说课案例包含了说教学背景、设计理念、教学目标、学习活动、方法策略、课堂评价、反思、板书八个方面的内容。你觉得哪些部分是最值得学习的？哪些部分最能反映当前教学新理念？

（2）上面的说课案例具有什么特征？请用一些关键词描述这些特征。

（3）蔡老师的说课案例中哪部分体现说why？

第三章

英语课堂观察和反思

第一节　课堂观察的意义和课堂观察类型

　　课堂观察（classroom observation）是教师教育和教师培训的重要内容之一。课堂观察是评课、议课的前提，没有观察就不能评课，评课和观课密不可分。课堂观察是教师专业成长的重要基础，师范生在职前就要学习如何进行课堂观察，发展课堂教学能力。在职教师也需要通过课堂观察向同行学习，有效提高自己的教学能力。

　　长期以来，我国的课堂观察处于"原生态"状态，存在着观课教师不做准备、不理解听课教材理念、不了解授课教师教学目标、没有具体听课目标等现象。教师观课缺乏理论意识，方法和手段相对落后，技术路线不清晰。这些影响了观课效果，制约着教师课堂教学能力的提高。

　　教师在授课时不能冷静和客观地感知课堂里发生的所有事情。授课者常常处于当局者迷的境地，耽于某种习惯、工作方式以及说话方式而不自知；授课者看不到自己的不足；授课者总是回避自己不擅长的方面；授课者跟观课者观点存在差异等。因此，有必要邀请值得信任的同事来观摩自己的课堂，发现自己并不知道或知之不多的东西。斯克里温纳认为，观察其他教师的课堂有助于更好地培养自己选择的意识，并为个人反思和后续的研讨提供有用信息或启示。课堂观摩和后续的课例研讨是观察者和教师学习的工具。在诚恳、互相尊重和相互支持的气氛中进行课例研讨是教师成长的宝贵路径。

　　斯克里温纳提出五种类型的课堂观察：培训型观课（training observation）、发展型观课（developmental observation）、评估型观课（assessment observation）、数据收集型观课（data collection observation）和同行观课（peer observation）。

　　（1）培训型观课的目的是帮助受训者认识授课者现在的教学技能水平以及需要改进的地方，它服务于某一特定的目标。

　　（2）发展型观课是观课者自发的活动，观课者自己确定哪些方面的反馈是最有用，最能帮助自己专业发展的。

（3）评估型观课是上级领导或同行根据一定的质量标准来观摩课堂，以评价授课者的教学。

（4）数据收集型观课是观课者为了调查课堂的某些方面而进行的课堂观察，比如，通过观察找出教师所提问题的种类以及比较男生和女生课堂的参与度等，其收集的数据往往用于量化研究。例如，课堂上教师或者学生某种行为的频率和数量。数据收集型观课者通常是同行或者研究者。

（5）同行观课的目的是互相学习。通过交流和讨论，观课者和授课教师相互获益。

高效的课堂观摩需要系统的培训。课堂观摩要解决观什么、如何观的问题以及如何记录观察所得等问题。有效的观课一般有下面的程序：观课前的准备工作。为了取得更好的观课效果，观课者需要提前了解下列信息：①授课班级学情。包括学生水平、学习状态、近期存在的问题等。②授课课型。常规课（by-the-book lesson）、即兴课（wing-it lesson）、试验课（experiment lesson）、展示课（driving test lesson）、代表课（representative lesson）。③观课类型。培训型观课、发展型观课、数据收集型观课、评估型观课、同行观课。④观课目的。包括观课者计划好的观察点和评论点。⑤观课方式。观课者参与课堂、观课者隐藏自己、观课者做笔记、观课者录像。

选取或确定观察点。观什么是指课堂观摩的观察点，观察什么取决于观课的目的。就观察点而言，韦津利认为，课堂的观察点可以落在下列七个大的方面：学习者、教师语言、学习、课堂、教学技巧和策略、课堂管理以及教材和资源。

不论何种类型的课堂观摩都可能是有益的学习。但要使课堂观摩活动效果最大化，还需要在观摩后有评课、议课活动，即有讨论及反馈环节。

第二节　课堂观察任务和观察点

　　课堂观察需要观察者提前确定观察点作为观察的任务，而信息的收集、后续的讨论及反思都可以围绕观察点进行。理查兹把观察任务具体化为一些观察时需要回答的问题：

（1）What are the main goals of the lesson?

（2）What is the most important thing the students learned from the lesson?

（3）What do you think was the most successful part of the lesson?

（4）Was there anything about the lesson that was not very successful?

（5）How do you feel about the lesson as a whole? （略有改动）

理查兹列举了一些教师关注的课堂观测点：

（1）课堂结构。

（2）教师的时间管理。

（3）学生完成任务时的行为。

（4）完成任务的时间。

（5）教师提问和学生回答问题。

（6）教师的讲解。

（7）教师的行动区域。

（8）学生对子活动的行为。

（9）课堂互动。

（10）教师使用教材的情况。

（11）新教学活动。

（12）小组活动。

舒尔曼在一段关于教学技能的表述中也提到可以观察到的教学行为：

（1）课堂组织和课堂管理。

（2）清晰的讲解和生动的描述。

（3）布置活动和检查活动的完成情况。

（4）提问和探讨问题的有效互动。

（5）回答问题和做出反应。

（6）表扬和批评。

诸如RSA Diploma之类的语言教师证书课程把下列的教学技能当作评估语言教师的基础，因此，就观察教师的教学技能而言，它们也可用来当作课堂的观察点：

（1）计划交际互动活动。

（2）组织交际互动活动并为其提供便利。

（3）判断课堂上准确性活动和流利性活动之间的平衡。

（4）对学习者偏误的意识。

（5）恰当对待学习偏误。

高尔和沃尔特斯认为教学技能应该包括下列技能：

（1）呈现语言。

（2）组织控制性练习。

（3）检查学习情况。

（4）引发对话和叙述。

（5）使用对话进行教学。

（6）运用文本进行教学。

（7）设立交际性活动。

任务：

从观察教师教学技能的角度来看，可以设置哪些观察点？试着把这些观察点归类。

第三节　课堂观察工具

　　课堂观察需要借助一些工具和手段。一线教师听课、观课时常常携带学校或科组统一印制的听课手册或听课记录表，以便记录、收集课堂的信息。大多数的课堂观摩者会采用下列两种形式之一的记录方式：①用文字描述课堂事件或特别之处。描述可能是总结性的，也可能是针对局部的、细节性的信息，例如，课堂中的亮点或者不足。②用观察量表或者编码系统来记录课堂的细节。

　　课堂观察时教师可做人种志记录来记录课堂里的主要事件和影响。这种记录通常是简短的、提纲式的记录，例如：

T enters...greets whole class from the front of the room. T announces what the lesson is going to be about today. T reminds SS how this lesson follows on from yesterday's ... T drills new pattern...S asks questions about the form of the verb in pattern on board...T explains. S seems to be satisfied but another S continues to ask similar questions...

　　课堂上充斥着复杂的教学事件，许多不同的活动在同一时间发生，全方位的课堂观察是没必要的，也是不可行的。因此，课堂观察要有重点。为了提高课堂观察的效率，观察者需要借助观察量表之类的观察工具，例如，当观察的重点是课堂提问的情况时，可用表3-1来记录和收集观察到信息（在相应的栏目打√）。

表3-1　记录信息表

问题序号	问题类型		回应方式		答案的形式	
	事实性问题（factual）	推断性问题（inferential）	指定回答（invited）	自荐回答（voluntary）	用关键词作答（key words）	详细作答（elaboration）
1	√		√			√
2		√	√			√
3		√		√	√	
4	√		√			√
5	√		√			√
6		√	√			√
7	√		√			√
8		√	√			√
9	√			√		√
10		√		√	√	
11	√					√
12		√		√		√

　　在没有现成的量表可供使用的情况下，课堂观摩者可根据自己的观察重点来设计和制作适合自己使用的观察量表。观察表的制作既要有理论支撑也要基于观察的目标。比如，表3-1的理论支撑是关于课堂提问的理论，观察目标则是课堂提问和回答情况。

　　为了让观察者和被观察者能够较大程度地获益，观察者在课堂观察前要就观察点进行深入的、系统的思考。以教师提问这个观察点为例，观察者要思考下列问题：

　　（1）提问的原理是什么？

　　（2）哪些提问行为是有效的？哪些是无效的提问行为？

　　（3）提问的主要目的是什么？

　　（4）什么问题对学生来说最简单？什么问题对他们来说最难回答？

　　（5）期待学生怎样回答？简答还是细答？

　　（6）怎样鼓励学生提问题？

　　在对观察点有了成熟的思考后观察者即可着手研制观察量表。这样的观察表能够有效地搜集被观察者的相关信息，为后面的讨论和反思打下了扎实的基础。

此外，课堂观察可以借助录音、录像等设备。借助录音、录像设备，听课者能够在观摩课后更详细、更系统地整理所需信息。

课堂观察可以在课堂上进行，也可以在课后观看课堂录像。有的观摩者会在观课后把录像或者录音转写成课堂实录，作为本人或同行后续深入学习或研究的资源。著名特级教师王崧舟说他喜欢收集课堂教学实录，特别是有代表性的名师实录。首先，他把实录还原成教学设计，然后把教学设计还原成教学理念，再把教学理念还原成教学设计，最后把设计再还原成实录。通过这样一个来回还原的过程（如图3-1所示），使自己在课堂教学中既有教学思想，又有教学技术，因而能够挥洒自如，即"上得了天，下得了地"。王崧舟把这个过程形象地称为"独孤九剑中的第一剑"。

图3-1 课堂教学实录还原

在本书的评课实践中，笔者在评课前基本上都提供了所评课例的课堂实录。这些实录帮助师范生学习如何进行教学设计、如何实施教学，特别是如何组织课堂语言等。

第四节 课堂观察后的反馈和反思

评课、议课是根据课堂观摩的目的进行的研讨活动。在此期间，观摩者会就所观课例进行讨论和评价，这个时候观摩者变成了评课者；授课教师会独立反思或者结合评课者的反馈进行反思；观摩者和授课者进行观点的交流等。评课、议课在某种程度上是课例研究活动。

　　实际上，评课、议课是观课者给授课者提供对其教学的反馈；反馈是观课活动的重要价值之一；反馈可以包含评价的成分。如果没有反馈，那么观摩课活动的价值就会大打折扣。评课或议课是信息差、意见差和价值差原理的运用，这种活动开展起来不难，因为不同观察者之间以及观察者与授课者之间存在着信息差、意见差和价值差。不同层次的教师在评课存在着观点差和价值差。理查兹发现，在评论一节课最精彩之处时，新手和有经验的教师评价的角度是不同的。新手更多地从教师的角度来看课堂上最有效的教学，而有经验的教师则倾向于从学生最能获益的角度来看。

　　观察者在观察后的议课阶段可以把评议的重点放在这三个问题上：

　　（1）这节课什么地方最精彩？（What worked best in the lessons?）

　　（2）这节课哪一部分效果最差？（What was the least effective part of the lesson?）

　　（3）如果你有机会上这节课，你会怎么上？（What would you have done differently if you had taught the lesson?）

　　授课教师也可为自己的教学提供反馈，即自我反馈（self-feedback），以便改进自己的教学。自我反馈可以是热反馈（hot feedback），也可以是冷反馈（cold feedback）。教师自我反馈有助于提高分析自己教学的能力及教师专业发展。下面是斯克里温纳提供的两个例子。

Hot feedback

The oral practice seemed to work well. The students got really involved and didn't want to stop. I noticed that I was concentrating on students to my right; I rather left out the five sitting near the door.

Checking the homework with the whole class was very dull. There must be a better way to go through all the answers.

Cold feedback

What was successful: the lexical game—fast and fun—they practised a lot of words. I felt more confident in this lesson; I'm beginning to get used to the way this class works.

To work on: I could be clearer with instructions. They were definitely confused at the start of the game. I talked rather a lot. I noticed myself talking about their answers when I got impatient—I'll try to watch for that in the future. I don't think

Joanna said any thing during the whole class . I must have a chat with her and find out if everything's OK. Perhaps I could ask questions direct to named individuals, rather than general questions to the whole class.

如果发觉写自我反馈有困难，也可以采用下面的这个自我评估模式。这个模式包含三个部分：回忆课堂、反思课堂、总结课堂和规划未来教学。回忆部分主要是回忆课堂上发生的事情；反思是寻找课堂上成功的东西；总结和规划部分是基于经验得出结论并找出可以促进自己未来教学的东西。每次上完课后，授课教师可以从这三部分中各取一个问题进行反思。下面是斯克里温纳提出的自我评估模式的三个组成部分，非常值得一线教师和学习教学者借鉴：

回忆课堂

（1）列举课堂里你做的几件事情。

（2）列举课堂里学生做的几件事情。

（3）记下课堂上学生给你的任何评价或反馈。

（4）记下课堂上你与单个学生之间重要的互动。

（5）根据你的记忆归纳该课的主要课堂环节。

（6）教师做事和学生做事的比例如何？

（7）列举基本按照你的计划发生的几件事情。

（8）列举不按你的计划发生的几件事情。

（9）回忆你能够清晰地做出课堂决策的时刻。你选择什么？你舍弃什么？

反思课堂

（1）记下这节课的几个亮点。

（2）这节课的高潮在哪里？你为什么觉得它好？

（3）你能从学生的角度回答相同的问题吗？

（4）列举你认为学生学有所得的几个具体的节点。

（5）在哪些节点你还可以更清晰一些？

（6）课的哪一部分最能使学生投入学习？

（7）哪些活动最能给学生带来挑战？

（8）哪些活动耗时低效？

（9）在什么时候你感到最不得心应手？

（10）你取得预期的目标了吗？

（11）学生达到你的预期了吗？

总结课堂，规划未来教学

（1）假如再教一次，你还会这样教吗？

（2）假如再教一次，你会做出哪些改变？

（3）关于教学设计，你学到了什么？

（4）关于教学程序和技巧，你学到了什么？

（5）关于学生，你学到了什么？

（6）关于自己，你学到了什么？

（7）关于学习，你学到了什么？

（8）列举你对未来教学的打算以及行动计划。

（9）从学生的角度描述一下作为教师的你。作为你的学生他们的感觉如何？

（根据斯克里温纳原文内容转述）

理查兹认为，观摩别人，是为了反思自己，而不只是把注意力集中在别人的教学行为上。他提出了三步式的课堂观察（Three-way observation）：①教学新手和有经验的教师结对；②每一对教师开展同伴课堂观察；③每节观摩课结束时收集学生、授课教师、观摩教师对该课的感受。课堂观察的最有用的结果是它使有经验的教师充当经验尚浅教师的导师。他还认为，如果课堂观察者的角色只是收集课堂教学信息而不是作为评价者的话，那么课堂观察的价值就更高。

批判性反思教学把研究和反思当作教师发展过程的核心。发展研究技巧和反思技巧目的是使教师从依靠直觉教学、本能教学、根据常规进行的教学走向反思性教学和批判性教学。

近年来，我们对课堂观察在教师教育中的作用的理解已经发生了改变，因为课堂观察的重点已经从技术教学观统辖下的观察优秀教师的教学行为和教学技能转向对观察到的行为背后隐含的复杂意义的理解。

任务：

（1）选取三个观察点，以小组为单位观摩一节课并围绕这三个观察点进行讨论。

（2）观察一节课并将该课录音，把其中三个重要片段转写成文字。

（3）观察一节课，写一个含有回忆课堂和反思课堂的小报告。

第四章

英语评课的理论

第一节　评课的目的和意义

一、评课的意义

评课也称议课。简单来说，评课就是评课者对所听的课程或者所观察的课堂进行的讨论及评价活动。评课者对一节课或者一节课中某些环节的评价通常包含两个部分：评价语和评价依据。评价语包含评价者的态度，评课是评价者的情感系统、裁判系统和鉴赏系统对事物价值的评价。

评课在不同的环境下有不同的目的和功能。在中小学的教研中，评课往往有诊断的功能。对于在校的师范生来说，评课具有学习的功能，掌握评课技能，学会如何看一节课的优缺点对师范生的教学能力的形成具有反拨作用。而对于中小学一线教师来说，评课、议课是教研活动的主要载体和形式，在一些地方，评课是教师职称评定的考核内容之一。目前，在中小学外语教学中，评课的评价功能正在逐渐向诊断功能转化。评课、议课是每一位在职教师必备的专业技能，也是职前师范生必须掌握的技能。

评课的更深层次的意义在于使授课教师在借鉴别人评课的基础上能够进行批判性反思，能够对自己的课堂进行系统的思考，从中挖掘教学的内涵和意义。

一般来说，英语评课就是讨论和评价一节课的优、缺点。有建设性的评课是评课者在提出自己对课的看法的基础上指出如何改进不足之处，有的评课者甚至指出如何重构一节该课。特级教师余映潮主张将评课分为四个步骤：一谈课堂流程，二谈一个突出的优点，三谈一点建议，四谈一个新的教学设计。

二、评课需要知识和能力储备

评课需要评课者有一定的知识和能力准备。只有有相关的知识和能力储备，评课才能准确地抓住课堂教学的优点和不足之处，才能起到真正诊断课堂教学、促进教师专业发展的作用。只有专业的评课，才能真正使授课教师受益和信服。作为外语师范生来说，首先要掌握学科知识和学科教学理论。只要掌握了学科知识，你才能判断教师在教学这些知识时是否科学，是否正确，深度和广度如何。只有掌握学科教学的理论，你才知道如何进行的语音教学、语法教学、词汇教学、文化教学、听的教学、说的教学、读的教学、写的教学，等等。掌握英语有效教学的特征和标准也有助于评课。对于一线教师来说，他们不但掌握了学科知识、学科教学知识和技能，还积累了一定的实践性知识，有的教师甚至已经形成了个人教学理论，这些都是他们评课的基础。他们需要学习新理论，不断开阔自己的教学视野。

不管是师范生还是一线教师，都要掌握有效课堂的特质标准，都要掌握国家颁布的《英语课标准》，因为它是英语教学的指南和"圣经"。我们的英语课堂教学以及评价，都要以《课标》为准绳。

第二节　评课的依据和方式

英语评课的依据主要来自《英语课程标准》、英语教学理论以及教师的实践知识。用来作为评课依据的英语教学理论一般包含教学方法、教学原理。此外，评课的依据也来自语言学、语用学、篇章语言学、第二语言习得、教育学、心理学等上位学科或相邻学科的理论。

各个版本的《英语课程标准》一直是基础英语教育、教学评课的依据。《课标》设定的英语课程的总目标、提出的教学理念、建议使用的教学方法，以及课堂教学的实施和评价、课程资源的开发和利用等都可以用来作为评价课堂教学的依据。在当下的不同学段、不同层次的教研活动中，人们倾向于用学科核心素养来看教师在培养学生的语言能力、学习能力、思维品质和文化意识方面的方法、策略和成效。而在看思维品质和思维能力的培养时，又会把它跟布鲁姆的教育目标层次连接起来，与英语课堂教学中的问题设计的思维层次、思维的外显工具思维导图的使用、教育信息技术手段的运用等结合起来。下面是一个以2011年版的英语课程标准为依据的评课案例：

我们现在谈核心素养不是说就要丢掉我们2011年版《课程标准》上的一些好的核心理念。其中课程理念当中有一句话，就是六大理念当中有一个是"面向全体学生，关注全体学生""关注语言学习者的不同特点和个性差异"，因为我们这个不是精英教育，在义务教育阶段是全民教育，我们希望孩子们一个都不能落下。那么我们在进行课堂教学设计的时候，对能力发展或者培养要考虑梯度和活动形式的问题。比如这个一问一答，其实反映了这个活动。我们抛出问题之后，可以更多地让孩子们discuss，group work，让孩子们有更多时间在一个很安全的心态环境下去跟伙伴讨论，能去触摸这些知识，让他们心里有一些准备之后来回答。所以，如果用这种方式，最终我们看到的不只是班上两三个孩子一直在跟你互动，应该是全体学生的投入。（根据案例集光盘转写，略有改动）

在对照式评课中，评课者以某一种教学理论为标尺，然后对照课堂教学实际而做出判断，即哪些安排是合理的、哪些环节是不符合原理的。例如，在评课中，评课者会根据英语阅读教学理论和二语习得理论来判断阅读活动的设计和安排是否合理，是否有亮点，是否有新意，等等。具体看教师是否在读前激活学生关于文本话题的背景知识，激发学生的阅读动机；是否在读中先让学生读懂文本大意，再读细节，接着开展深层次阅读，活动之间是否有关联、是否有层次性；是否能够有效训练学生的阅读技能和阅读策略；是否培养学生理解信息和处理信息的能力；读后是否设计了能够激发学生兴趣和参与的输出活动等。就整个阅读课而言，我们还要看阅读教学活动在形式、手段、工具、方法上是否有创新；教师是否有综合视野以及教师是否设计了多元阅读教学目标；整节课是否遵循从输入到输出的逻辑顺序，等等。

对照式评课有助于教师对教学理论进行学习，使参与者对新的教学理念有更直观和更具体的理解。但它的不足是评课者往往把教学理论当作唯一的评价标准，没有考虑理论和课堂实际并不完全对称，因此，评价的框架和视野会受到限制，评价结果可能有偏颇。

诊断性评课或原因剖析式评课是对照判断式评课的深化，评课者能够中肯地指出课堂教学中的不足是什么原因造成的。诊断式评课有助于教师找准毛病，改正缺点。例如，在评论第十二届初中英语课堂教学观摩课I'm more outgoing than my sister时，评委1这样点评：

今天导入的这首歌花了两分钟，结果只问一个问题：What is it about? 听两分钟的歌，回答一个问题，你觉得划不划算？听两分钟的歌曲可以，但你要保证学生听到什么，第二要根据听的内容至少设计两三个问题，然后对后面的教学有帮助。如果只是引入friends这个话题，我觉得这两分钟用得不太划算。另外一个：当你要学生Read the passage and answer the questions: Who are their friends后，让学生Find the sentences about the differences。我认为当我们读课文的时候？我们是Find the differences and similarities。我们是找信息，不是找句子。（根据课堂教学案例集光盘转写，略有改动）

献计献策式是用建设与创立来代替浅层次的判断和分析的评价。献计献策评课对评课者的要求较高，着眼点在于能够为评价对象提出建设性的建议，它比前面的两种评课方式更进一步。但被评课者对评课者的"计"和"策"要进一步反思，以便能够把他人的建设性意见内化成自己的教学能力的一部分，而不只是停留在借助外力的层面上。在评论第十二届初中英语课堂教学观摩课I'm more outgoing than my sister时，评委1就这样说：

如果我来设计教学，我会跟学生说：你们认为朋友到底该一样还是不一样？学生发表意见。然后让学生读课文，看这三个人怎么说。说完以后，这三个人怎么去证明他们的观点的？然后过渡到细节。

评委2这样说：

你这节课设计的主线我用四个关键词来总结：differences, similarities, opinion, support。如果我来设计，我的主线是：话题是friends，然后是friendship。我会遵循从总到分再到总的思路。首先我们要提出的是关于friends的这三个观点：1.Friends should be the same; 2.Friends should be different; 3.I don't care。如果用这种思路，我认为可以把复杂的东西变得更简单。这是我对这个教材的解读。我讲的问题是主线和思路的问题。关于朋友这个话题，学生非常熟悉，有话可说，有话能说，有话想说。（根据课堂教学案例集光盘转写，略有改动）

在发现式评价中，评价者本人有见微知著的敏锐观察能力与洞察力，能够发现人之所未能发现，评课常常有一种"于无声处听惊雷"或"那人却在灯火阑珊处"的感觉。这是一种较高境界的评课，能够引发思想认识方面的精华，这种评课需要评课者具有很深的功力。独创发现式评价具体可表现为以下几种情况：①发现原创性亮点；②发现普遍性现象；③发现个性化品质；④发现根源性问题；⑤发现阶段性嬗变。

第三节　评课的视角

评什么取决于几个要素：在什么情况下的评课；评课的目的是什么；谁是评课者。评课之前先要观课，因此，评什么也取决于评课者的观察点。观察点可以是根据评课目的预先设定的，也可以是随机选择的。前者涉及评课者的有意注意，后者则是下意识的活动，这种下意识活动受评课者的知识、经验等所影响。但是，有一些评课点并非来自观察点，因为不是所有的东西都是外显的，都是可以观察得到的。从理论上来说，英语课堂上任何跟教学相关的因素和变量都可以作为我们的评课内容。实际上，评什么最主要取决于开展观课评课主题和目的。

一、评课的视角取决于评课者的课程观

课程观指的是对本门课程性质的定位，比如，英语课程是一门语言课，是一门外国语言课。从宏观的角度看，英语课程属于人文课程；从中观的角度看，英语课程属于大语文课程；从微观的角度看，英语课程是外语课程，不是母语课程。课程性质决定了课程内容和课程实施方法。那么，我们评课时就应该立足于本门课程的性质和特点来做出判断和解释。外语课需要兼顾语言的工具性和人文性，而在工具性和人文性统一的基础上，我们还要往前走一步，我们需要认识到工具性是语言的本质属性，而人文性是语言的重要属性。因此，在英语课堂上，我们在培养学生语言能力的同时也要培养学生的文化意识和思维能力。在评课时，我们不但要关注授课教师对学生语言能力的培养，也要关注其在培养学生文化品格、思维品质方面的作为；关注教师是否在英语课中进行全人教育。

把英语课程作为语言课来看，意味着在课堂上教师要创设情境和机会，让学生进行大量的语言练习和语言运用，让学生在游泳中学游泳，而不是把大

量的课堂教学时间用于对语言知识的讲解。在组织对子、小组活动时，教师主要考虑如何在单位时间里提高学生语言练习和语言运用的量和质，而不只是通常意义上的观点的分享和共同探讨解决问题的办法。当然，如果小组活动能够既让学生用语言来做事，又让他们通过做事来学习和运用语言，那是最理想的了。

二、评课的视角取决于评课者的教学观

教学观指的是教师对教学的本质的理解，典型的教学观有以下三种：科学——研究观（science—research conceptions）、理论——哲学观（theory—philosophy conceptions）和艺术——技艺观（art-craft conceptions）。

教学的科学——研究观的教学主张是：①理解学习原理；②基于学习原理设计学习教学任务和活动；③监控学生完成任务过程中的行为以便观察目标是否达成。

教学理论——哲学观的教学主张是：①理解理论和原理；②根据教学理论来设计大纲、选择材料以及安排任务；③对教学进行监测以观其是否符合相关理论。

教学艺术——技艺观把教学视为艺术和技艺，它的教学主张是：①把每个教学情境都视为独一无二的；②确定每个教学情境的特殊特征；③尝试不同的教学策略；④发展个人化的教学方法。

每位教师都有自己的教学观，他们的教学观也许是上面几种教学观中的一种或者几种的混合。教师的教学观不但影响他们自己的教学，也影响他们评课的角度、方式、内容和标准。比如，持教学艺术——技艺观的教师评课时可能会评价教师的教学风格；持教学理论——哲学观的教师在评课时可能会更关注授课教师是否依照教学理论来进行教学。

教学是个多维度的过程。舒尔曼指出，教学至少包含五个要素：视野、设计、互动、结果以及分析。视野指教师具有的教育教学思想和理念，先进的思想和理念通过教学设计进入教学实践，并通过师生互动和生生互动产生一定的教学效果。但教学总是被片面地理解为师生之间的课堂互动。教学过程的多维度决定了评课的视角和内容的多维度。

三、评课的视角也取决于评课者的教师观和学生观

传统的教师观把教师视为知识的传授者和课堂教学的权威，这样的教师观导致了课堂以教师为中心。而相对应的学生观就是学生是知识的接受者，是知识的容器，学生在课堂上处于被动的地位。现代的教师观则把教师定位为为教学提供便利者，现代学生观把学生当作学习的主体。

在外语课堂教学中，教师扮演以下几种角色：语言的输入者、讲解者、语言活动的组织者、语言活动的提供便利者、语言活动的指导者和反馈者，等等。学生是目的语的学习者和语言运用的尝试者。

可以说，教师观和学生观是密不可分的，有什么样的教师观就有什么样的学生观。持教师中心观的教师必然是排斥学生中心观的，持学生中心观的教师必然是排斥教师中心观的。

评课者的教师观和学生观决定了他如何看待和评价教与学的有效性。例如，教师是否为学生提供优质的学习资源；教师是否帮助学生对学习材料进行个人意义的构建；授课教师是否把课堂控制得太紧；教师的讲解是否精炼；教师是否培养学生的学习策略；教师是否能够适时给学生提供帮助或者反馈；教师的反馈是否能够促进学生的发展；教师是否能够激发学生的正面学习情感。从学的角度来看，学生的课堂参与是否积极主动；学生是否敢于在课堂冒险尝试语言的运用；学生是否能够主动去构建语言规则和语言使用的规则；学生是否能够自主运用学习策略；学生是否能够与同伴合作；学生能够在有需要时向教师或同伴求助；学生的思维是否得发展，等等。

四、评课的视角也取决于评课者的课程资源观和教材观

英语课程资源具有多元及动态等特点。英语课程资源的多元性指的是它包括很多种类的教学资源；其动态性是指它在不断变化当中，教师可以通过各种渠道获得或开发新的课程资源，而不是被动接受已有的课程资源。首先，教师是课程资源的使用者，教师和学生都是已有课程资源的受益者。其次，教师也是课程资源的开发者。课程资源的开发，坚持简便、实用、有效的原则，注意开发多层次、多类型的英语课程资源，并不断更新和补充课程资源，满足不同层次学生的需求。教师也可以把学生当成课程资源的开发者。最后，教师和学生本身也可以成为课程资源。越自主的教师，越有可能把自己和学生都变成英

语课程的资源。

英语课程资源的核心部分是教材。人们对教材的地位一般这样描述：教材是教学的蓝本，但教材不是教学的根本。教师有权力对教材内容进行增删取舍，教师所选用的教材应该符合学生的年龄特征、心理特征和学科认知发展水平，具有科学性、思想性、趣味性、灵活性和开放性，教材应该做到题材多样、内容丰富、语言真实。教材应能激发学生学习的兴趣、开阔学生的视野、拓展学生的思维。在英语教学中，除了合理有效地使用教科书以外，还应该积极利用声像资源、报刊等，给学生提供更多的丰富、真实的语言学习和体验的机会。

《英语课程标准》（2017年版）提出，英语教材要突出对学生自主学习的引导作用，便于指导学生开展自主、合作与探究式学习。教材的练习设计应尽可能让学生去做事情，在做事情的过程中体验语言、感受语言、探究语言，从而学习和掌握语言。教材内容的编排方式有利于学生在语言运用中发现语言规律。教材要为学生提供学法的指导，帮助他们形成良好的学习习惯和有效的英语学习策略。教材要有利于学生拓展思维，培养创新精神和实践能力，有利于学生学会学习，获得自主学习的能力，为终身学习奠定基础。

此外，评课的视角和标准取决于评课者的知识结构、工作经历和经验。笔者曾问一位大学二年级的师范生怎样的一节英语课是好课，她的回答是"能让学生学到东西的课就是好课"。这位学生在大学二年级第二学期，前面所学的语言教学理论知识还不太多，她的答案来自她的直觉和自己的学习经历。可以说她评课的视角是学生的学，即从她作为一个学生的角度来看评课的标准：学生学有所得。对于高校的评课者来说，可能他们评课的视角除了受诊断的目的影响外，还受他们的教学或研究专长所影响，比如，如果该评课者擅长的是语音教学和研究，他可能会把视角落在语音教学方面。如果评课者是一线教师，那么评课的视角会受他的实践性知识和他教学兴趣、专长所影响。

评课没有绝对的标准，如果说评课有标准的话，那么这些标准落实在每一个跟教学有关的因素的标准上，如教师的语言、教师对教材的理解、教学活动的设置和安排、教学反馈和评价，等等。一节课没有百分之百的好，也许在理念上、设计上是好的，但可能在实施中会有瑕疵。抑或在实施的总体上是好的，只是在个别细节上有改进的空间。

第四节 评课的标准

如前所述，评课没有绝对的标准，但有相对的标准。有的标准是不变的，比如，英语课必须遵循外语教学的规律，这是绝对的标准。而有的标准是可以变通或调整的，比如，对于不同专业发展阶段教师所授的课程，评价的标准是有所不同的。对于名师的课和青年老师的课，在评课时标准是略有不同的。对于听说课和读写课，评课的标准也是同种有异。

著名教育家叶澜说，一堂好课没有绝对的标准，但有一些基本的要求，即一有意义、二有效率、三生成性、四常态性、五有待完善。所谓有意义的课，就是学生的学习真正发生的课。在这样的课上，学生学到了知识，发展了能力，有良好的情感体验并产生强烈的学习动机，主动地投入到学习活动中去。有效率的课就是不同层次的学生都学有所得，每位学生通过这样的课都发生了变化。生成性是指在课上教学并不完全按照教师备课时的预设进行，课上临时出现的问题成为教学的出发点，并把课堂的教和学引向深入；真实的课堂互动在某种程度是不可预知的，因此，在互动过程中常常能够产生新的教学资源。常态性指教师自己准备或设计的课，不是他人帮忙准备的课；不是反复磨合过的课，不造作的课，是原生态的课。有待完善的课是指没有十全十美的课，优质课也不例外。十全十美的课不是上出来的而是造出来的课，因而是不真实的课。孙泓在叶澜的好课的五个标准上归纳出好课的特征：扎实的课、充实的课、丰实的课、平实的课以及真实的课。

有生命也可作为评课的一个标准。深圳外国语中学的黄晓鸿老师认为教师要上有生命的课，每堂课都是生命与生命的交会，每一堂课都是全新的创造。他在课堂上会根据学生的逻辑线并依照学生的反应去进行课堂的生成，上课拒绝套路，因此他的每一节语文课都以学生雷鸣般的掌声结束。

什么样的英语课才是一节好课？虽然不同的人有不同的看法，但业界在这个问题上也已经达成一些共识。从宏观来说，一节好课在指导思想上应该是符合学科教学规律的，也是符合《课标》的理念和教学要求的。教学设计能够体现学科教学特点并且切实可行。从微观来说，好课对涉及的每一个教学因素都有比较到位的考虑。教学实施要做到有效率。

什么样的英语课算是成功的英语课？理查兹的一项对香港英国文化教育协会16名英语教师的研究表明，关于成功的英语课的标准，学生积极参与课堂以及运用语言是最多人认可的标准。其次是课堂要生动活泼、有趣。然后才是学生练习及使用目标语言、教学目标得以实现以及学生态度积极。

"后方法"外语教学的要求。一是学习机会最大化，课堂教学是创造和利用学习机会的过程，离不开教师的创意和积极参与；二是意图曲解最小化，尽量减少师生之间的意图被曲解的可能性；三是促进协商式的互动交流，鼓励使用目的语的有真实交际意义的师生交流和学生间交流；四是培养学习自主性，指导学生发现掌握个性化的学习策略和自我监控能力；五是增强外语语感，不仅注意语言形式结构，还要注意语言的交际价值和社会功能，增进对语言本质的认识；六是启发式语法教学，借助语料库中抽取的范例，引导、启发学习者注意语法结构形式；七是外语输入的语境化，提供语言输入的语篇上下文、交际环境和文化背景；八是语言技能综合化，听、说、读、写技能培养协调配合进行；九是语言教学的社会依赖性，语言学习只有跟社会政治、经济、文化等大背景结合才能提高效益；十是提高文化意识，鼓励语言学习者以自己的文化和教育背景为基础，积极创设学习机会，参与课堂交际。依据后方法时代对外语教学的要求我们可以构建21世纪英语优质课堂。

任务：

（1）你喜欢哪一种方式的评课？

（2）对于评课，你准备好了吗？

（3）基于自己的认识，建构一套关于优质英语课的标准。

（4）评课需要恪守一些职业伦理吗？如果需要，请提出几个建议。

第五章

英语评课的内容

第一节　教学理念和教学设计

一、教学理念

　　教师的教学理念决定教学设计的高度；教学设计、教学实施及实践体现教师的教学理念，优质课通常都能体现先进的教学理念。沙维尔森和斯特恩认为，教师的理论和理念充当过滤器的作用，可以帮助教师做出许多判断和决策。

　　英语教学中有哪些教学理念呢？从二语习得的角度来看，有下列这些理念：输入是二语习得的必要条件，但不是充要条件；互动促进习得；输入——互动——输出是二语习得的路径；意义磋商促进二语的发展，等等。从外语教学的角度看，有下列这些理念：以教师为中心的教学；以学生为中心的教学；以课程为中心的教学；隐性教学和显性教学；英语课程的双重属性；外语是通过"读"学会的；从英语阅读教学的角度看，有下列这些理念：阅读的综合视野；阅读具有多元目标；激活学生的图式有助于学生的阅读；互动模式是最有效的阅读模式；等等。不但教师有理念，《课标》也有自己的理念（2001年版；2003年版；2011年版；2017年版），《课标》的理念统领教师个人的理念。

　　教学理念是从哪里来的呢？理念主要是从教学理论中转化而来的，是教师接受和吸收了教学理论后结合自己的实践经验形成的关于教学的认识和信念。教师的理念还可能来自自己的学习经历、受教育背景以及文化背景等。伍兹把他所研究的教师关于有效教学的理念归结为源于教师自己作为学习者的经历以及作为教师的教学的经历。理念出现在教师的说课中，但是在课堂教学中不能直接被观察到，而是从教师的教学设计和教学行为中推测出来的。比如，一个教师在阅读课中没有直接教生词，而是在教师话语中反复使用这些词汇，因此，我们做出这样的推测：教师采用隐性教学的方式教词汇，她背后的教学理念是语言是默会的，即词汇可以通过隐性学习而学到。

教学理念带有教师的个人特征，因为它融合了教师个人独特的经验和思想并经过与具体情境的互动。因此，教师的教学理念已经区别于教育理论模式。这解释了为什么都是阅读教学，有的教师选择在阅读前教词汇，有的却在阅读中教词汇；也解释了有的教师的词汇的教学很有深度，有的却只是在堂上进行浅表化教学。在伍兹研究的两位教师中，一位教师的理念是教学必须跟着学生的兴趣走，因此，他的课堂决策是基于学生兴趣而做出的；而另外一位的理念则是教学必须先计划，教师必须跟着计划走，原来计划教什么内容就得教完它，因此，他做的事情是确保教完他计划中要教的材料。

由于教学理念统摄教学设计、教学实施以及课堂决策，因此，评课时高校学者或者教研员会从授课教师的教学理念入手去评析一节课或者课中的某些环节。例如，笔者当年在评析邓宁霞老师的写作课时，这样写道：

笔者十分欣赏这节课背后的教学理念：①作为输出的英语作文，应该建立在阅读等输入材料的基础上；②高中英语写作，关注过程应该多于关注结果；③图式理论在作文课的应用。

教学理念需要与时俱进。教学理念有新旧之分，也有先进和落后之分。教师要拥有先进的教学理念，必须不断学习新的教学理论，并将其应用到自己的教学实践中，结合自己的教学情境不断反思，以便逐渐形成自己的教学理念或者更新已有的教学理念。

理念再往前走一步就成了准则、信条或座右铭。准则是理念凝练而成的，它指好的或者理性的教学行为规则，特别是指那些以谚语或者格言形式出现的准则。一些参赛教师在赛课前会发表自己的教学座右铭，包括教师理念、价值观，可以用来诠释教师的责任、教学实施及其课堂决策。

二、教学设计和教案

教学设计的最大价值在过程而不在结果。教学设计的过程诠释了教学的本质——教学是一个涉及教学设计、学生反应和教师即兴教学三个因素的创造性互动过程。教学设计的过程是一个解构和重新创造的过程。不管要教的是教材中的内容还是教师自己收集的材料，教师在设计时要解决的问题是如何使这些潜在的教学内容变得可教、可学。教师借助对学生学习兴趣和已有的知识的了解以及自己的教学理念，构思如何使教学材料适应学生的需求并有助于实现自己的教学风格。

教学设计时要考虑什么活动或步骤是有效的。一节课的基本建筑材料是活动或任务，换言之，从形态上来说，一节课是由一个又一个的活动或任务构成的。所谓活动或任务，就是学生为了取得某一特定的结果而用语言进行的事情。结果可以是能够反映现实世界的结果，如学生角色扮演在火车站买票；或者是纯语言练习的结果，如在句子中用动词的现在完成时填空。

传统的教学设计把一节课看成是一系列的教师活动。从学习的角度来看，我们倾向于把一节课看成是一系列的学习活动。教师只有把注意力更多地集中在学生的活动上，才能更多地思考如何让学习真正发生，才能设计出真正有用的课。即使在呈现语言阶段，教师都要明白学生在做什么并且会产生什么结果。

好的教学设计，具有以下几个特征：体现新的教育思想和教学理念；目标明确且具可操作性；活动之间具有连贯性和层次性；教学活动、教学方法和教学手段具有创新性。

每个环节每个活动都有明确的目标。前面的活动是后面活动的基础，后面的活动是前面活动的发展和提高。而且活动环环相扣，抽掉其中的某个环节，整个教学设计就崩塌。传统的英语课往往前面的活动是一些以语言准确性为目标的活动，后面是较为复杂的以语言的流利性为目标的活动。一节循序渐进的英语课的活动态势是机械性练习——→有意义的练习——→交际性活动，活动安排的内在逻辑是从易到难，从简单到复杂。

《英语课程标准》（2017年版）提出了英语学习活动观，主张学生在主题意义的引领下，通过学习理解、应用实践、迁移创新等一系列体现综合性、关联性和实践性等特点的英语学习活动，使学生基于已有的知识，依托不同类型的语篇，在分析问题和解决问题的过程中，促进自身语言知识学习、语言技能发展、文化内涵理解、多元思维发展、价值取向判断和学习策略运用。

根据《课标》提出的英语学习活动观，以后在教学设计时教师会更加关注活动是否具有以下三个特性：综合性、关联性和实践性。因此，评一节课的教学设计的标准之一是看整节课的活动是否具有这三个特性。

好的教学设计能够基于学习科学、语言教学的新发展融入新颖的元素和理念，使教学活动能够更好地激发学生的课堂参与和思考，从而取得更好的教学效果。

好的教学设计有其适切性，同一内容对于不同的学生群体需要不同的教学设计。对于语言水平稍逊的学生，教学设计可能需要铺垫性的环节，教师要设计"手脚架"才能帮助学生顺利达成教学目标。在日常教学中，对于不同水平的班级施教，教师需要同课异构。

在课堂观摩中，我们发现公开课的教学活动往往看起来整齐、大气，过于注重课堂氛围而忽略对必要的知识点进行基础性学习，这是不利于学生学习的。

教学设计形之于文字就是书面教案，教学设计只保存在大脑中就是心理教案（mental plan）。经验尚浅的教师认为，教案具有管理和组织功能，即教学设计和教案有助于确保教师能够关注到课堂的不同要素，组织课堂结构和时间安排，提醒各种细节等。书面教案有助于教师系统地、确切地阐述其心理教案。心理教案越清晰，书面教案就越简单。有经验的教师更加注重教学设计的过程而不是结果，他们认为心理教案是对整节课思考的结果，旨在梳理问题、过程和策略。因此，有经验的教师多采用心理教案。经验尚浅的教师的教案大多详细，教案中描述了目标、活动、过程以及语言项目，在教学过程中他们扣紧教案，增加或删减活动主要出于时间方面的原因。而经验丰富的教师多采用提纲式的教案，他们的教案只列举要开展的活动作为提示，与经验尚浅的教师相比，他们更多地采取即兴教学。即兴教学是临时决策的结果，教师的即兴教学解释了为什么同一位教师执教同一内容的两次课很少一模一样。

无论是经验尚浅还是经验丰富的教师，在课堂上都会因临时的课堂决策而出现偏离教学设计的现象。教师偏离原来的教学设计主要原因如下：为了保持学生的兴趣和课堂参与而临时改变教学活动；在很多备选程序中选择最适合教学情境的那些；增加未经设计的活动；降低完成任务的难度；改变教学程序以便活动更具交际性；改变分组安排以提高教学的有效性；感到需要为学生提供更多的显性语言学习的机会，等等。而经验尚浅的教师还会改变原来的时间安排。归纳起来，引起教师做出偏离原来教案的决策的主要原因有四个：时间因素、情感因素（如兴趣、动机等）、教学因素以及聚焦语言。

理查兹把有经验的教师和经验尚浅的教师执行教案和做出偏离教案的决策的原理进行了归纳总结，详见表5-1。

表5-1　教案决策

	Maxims/Working principles
The less experienced teachers	Cover the lesson plan. Fit the teaching plan to match the time available.
The experienced teachers	Build on students' difficulties. Maintain active student involvement. Develop a language learning focus for the lesson.
Both the less experienced and experienced teachers	Provide students with sufficient guidance for tasks. Maintain a communicative focus to the lesson. Find the most effective grouping arrangement for tasks.

表格中描述的对象是一项研究中的香港英国文化教育协会的16位英语教师。

西尼尔认为，教师对成功课堂的意象（lesson image）通常对他们的教学设计产生巨大的影响。教师脑海里关于好课的意象影响着他们在备课过程中做出的选择和决定，很多教师教学设计时按照他们认为的好课的标准来设计他们的课程和课堂走向。

教学设计和教师课堂决策是议课、评课的内容。例如，在对第12届初中英语课堂教学展示课I' more outgoing than my sister点评时，评委2是这样评论该教师的教学设计的：

但是，我认为你的思路使你的设计显得有点学术化，如opinion，support，学生没有那么多的东西要说，因为这是初一的孩子。我个人比较主张reading有更高层面的东西，比如reading for pleasure，reading for thinking，reading for meaning。所以，这里有很多东西可挖掘，比如，里面提到Friends are like good books. What did you think friends are like? 可以启发学生的思维。另外，还有Friends are like a book. 可以通过追问，实现学生跟文本的互动，同时更重要的是激活他的思维，培养他的思维品质。后面的A true friend reaches your hand and touch your heart. 这个学生不一定理解，我们要引导学生去理解这句话，学生的观点是什么？（根据课堂教学案例集光盘转写，略有改动）

在点评阅读课Mickey Mouse时，评委2聚焦的第二点也是教学设计：

第二点，我觉得他的整个教学设计也比较合理，基本上实现了由浅到深、由表入里这样的过程。层次比较清晰，比如说读前的激活、导入；读中的三问：第一问涉及时间表、第二问让学生了解Disney Mouse的相关信息；第三问是Why is Mickey Mouse so popular? 这个我觉得非常好，是读中的活动。读后有两个步骤（同上）。

好的教学理念可能产生好的教学设计，而好的教设计则是走向好课的关键一步。理念统摄教学设计，教学实施落实教学设计，教学设计连接理念和实施。好的教学理念、优秀的教学设计和灵活高效的课堂实施是课程质量的保障，三者缺一不可。

任务：

（1）观察一节录像课，结合课型从新颖性、层次性来评价它的教学设计。

（2）观察一节课，找出支撑它的教学设计的教育、教学理念。

（3）观察一节课，讨论其教学设计中的亮点及有待提高的地方。

（4）下列哪种教案比较适用于新手：书面教案、心理教案、详细教案或者提纲式教案？为什么？

（5）教师为什么要在课堂中做偏离教案的决策？

第二节　教学目标和教学过程

一、教学目标

美国著名的教育家、心理学家布鲁姆指出，有效的教学是让有准备的教学达到一定的目标。目标是一切活动的出发点和归宿，教学要建立以目标为导向、以反馈矫正为核心的目标控制体系。英国语言教学权威吉姆斯克里温纳认为，教学是了解学习的目标并达成它。Teaching means (a) finding out where learning is, and (b) going there。华中师范大学吴伦敦教授认为，一节好课的前提是实现了教学目标。

教学目标要清晰、具体而且具有可操作性。预设的课堂教学目标不再被认为是教学任务完成得好坏的最重要的标志，教学目标的创设要基于文本解读和学情分析。而在制定教学目标方面，比较常见的两个问题是：教学目标宽泛，不具可操作性和可检测性；教学目标模式化，即课的教学目标适用于所有相同的课型。

有人说教学目标有课堂临时生成的目标，笔者并不赞成这个说法。所谓目标，就是计划当中的，它是课堂教学的导向，指引课堂教学去产生结果。如果课堂因某种原因而产生没有预设的结果，那么这种临时生成的东西应该叫生成性结果，而不是本末倒置的生成性目标。

在评课中教学目标是评课者的关注点，例如：

林老师这节课，我个人认为优点是：目标清晰，很好地实现了英语阅读教学的一些基本目标，例如，激发学生的学习兴趣，培养学生的阅读能力，提高阅读的技巧，兼顾了语言知识的学习，也启发了学生的思维。这是第一个优点。（根据案例集光盘转写）

二、教学过程

教学设计的结果是教案和讲稿（PPT），而静态的教案和讲稿始终要变成动态的课堂教学。有人将课堂比作舞台，将一节课的开头比作序幕，结尾比作落幕。序幕要引人入胜，落幕要令人感到意犹未尽。梅因格告诫教师，课堂教学切勿程序化。如果把一节课看作一系列事件所构成的连续体，那么在评价时要注意两个方面：一是活动的目的，如观察教师如何进行语言准确性和流利性的操练；二是观察教师组织教学的手段，即教师掌控课堂的程度和给学生课堂自主的程度。

导入的主要目的是激发学生的学习动机或学习兴趣，引起学生对即将学习的内容的注意，为即将到来的学习做准备。导入的手段要新颖；导入的内容跟主题密切相关；导入要直截了当。导入只是一节课的序幕，不宜过分铺陈。常见的导入方式有画画、用投影仪投出图片、播放一段视频、讲轶事、陈述一个能够引发学生回应的观点，例如，教师说：I think smoking is very good for people，提出能够引发学生回应的问题；例如，教师说Have you ever seen the shooting stars on our campus? 在黑板上的word-cloud中间写上一个词以便引发学生加上相关的词汇，等等。

导入的直击性和关联性一直是评课者的重要关注点。例如，评委1在点评

Mickey Mouse一课时说：

导入环节……你觉得这样做是否有点绕？我也非常重视导入环节，所以每次点评都提到这个问题。如果不说自己叫××，不说你长得像功夫熊猫，就不能引入Mickey Mouse 这个话题吗？教材有个非常好的引入环节，Discuss the following questions with the partner：Do you like to watch cartoon？What is your favorite cartoon？Why do you like it？你觉得这三个问题怎么样？可以用来导入吗？你为什么选择不用它们呢？

在对阅读课Should friends be similar or different？进行点评时，评委1也对导入的有效性进行质疑：

今天导入的这首歌花了两分钟，结果只问一个问题：What is it about？你觉得听两分钟的歌，回答一个问题，你觉得划算不划算？花两分钟时间听一首歌可以，但你要保证学生听到什么，第二要根据听的内容至少设计两三个问题，然后对后面的教学有帮助。如果只是说引入friends这个话题，我觉得这个两分钟用得不太划算。

一直以来教学过程都是评课的重点。除了热身和导入，传统教学模式的教学过程还包括呈现、练习、运用、拓展等课堂环节。而听、说、读、写这四个传统课型都可以用PWP模式（Pre-stage，While-stage，Post-stage）来进行教学。以阅读课为例，阅读课的教学过程有读前、读中和读后三个阶段，每个阶段里面都有具体的活动安排。

在教学过程中，教学方法和教学策略的选择和运用是否恰当也是评课的依据，是重要的着眼点。只要方法和策略选得对、用得对，就能产生好的教学效果。比如，一节口语课运用3P模式或者运用TBLT，可能会产生不同的效果；用全班教学的方式策略或是运用小组合作学习的策略，对学生的口语能力的训练力度也是不同的。又如，写作教学采用成果写作教学法或是过程写作教学法，不但理念不同，侧重点不同，教学过程不同，而且产生的结果也是不相同的。理念先进且符合学生实际需要的教学方法才是有效的方法，因而也是好的方法。

章兼中教授曾经提出英语课堂教学"多信息、快节奏、高密度"的教学原则。这条原则在某种程度上反映了有效教学的要求。一堂好的英语课要让学生吃得饱，所以需要多信息；多信息实现的手段或者条件是课堂节奏相对要快，活动密度也相对要高些。用现在的观点来看，"多信息"不但指输入，也指输出。优质的英语课堂，不但要有大量的输入，也要有大量的输出。相反，输入不足、节奏缓慢、活动稀疏的课谈不上是好课。当然，教学规则都是有其适用情境的，如果对基础比较薄弱的班级或学生，输入、节奏、密度的评价要求是适当，合适的才是最好的。

对教学过程的评价还要看其是否体现科学性、教育性和艺术性。教学的科学性指教授的内容正确，没有偏误。如培根所言，知识就是力量，但不正确的知识就是负力量了，可能会给学生带来危害。教学的科学性是教学的基础和底线，我们不能离开科学性去谈教育性和艺术性。如前所述，教学是有境界之分的，有的教学只是达到教学要求的底线，有的则达到艺术的境界，如在教师语言、教学技能、教学机智等方面已经能够给学生带来美的感受。

任务：

（1）观察一个课段或一个活动，找出它的教学目标。

（2）观察一个教学活动，找出它的教学目标。

（3）观察一节课，评价它的教学目标。

（4）观察一节课，评价它的教学过程的科学性、教育性和艺术性。

第三节　教师的语言及其功能

一、教师语言

教学技能包括教师的语言交际技能。因为教学的主要媒体是言语，因此，有效交流的能力通常被视为一名好教师必备的技能。当夸奖一个人天生是当教师的时候，人们往往不但指该人口头表达能力强，而且还指人在清晰表达、有效表达方面是有能力差异的，有的人能够更好地表达自己。库珀认为，教与学过程的本质是师生之间的有效交际，离开交际，教与学根本不可能发生。

RSA证书项目把教师语言交际技能当作很重要的技能，因此把它当作考核考生的内容，例如：

—— personality，presence，general style

—— voice—audibility，ability to project，modulation

—— voice—speed，clarity，diction

—— ability to establish/maintain rapport

教师在课堂教学中的话语属于教学话语（instructional discourse）。教学话语的功能有这些：讲解；发出指令、宣布规则；引起注意；提问；重复或者重申说过的内容；允许和拒绝学生的要求；发出警告或者给出建议；给出理由或者解释；反馈；布置作业；等等。履行上述功能的语言也叫元语言。教师语言包括作为输入的语言和元语言。在英语课中，教师语言既是教学的媒体，也是目的语语言输入的重要源泉。

在英语课堂教学中，教师的语言在质方面首先要做到清晰、准确、流利。其次是风趣幽默，具有一定的教育性和感染力。在量方面要尽量减少教师话语时间（teacher talk time），教师说得越多，学生开口的机会越少，教师不要用教师语言把课上的每一分钟填满。教师一方面要减少自己说话的时间，另一方面要给学生留白，要留给学生安静思考、策划在课堂上说什么而且怎么说的时间，以便最大程度地发挥学生作为学习主体的作用。

在英语课堂教学中，经常出现教师迫不及待地在学生没说完时帮他们完成句子的现象。这种"加尾巴"的做法不但没有好处，反而会产生反作用（counter-productive）。学生必需自己完成句子，当他们无法自己完成句子时，他们需要的是那些能够让他们用自己的词语和语句去表达自己思想的帮助，而不是有人替他们完成话语。

教师语言能力影响着教学专长的许多方面，包括教学技能和学科知识等，因此，教师的语言能力经常是评课的内容之一。下面的一段全国初中英语课堂教学展示的专家点评就是一个例子：

谢谢美丽的王老师给大家带来一节颜值非常高的课。借用我们教授的一句话，这个"颜值"除了指我们容貌的颜，也是我们语言的言。感觉到王老师的语言能力也非常强。我们本身是一个英语课，是一个语言的课。老师的语言素养也会潜移默化地去带动学生，这是一个潜移默化的培育。（根据案例集光盘转写）

二、教师指令语

教师语言包括教师指令语。教师指令语通常包含几个层面的信息：做什么，如何做，用多少时间做，达成什么结果等。教师指令语要清晰、准确、简洁。教师要确定学生最需要知道的内容，并言简意赅地表达出来。因此，教师指令语不宜太复杂。例如，如果教师想让学生停下某个活动，他可以直截了当地说：Stop now, please!

有时很简单的指令语也未必能让学生明了，因此，教师在给出指令语后要适当检查学生是否明白。要检查学生是否听懂教师指令语不能简单地问 "Do you understand? " "Are you clear? " 或者 "Did I make it clear? "，它们在某种程度上是没用的，因为很多时候学生不明白也会说 "Yes! "，原因可能是：①有些不懂的学生为了保全面子会说懂了；②有的学生不想浪费全班的时间而做出肯定回答；③学生认为自己是懂的但实际上并不懂。因此，教师得到的回应可能是虚假信息。明智的做法是请一两个学生重复教师的话语，例如，问学生 "×××, what are you going to do next? " 或者让学生演示一下，抑或让他们用自己的话语解释一下对教师的话语的理解。这也是一种师生之间的意义磋商，可以使课堂更具交际性。学生可以把这种意义的磋商技巧迁移到真实的交际活动中去。此外，要确保学生能够执行教师的指令，教师也可以就指令语中的"如何做"亲自演示或示范。

T: Well, I'm gonna ask you to get into pairs, but before that there are some things we've gotta work out. So just jot down if you've got a pen, could you write this? Then when we've finished that we're going to do the next thing which involves more...

好的教师指令语具有权威性和力量，教师指令一出，学生就会执行。如果学生不执行教师指令，那么教师就要对指令语进行反思了。

三、教师提问和问题

教师语言包括教师提问。提问是教学中的唤起技巧，是典型的课堂话语结构IRF（Initiation—Response—Feedback）的一个部分。乌尔指出，作为语言教师，提问的目的是促使学生使用语言积极参与课堂语言材料的学习。因此，有效提问技巧是能够引发即时的、相关的、能够驱动学生的、完整而充分的答案。乌尔提出有效提问的几个标准：

（1）清晰：学习者能否立刻理解问题的意义，并且知道需要什么样的答案？

（2）有学习价值：引发的思考及答案能否对进一步的学习目标有贡献？抑或问题只是用来填塞时间、跟学习无关或者没有用处？

（3）有趣：是否有趣、具有挑战性、能刺激学生？

（4）具有可及性：是否是全班大多数学生都能回答的问题？还是只有那些成绩好、自信、知识面广的学生才能够回答的问题？

（5）拓展性：问题能否引起拓展或引发不同的答案？

（6）教师反应：学生的回答是否受到尊重？当学生做出不太确切的回答时是否受到教师的奚落或嘲笑？

教师提问的载体是问题。辛克莱和库尔特哈德认为，问题是课堂话语中最常见的话语类型。英语课堂上的问题有许多功能，如教师检查学生的学习情况、设置学习任务、启迪学生思维、组织和推进课堂教学活动等。

从不同角度分，问题可以有不同的种类：

肯定与否定问题（Yes/No questions）：即只需用yes或者no来作答的问题，这种问题一般没有太大的思维空间。如果需要激发学生进一步思考，教师可以在后面加上why问题。

开放性问题（Open-ended questions）：即没有固定答案的问题，这种问题有助于培养学生思维的发散性和创新性。

展示性问题（Display questions）：展示性问题不是真问题，而是为了引出某一语言结构或句型而问的问题。这种类型的问题没有涉及真正的信息交换。韦津利则认为，展示性问题是需要回答者用已有信息作答的问题，有助于培养学生对知识的识记和再认能力。在阅读课中那些能在文本中找到答案的问题也属于展示性问题。

参阅性问题（Referential questions）：即没有预设答案的问题或者是需要用新信息来作答的问题，此类问题被认为是真问题。朗认为，教师应该多问参阅性问题。

非回忆性问题和想象性问题：指不需要找寻已有信息而通过推断、给出建议或判断而能回答的问题，如：What do you think the author implies？

在英语课堂上，教师构设问题需要考虑下列的因素：学生、年龄语言水平、认知水平和课型等。一般来说，学生的年龄和他们的语言水平及认知水平密切相关。学生的语言水平决定了他们是否能够理解教师提出的问题，这是做出正确回答的前提。认知水平是会影响学生回答问题的能力的另外一个因素，如果学生的认知水平低，就难以回答需要高级思维关于语言水平的问题，教师尽量避免在面向语言初始学习者的问题中使用大词复杂的语言结构。在认知负担方面既要考虑所提问题的功能，也要考虑问题所涉及的认知层次，即问题是检查学习者对所学知识的记忆、理解、应用、分析、评价还是创造。

课型也部分决定了问题类型。在阅读课中，教师一般会设计三个层次的问题：

（1）能够在原文中找到答案的问题，也叫事实性问题，其对应的阅读层次是read the lines。例如：What is this story about? / What does his mum say? 等。

（2）经过推断才能找到答案的问题，对应的阅读层次是read between the lines。例如：What is the intention/attitude of the author?

（3）超越文本的问题，对应的层次是read beyond the lines。例如：What do you think of...?

此外，影响问题类型的还有课的阶段。在一节课的不同阶段教师所提问题的性质也是各不相同的。

有效提问需要技巧。不同类型的问题有不同的功能，教师要尽量做到提问能够启迪思维，激发学生的学习兴趣和动机，从而提高课堂教学的效果，有助于英语学科核心素养的培养，即通过提问，能够有效提高学生的语言能力、语言学习能力、文化意识和思维品质。在外语课中，教师要善于运用问题来帮助学生培养思维品质和思维能力，如思维的逻辑性、批判性、创新性以及发散思维能力、批判性思维能力和创新思维能力等。

有经验的教师善于运用问题来组织教学及推进课堂的发展。在很多英语优质课中，教师在熟悉教材的基础上把教学内容转化成为一个又一个的问题，即形成问题链。这些问题环环相扣，能够引起学生的有意注意和积极思考，而回答问题的过程就是学生学习的过程。教师在教学时或指定学生回答，或者让学生自荐回答，形成比较好的课堂参与状态和思维状态。这样的教学方式不但增加了师生互动，也培养了学生的问题意识。

教师在等待学生回答时应给他们留足思考时间。不少教师为了赶进度或避免冷场，在提问后迫不及待地收回回答问题的机会，这是不利于培养学生的积极学习情感的，因而是不利于语言学习的。

此外，值得一提的是，在全英教学的课堂中，我们发现教师提问的能力尤其是追问的能力受到教师的口语能力的限制。有的英语教师虽然有追问的意识，但不敢在课堂上追问就是因为其语言能力不能支撑其追问的需要，因此没能引发更多的课堂生成，也没能通过追问推动课堂教学向纵深发展。有效的提问，不但取决于问题提出的方式，也取决于教师的口语能力。

四、教师反馈

教师语言包括教师反馈语。教师反馈语是教师对学生的语言产出做出的反应。语言产出至少应该涵盖两个方面的内容：产出的内容和产出的语言。也就是说，教师的反馈可能针对学生产出的内容，也可能是针对产出的语言。实质上，教师反馈也是一种教学评价，即教师对学生的学习行为的评价。针对语言的准确性的反馈对检验假设及发展隐性语言知识是不可或缺的。学生通过教师的反馈来检验自己关于语言及语言使用的假设是否成立，如果假设不成立，学生会做调整，并构建新的假设。目前，教师资格证考试中面试部分把考生在上课时是否有教学评价当作一个评分点。

教师在课堂教学的一个重要作用是给学生提供反馈。反馈是课堂教学的价值之一，反馈是学生学习取得进步的源泉。没有教师的反馈，学习者难以改进自己的学习，也不能有效评估自己的学习的效果。

反馈语可分为肯定反馈语、中性反馈语和否定反馈语。肯定反馈语如"Perfect！""Wonderful！""You did a good job！"等表达了教师肯定的态度，一般来说对学生具有鼓励作用。中性反馈语不对学生的语言行为或答案做出价值判断，教师用"Uhuh！""Mhm！"等表示教师在倾听学生说话，但不表明自己的态度。而否定反馈语如"I don't agree！""I don't think so！"等表达了教师的不认可。否定反馈语被认为会削弱学生的学习动机。

然而，布朗认为，反馈不只是为了鼓励，空洞的、不假思索的鼓励常常是无用的。例如，有的教师会习惯性地说"Good！"或者"Excellent！"，甚至对于很一般的语言行为都用上这样的评价语。实际上，对一些学生来说，这些评价语根本起不到鼓励的作用，他们更想听的是"Good！I think your answer is better than mine because you used a sentence！"真诚的、有效的反馈语最好既包含评价语也包含信息内容，这些信息内容可以是"好"或"不好"的理据，也可以是改进的方向，而这种反馈语则被称为信息型反馈语。换言之，在反馈环节教师最好能够对学生的语言产出提供信息型反馈。

教师反馈语具有三种价值：动机、认知和语言。正面的反馈或评价能够激发学生的学习动机，而负面反馈则可能降低学习动机，这就是反馈的动机价值，也即情感价值。反馈的认知价值指通过教师的反馈，学生明白对错。这是反馈的认知价值。如果学生的语言产出是对的，甚至很精彩，那么教师有时会指出"对"和"精彩"的理由。如果是错的，教师则会指出正确的说法，这就是反馈的语言价值，即通过教师反馈，学生在语言方面可能取得进步。因此，教师反馈至少应该包含教师对学生语言行为或结果做出基本的价值、态度判断：对或错，认可或否定。然后在条件允许的情况下提供进一步的信息：为什么是错的，需要如何改进等。

扎梅尔提出，具有下列情形的反馈是最有效的反馈：当反馈指出产出语言的关键特征；当反馈提供的信息能够让学生自己发现语言的规则和原理；当反馈能够降低学生选择的多种可能性。扎梅尔的有效反馈直指反馈要有针对性和直击性，好的反馈能够清晰、准确地传递教师的态度和意图。

理想的反馈范式应该包含四个组成部分：教师提问+学生回答+教师反馈+学生回应教师反馈，即teacher question + student response + teacher feedback + student response to feedback（下称TQ+SR+TF+SRF模式）。而实际教学中，由于课堂时间压力或者教师未能认识到学生需要把教师的反馈结合到自己答案中的重要性，一般都会略去学生回应教师反馈这个部分。因此，部分学生未能通过教师的反馈习得语言的正确用法，未能很好地内化教师的反馈并发展自己的语言能力。这说明了为什么有的学生这次错了下次也犯同样的错误。如果学生没有内化教师反馈语中的信息，那么就是我们通常所说的学习没有真正发生。任务型教学的新的教学模式就是在post task阶段，即language focus之后加上一个task repetition的环节，让学生把做过的任务再做一次，其主要目的就是让学生有机会把教师的反馈结合到重做的任务中来，把任务做得更好，以期学习真正发生。总之，TQ+SR+TF+SRF反馈模式不是教师在唱独角戏，而是把学生也引入反馈活动中，充分发挥了学生学习的自主性。这对学生的影响是深远的，习惯这个反馈模式的学生，将意识到重构自己话语和答案的重要性，真正做到从反馈中学习。这个反馈模式在写作教学中的运用是：学生写作——→教师反馈——→学生重写——→教师反馈。

在课堂观摩中，我们发现有的教师在反馈环节只是大声重复（echo）学生的答案，而没有做出自己的判断或表明自己的立场。这样的反馈属于零反馈。那么，这种echoing有没有教育价值呢？有几种情况中的echoing是有作用的：①当学生的答案有问题时，教师用升调重复学生的答案，暗示教师对学生的回答有疑问或不认可；②当学生的回答不够响亮或者语音较差时，教师为了全班学生能够听清楚答案而重复；③当教师认为这个话语很重要，重复能够起到强化的作用。而如果教师对学生的每个答案都重复的话，那就不是优质的反馈了。这种行为可能跟教师的教学理念有关系，也可能是教师的下意识的行为。总之，如果教师在课堂上经常重复学生的答案，这种echoing在很大程度上是在浪费宝贵的教学时间。另外，那些已习惯于接受有态度和价值判断的教师反馈语的学生可能会感到不满意或失望。韦津利认为，教师仅仅重复学生的话语，而不对其做出任何回应，不仅不能推进师生之间的交流，反而使交流进入死胡同。

如果教师非要重复学生答案，那么可以在重复学生话语时，采用部分省略或改变语调等方式，会引发学生的思考，引导学生进行自我纠正。

如上所述，反馈既针对学生产出的语言本身，如语言是否准确、得体、适切等；反馈也针对所表达内容，如教师是否认可学生回答问题的内容等，如有的教师说："I can't agree with you more！"优秀教师在进行反馈时能够自成风格，有的简洁严谨，有的机智、幽默，有的严肃守正，有的宽容大度。教师的反馈风格跟他的语言学习观、个人性格和教学风格密切相关。

有的教师视反馈为鸡肋，把反馈看成是对答案，而对答案是很枯燥乏味的事。然而，教师反馈绝不仅仅是对答案，对答案可以变成反馈讨论会。现在练习的答案不仅仅掌握在教师的手中，学生也会有答案。在信息时代，提供答案的事也可以由智能平台来做。教师只负责平台或机器做不了的事情。

任务：

（1）观察一个课段或一个教学环节，看看学生活动结束后教师是否有反馈。

（2）观察一节课，找出教师在不同教学环节的反馈模式和特点。

（3）观察一节课，看看教师的反馈是否存在重复学生答案的现象。

（4）观察一节优质课，看看教师使用反馈模式是否是TQ+SR+TF+SRF模式。

五、课堂纠错

如果学生的语言产出有不妥之处，那么教师反馈会涉及示错和纠错。错误也叫偏误，是学生中介语中的存在的现象。如何对待学生的语言错误反映了教师的语言学习观。能够宽容学生语言错误的教师认为语言学习是一个不断试错的学习过程，因此，鼓励学生在课堂上敢于冒险进行语言练习和语言运用的尝试。纠错过多会打击学生学习的积极性，所以对学生的语言错误必须区别对待，有选择性地纠错。

在口语活动中，当语言练习的目的是发展语言的准确性时，那么可以立即纠正学生的错误。而在以培养学生语言的流利性为目的的活动中，教师一般不在活动中纠正学生的错误。教师会在活动结束后指出重要的、严重的语言错误，并让学生自行改正。

为了保护学生的学习动机，教师一般不会直接说 "You're wrong! You made a mistake! You should say...!" 之类的话语，而是用语调重复错误处或者提示等方式示错并让学生自行改错，或者通过教师重构正确话语的方式来改错。在下面的两个师生对话片段中，片段1就是教师示错、学生改错，而片段2则是教师重构话语。

片段1：

T：They have no chair to sit down with or there was a broken chair?

S：There was.

片段2：

S：They buy a big lamp.

T：They bought a big lamp and...

教师对待错误的策略：策略地示错，有选择地纠错。最好的对待错误的方式是教师示错，同伴改错或者学生自我改错。注意学生说出正确话语时，究竟是仅仅重复了正确的话语，还是在头脑中进行了重新加工，还要注意教师在纠错时是只顾语言形式，还是也注意到学生所表达的意义或概念。

针对纠错问题，如果是教师纠错，人们担心的是学生能否把教师的改错结合进自己已有的知识体系，并内化成其自身的能力。这个担心不是毫无道理的，因为有些知识点教师在改错时多次重复，但学生在下次的语言产出还是会犯同样的错误。从这个角度来看，先引起学生对语言错误的注意，然后让其自行改错的做法更有助于学生内化语言知识和发展语言能力。

六、教师启发

在英语课堂上，经常是教师提出问题，然后学生回答问题。而当教师意识到问题较难回答时，就会犹豫是直接告知答案还是进行一番启发。教师可能在学生回答问题前或者回答问题中给学生以启发。那么如何启发呢？比如，提供提示（prompts）。在2018年全国小学英语课堂教学展示课中，钟秀清老师在举例说明她对所住宾馆的评价后问学生她评价的是什么，为了帮助学生回答问题，她给出了提示：是在评价淘宝还是城市？

I stay in Jiangwan Hotel these days. It's a wonderful stay. And the house-keepers there are very helpful and nice. They help us clean the room and make the bed. What about this comment? What was the comment on? On Taobao? On a city? What's the comment on?

接着钟老师问学生顾客对管家Ms. Bloom的评价如何，同样也给了提示：好评还是差评？And that's the housekeeper. She's Ms. Bloom. How was the comment? Good or bad?

通过提示，可以让学生明确思考问题和回答问题的方向，增强了他们回答问题的信心，从而提高他们参与课堂的热情。

第四节　教师的学科知识及能力

理查兹认为，外语教师的学科知识包括以下这些方面：语音、句法、二语习得、课程与大纲设置、话语分析、社会语言学、TESOL方法分析以及测试和评估，等等。教师的学科知识是形成教师思考和决策能力的基础。

一、教师的英语语言知识和能力

教师的英语语言知识包括语音知识、语法知识、词汇知识等。教师的英语语言能力指的是其听说读写译的能力。语言能力不足会影响语言教学的技能，比如，语言能力差的教师很难进行有效提问或者为学生提供可以理解的解释。

大量的课堂观摩告诉我们，优质课的教师通常都有共同的特征：英语语音、语调佳，口语流利且有感染力。在国家级的英语课堂教学展示中，英语语音带有地方口音的授课教师绝少，这说明经过层层选拔最后能代表各省进入课堂展示的教师的语音能力都是比较高的，而且整体的口语能力也相对较高。

二、教师二语习得的理论知识

克拉申提出五个理论：①习得/学习理论；②输入理论；③监察模式；④情感过滤假设；⑤自然顺序。其中，可以用于评课的主要用输入理论和情感过滤假设。输入理论可以从量和质的角度来评价教材和教师语言。例如，教材的内容应该是可以理解的，同时也要尽可能地满足其语言水平要略高于学生现有语言水平的要求；教材要有趣，要跟学生学习和生活相关；输入要有足够的量，等等。情感过滤假设在某种程度上解释了为什么同一教师、同一教材和相同的教学活动教出来的学生语言能力是不同的。因为情感因素是有个体差异的，因此它们在某种程度上导致学习结果的不同。

输入——互动——输出模式。这个模式带给我们的启迪是教师在教学设计时要考虑如何对学生进行输入，如何提供互动的机会，如何组织学生的产出活动。

信息加工模式。由下而上模式，自上而下模式，以及互动模式是听力教学和阅读教学中常用的三个信息加工模式，是我们用以组织输入性教学活动的原理，也是我们用于评价听力活动设计和阅读活动设计是否科学、合理的依据。

社会文化理论。以维果茨基为代表的社会文化理论认为，社会语言经历孕育着语言习得的起源；学习在社会中发生；学习者的发展根植于环境而不是学习者个人。维果茨基提出了最近发展区的概念，最近发展区指的是学习者目前在他人帮助下完成任务的能力和学习者当下独立完成任务的能力之间的距离或空间。另一位学者布鲁纳提出了"手脚架"的概念，指来自教师或有经验的同伴的帮助或支持。社会文化理论和外语合作学习理论为小组学习、团队学习提供了理论支撑，也是我们评课时常用的理据。

三、文本分析能力

文本分析又称语篇分析。语篇是英语教学的基础文本和学习资源，狭义的文本分析，就是对语篇意义的解读。文本解读的目的在于把握主题意义，挖掘文化价值，确定合理语境，梳理结构化知识，并通过分析文体特征及语言特点，发现其与主题意义的关联，从而确定教学的重点。

分析语篇要基于对语篇的研读。研读语篇就是对语篇的主题、内容、文体结构、语言特点、作者观点等进行深入的解读。处理语篇时可以问这三个问题：① what问题：语篇的主题和内容是什么？② why问题：语篇的深层意义是什么？即作者或说话人的意图、情感态度或价值取向是什么？③ how问题：语篇具有什么样的文体特征、内容结构和语言特点？作者为了恰当表达主题意义选择了什么样的文体形式、语篇结构和修辞手段？

why和how的问题通常没有统一的答案，对语篇深层意义和问题结构的解读更多取决于教师的教育背景、生活阅历、认知方式，以及教师在与语篇互动的过程中所表现出来的分析和探究能力。因此，每个人都可能会给出不同的解读和阐释。

如何在研读语篇的what、why、how的基础上对语篇进一步研读？2017年版《课标》提出，可以关注语篇的选材出处和发表时间，分析作者或说话人的立场、观点和写作或表述风格，以及特定时期的语言特点和时代印记等。研读语篇可以帮助教师多层次、多角度分析语篇所传递的意义，依据语篇的主题意义、文体风格、语言特点和价值取向，设计合理的教学活动，同时利用作者视角、写作背景和时间等信息，帮助学生深刻理解语篇，把语言学习和意义探究融为一体，实现深度学习。深度解读语篇有助于教师设计高阶思维的问题，从而开展有深度的教学，摆脱外语教学浅表化和低智能的诟病。换言之，深度教学有赖于教师对文本的深入解读。

对于教材中的情意目标，戈向红认为，教师们大都能够从人物情态、文本情趣、话题情缘三个纬度剖析、整理、解读教材的情感内涵，从而使教材充满亲和力，让课堂富有感染力，让学习富有吸引力。这说明教师的文本能力在不断提升。

王蕾认为，教师对文本解读水平决定了有效的教学设计；一位教师如何分析语篇，就会产生相应的教学设计。文本解读能力高的教师在教学设计时具有优势，能快速抓住文本的主要特征，围绕文本的主题意义设计活动和开展教学。本书评课案例中The Olympic Games就是一节体现教师具有较高文本解读能力的阅读课。有效的教学设计，能增加学生的学习体验程度、认知发展维度、情感参与深度以及学习成效的高度。教师一般会在教案中简单进行教材分析，因此，我们只能通过教学设计、教学过程、教学效果去反推授课教师对文本的解读是否到位。例如，从活动设计缺乏内在逻辑和关联，教师没有对内在知识结构进行提炼和整合可以看出教师对文本的解读深度不足。从缺少育人价值我们反推，有的教师只把文本理解成语言知识和语言技能学习的载体等。

文本分析发生于教师备课环节并体现在教师的教学设计中，在授课时我们观察到的是教师文本的结果——基于文本分析的教材处理和教学活动设计。

目前，在评课环节，文本分析和文本处理已经进入观课者和评课者的视野。2018年12月，在厦门举行的小学英语课堂教学展示中，西南师大杨晓钰教授就着重从文本分析和文本处理的角度来评钟秀清老师的Guest Comments一课。下面是杨晓钰教授的点评。

1. 关于文本的处理方式。这节课是Read and Write.。一般有三种方式来处理文本。① Read，通过阅读去了解文本的大意、信息以及作者的意图。然后有个微输出，也就是写的部分只是一些句型，这也是教材有时候的活动；②帮助学生找结构以及语言点，然后进行仿写；③在阅读以后，能够理解文章的大意，作者的意图，然后根据这篇文章进行评价。那么今天这节课用了第二种模式。老师先通过具体案例讲解结构，再进行仿写。

2. 文本本身的处理方式，根据文本特征来做，大家可以看到，第一个重要的几个点，一个是opinion，第一句话一定要点出opinion；第二个一定要给出facts，这个bad为什么是bad你要给我理由。所以说，批评思维不是随便说好或者不好，而是要用事实说话。所以才会有后面的仿写，要给good or bad，一定要在前面的框架提取opinion到facts，到最后我们才说I'm sorry that...给出一些理由。大家看，文本特征有几个东西。一个是but的使用，有很多个but。这个课上不但要阅读，还要看文本特征。孩子只有知道文本特征才能做最后的输出。

3. 几种形式的comment。如家具，那个鱼骨是一个颜色，如果分不同颜色，就能知道它的分类。我们在评价的时候，要么就涉及家具的问题，食物的问题，环境的问题。所以将来学生要投诉什么，会分类进行，不是直接从课本提取信息就行的。另外，可以从人物的角度，从不同的角度，深度地解读。这个课的目标还是很清晰的，真正地做到实现核心素养的要求。看它的语言能力。其实语言能力包括对语篇的理解，文本的解读，还有其他的，如理解的能力。孩子能够读，能够找到框架，然后基于框架去写作。这是非常不错的。大意理解，细节理解以至于对整个语篇的理解。（据案例集光盘转写）

文本解读包括对非连续性文本（下称非连文本）的解读。非连文本又称"间断性文本"，是指由逻辑、语感不严密的段落层次构成的阅读文本形式。非连续性文本来自国际PISA阅读素养测试项目。学会从非连续文本中获取我们所需要的信息，得出有意义的结论，是现代公民应具有的阅读能力。

非连文本的表现形式。非连文本作为文本的一种类型，它既有文本的基本共性，但在语言和结构的组合上又区别于其他文本形式。非连文本在生活中十分常见，一般包括图表、目录、说明书、广告、地图、索引、凭证单、清单、时刻表、宣传标语、对联、短信、网络跟帖、建议、辩论词、颁奖词、演讲词、开场白、结束语、串联词、推荐语等。

非连文本的特点。非连续性文本在结构和语言上不具有完整的故事性，但是它比叙事性文本更能够直观地表达文本要传递的基本信息，具有概括性强、醒目、简洁等特点。非连续性文本能够简洁系统地呈现文本的关键信息，其阅读具有短、简、快的特点，能够大大缩减读者的时间，提高阅读的效率。非连续性文本主要是为了客观说明某一事物或事件。由于作者不加上自己的感情色彩和思维方式，读者在阅读的过程中只需根据自己的需要和判断，就能很方便寻找出有价值的信息。

非连续性文本的教学还需要得到国内语言教学界更多的重视。在国外，这方面早就引起了重视，外国的小学生在教师的指导下学会了看地图、阅读说明书等。在《英语课程标准》（2017年版）的语篇类型的内容要求部分，出现了产品介绍、宣传册、目录与指南、表格与图示、讲座、博客、广告等非连文本形式，但它们没有被明确地定位为非连文本，只是在语篇类型的教学提示部分，出现了一段含有非连续性文本的表述：

不同的语篇类型为学生接触社会中丰富的语篇形式提供了机会，也为及时组织多样的课堂活动提供了素材。教师和教材编写者在选择语篇时，应注意长短适中、由易到难，尽量涵盖实际生活中各种类型的语篇，包括多模态语篇。此外，还应注意文学性和非文学性语篇的合理比例，在确保选择一定比例的文学性语篇的同时，注意为学生提供体验非连续性文本的机会，提高他们对非连续性文本的能力。语篇的选择还需要考虑该语篇在促进学生思维、体现文化差异、形成正确价值观等方面的积极意义，使学生一方面能够接触到真实、多样的语篇材料和语篇形式，以便更好地适应未来学习、工作和娱乐。另一方面，通过学习语篇所承载的文化和价值观等具有深刻内涵的内容，使学生学会欣赏语言和多模态语篇的意义和美感，丰富生活经历，体验不同情感，树立正确的世界观、人生观和价值观。

虽然，2017版《英语课标》已经明确提出要提高学生对非连文本的解读能力，但非连文本的教学还没有系统地展开，英语非连续性文本的教学和研究还没有得到应有的重视。2019年上半年高中学科教师资格考试面试试讲题目中，开始出现"非连文本"的教学策略了。

一节好课，不但体现在教师有先进的教学理念、高超的教学设计和教学实施能力，而且体现教师有较高的学科知识素养。因此，教师的学科知识素养也是评课的内容之一。笔者认为，上好一节英语课，教师的学科知识素养起着至关重要的作用，学科知识素养是决定课的科学性和深度的关键因素。

第五节　学生的学习

一、学生的学习

"让学习真正发生，让思维真正发生"是当下基础教育界的流行语。为什么要倡导"让学习真正发生"呢？它是针对课堂上假学现象提出的。假学是指表面上看课堂热热闹闹，一派生机勃勃，其实学生没有学到东西。其实质是教师的教没有促成学生的学。

学生是学习的主人，教师是促学因素，是学生学习的激发者和提供便利者。传统的学习主要指学生向教师的学习，而现在的学校教育也倡导学生向同伴学习，但如威多森所言，学习者作为学习资源的集体潜势还没有被利用。为了实现学生作为学习资源的潜势，我们在课堂里要多组织和开展小组学习。当然，在全班活动中学生也可以互学。在东莞松山湖学校韩松锦老师的Why Don't You Talk to Your Parents课上，出现了很明显的学生互学的证据和效果。请看下面三个片段：

片段1：

S1：I am Mary.

S2：I am her mum.

S1：May I have a talk with you?

S2：Of course.

S1：Mm，I don't want to go to a after-school class.

S2：Why?

S1：I don't want to go！I want to do sports on weekend！

S2：Do sports on workday.

S1：I think it's very tired to do sports on weekday. I need more time to have a rest. And I want to get up late in the morning on the weekends.

S2：Getting up early is good for your health，you know！

S1：I promise I will study hard and get better marks. And I want to go to cinema or park with my friends on weekend.

S2：Listen！After-school classes can improve your study.

S1：But study is not the only thing in my life.

S2：OK，OK，I agree with you. But you should promise you keep a good mark.

S1：OK. Thank you！

片段2：

T：So they tell us many reasons. Please remember one sentence she said：study is not the only thing in your life，right？OK，now let's welcome the next group. Come here.

片段3：

S3：Mary，come here.

S4：OK，Dad！What's wrong?

S3：Could you tell me why you failed in the exam again？Tell me why?

S4：I...

S3：I am very angry with you!

S4：OK.

S3：I am very worried about your study! I am worrying about your future!

S4：Fine，Dad!

S3：I think you must ...

S4：Oh，Dad! Calm down! Calm down! As you know our students must get up early in the morning. And we have too much homework，so don't angry with me. Please!

S3：But I think you，you must go to the after-school class.

S4：So tired!

S3：This is，this is...

S4：What can I say?

S3：Reason! You need a reason.

S4：You know，as my classmates said，after-school classes is not the only thing in my life. You know，I promise you I'll get up early in the morning at first. And I'll get good grades in my next exam. I promise you，my dear Papa.

在片段1中，学生在小组角色扮演活动后派代表到课室前面进行展示，学生1扮演Mary，学生2扮演Mum。Mary的妈妈要她去参加课外补习班，Mary说她不去。而妈妈认为课外班有助于提高学习成绩，Mary回应她妈妈说：But study is not the only thing in my life（学习并不是生活中唯一的事情）。

在片段2中，授课教师韩老师在给学生反馈时说：Please remember one sentence she said：study is not the only thing in your life，right? 教师的反馈肯定了上面学生的观点：学习并不是生活中唯一的事情。教师的这个反馈语对全班学生来说有着提高意识的作用，把全班的注意力集中到同学的精彩语言上。

到了片段3，一对男生也到前面来扮演Mary和她的Dad，任务跟前面的学生一样。Mary的爸爸要她上课外补习班，Mary不愿意去，可是她爸爸认为她必须去，不去要给个理由。这时候Mary学以致用，说：You know，as as my classmates say，after-school classes is not the only thing in my life（您知道啦！就像我那位同学刚才说的，学习并不是我们生活里的唯一事情）。这个时候，全班响起了热烈的掌声，大家都为这个学生机智精彩的回应喝彩。显然，这个学生能够把从同伴那里学来的话语应用到自己的说理当中，这是课堂的一个生成，这个生成正是学习真正发生的证明。

那么，教师如何了解学习真正在发生或者学习已经发生了呢？教师需要发展能够监测学习是否发生的策略。真正的学习是从问题开始的，教师经常采用的学习检查手段是提问。在观察教师检查学习的微技能时，我们可以借鉴表5-2的问题。

表5-2　教师检查以及学生回应的相关问题

Question 1	Question 2	Question 3	Question 4	Question 5	Question 6
How does the teacher check?	What does the teacher check?	Why does the teacher check?	How does the student respond?	What follow-up is there?	What did the learning check achieve?

（根据韦津利表格改编）

另一个手段是通过任务完成过程及结果对学生的语言行为和学习情感等进行评估。

英语课堂上的学习包括语言能力的学习、学习能力的学习、文化意识的学习、思维能力的学习。真学习就意味着学生语言知识和能力得到增长；学生学习能力得到提高；学生文化意识得到加强；思维品质和思维能力得到改善和提高。

当我们评一节英语课学生的学习时，我们可以把着眼点放在学生的学习素养、学习过程、学习能力以及学习结果上。学习素养包括态度、习惯、积极性等。学习过程包括感知知识、接受知识、建构知识和内化知识等过程。学习能力包括学习策略。学习结果包括语言结果和非语言结果。

二、优秀外语学习者的特征

埃利斯试图描述怎样的学习者是好的学习者。埃利斯认为，好的语言学习者有以下特征：

（1）能够适应小组学习机制，在小组学习中不会感到焦虑和压抑。

（2）寻找一切能够运用目的语的机会。

（3）利用一切机会聆听目的语或用目的语回应听到的话语，不管这话语是否是对自己说的，这个时候学习者关注的是语言的意义而不是形式。

（4）通过跟目的语使用者直接接触学到东西，这个时候学习者关注的可能是语言的形式。

（5）在学习语法的初期，成人或者青少年学习者要比幼儿适合学语法。

（6）具有足够的分析能力，能够感知目的语的特征，对它们进行分类和储存并且能够监察语言错误。

（7）做好冒险进行语言尝试的准备，即使这种尝试会使自己出丑。

（8）具有强烈的学习目的语的理由。

（9）能够适应各种不同的学习环境。

在评课时我们常常会提到学生的素质和能力，这些素质和能力在某些意义上说明了他们是否是好的英语学习者。从以学评教的角度来看，如果一节课涌现了一批优秀的学习者，或者该课大部分学生具有上述优秀外语学习者的若干特征，那么这节课很可能就是一节优质课了。因为在这样的课堂上，教师成功地营造了让学生感到安全而敢于冒险进行语言尝试的学习环境，成功地设计了能够激发他们学习动机的学习任务和合作学习机制。所以，我们在评课时可以把落脚点放在考察学习者的学习品质上。

三、学习者的学习动机

二语习得研究表明，动机是影响习得结果的因素之一；最成功的学习者是那些既有语言学习天赋又有高水平的学习动机的学习者。在外语学习中，学习动机影响语言学习的效果。在各种路径的二语习得研究中，只有认知法认为动机在语言学习中不起重要作用。

不同的角度，学习动机可以有不同的分类；从动机的来源来分，动机可以分为内在动机和外在动机；从动机的用途来分，动机可分为工具型动机和综合型动机等。内在动机跟学习者的兴趣、需要有关；外在动机跟外部因素有关，如与家长、教师和同伴的期望和激励有关。外语工具型学习动机指学习者因为语言的实用性而产生的学习需要。简单来说，持工具型动机的学习者学习外语是因为外语能够派上用途。综合型动机指为了增进对目的语文化的理解及认同、跟目的语国家人士交流及联系，或者融入目的语文化而产生的学习需要。就工具性动机和综合性动机而言，现在的外语学习者兼有这两种类型的学习动机。也就是说，大多数的学习者不再只支持有一种动机。布朗还把动机分为整体动机、情景动机以及任务动机。其中，总体动机对应于加德纳和兰伯特提出的综合型动机，它跟学习者对学习目标的总体定位有关；情景动机跟学习情境有关，比如课室环境还是自然环境；任务动机跟完成某个任务有关。

动机水平越高，学生对学习的投入程度越高。动机水平影响学习者的预期角色。具有高水平学习动机的学习者更容易跟教师角色进行协同，更可能在各种学习过程中跟教师同步和合作。学习动机跟学习兴趣一样，不是静止不动的。相反它是动态的，有一定的波动性。德尔涅伊和麦金太尔等把对动机的研究放在动态系统论（DST）的框架之下。学习者个体的学习动机、一个班组的学习动机，乃至整个社会的学习动机都会发生变化。虽然说学生在一节课的动机相对来说是稳定的，但教师要有动机变动的意识。日积月累，一节课的学习动机也会对后续的学习造成影响，教师要以课为单位激发或保持学生的学习动机。

动机是否可以观测？动机跟态度和语言熟练程度一样，是构念，而构念是看不到的典型特质，不能直接被观察到。但是，我们在评课时会说在这位老师的课堂上，学生学习动机很高，学生积极参与互动，学生主动向教师提问，等等。那么，我们从何知道学生动机的强弱呢？实际上，我们是通过学生的外在表现来推知学生动机水平的高低的。学习动机经常表现在以下的学生课堂行为中：学生回应教师的积极性、参与任务的热情、遇到不确定事情时发问的意愿以及对其他学生的容忍度等。

如何提高学生的学习动机是我们观课后需要反思的问题之一。在外语课堂教学中如何培养、激发或者提高学生的学习动机呢？首先，学习动机跟学习者的目标有关，因此教师要引导学生去建立自己的目标。其次，学习动机跟学习者的个人需要、兴趣或者外部期望有关。教师要从激发兴趣入手，针对学习者的需要开展教学活动，并采取以表扬、激励为主的反馈方式，激发或维持学生高水平动机。此外，有些学者认为学习动机的变化跟学习者所处的具体情境和所从事的活动有关；有学者认为学习动机主要来自交际本身，来自交际的成功；学习者表达自己的需要和成功表达的喜悦驱动了二语习得，因此，教师要利用各种手段创设有利的学习情境，精心设计跟学生的学习和生活密切相关的，对他们来说有一定挑战性的学习任务，这样既可以促进语言能力的发展又能让他们体验成功的喜悦，从而产生学习的内在动机。

例如，在第八届全国小学英语课堂教学展示课中，王红老师授课的课题Life in the Future。在该课的最后一个环节，王老师设置了一个Talk Show活动。

在展示时，学生的表现充满想象力和创造力，请看下面的片段。

S1：I hope the dinosaur will come back and will be my pet. I will play with them. I think they are cute and lovely.

S2：I don't agree with you. Maybe the dinosaur will eat you. I think we will fly a spaceship.

T：A spaceship?

S：Yes.

T：Great.

S3：I agree with you. I think we can eat magic pills. If you can eat a magic pill.

T：Pills，oh. So which person would you like to be? Superman or...?

S3：Harry Porter.

T：Harry Porter. Oh，so great. So boys and girls，do you agree with him? You have your opinion. The boy.

S4：I agree with Yang Zeqi.

T：Who?

S4：Er I agree with Yang Zeqi because I like变形金刚. I want to eat 擎天柱pills and I'll be 擎天柱.

T：Wow，that's great. I like your idea very much...

在上面的片段中，第一组上来展示Talk Show的学生对未来有丰富的想象，如第一位学生想象恐龙会重新出现并成为自己的宠物；第二位学生则想开宇宙飞船；第三位学生说想吃神药然后变成哈利·波特；而一位组外的学生主动抓住话题说他想吃擎天柱药然后变成擎天柱。如果没有这个环节，我们就无法了解孩子们关于未来生活的缤纷的想象。因为任务设计得恰到好处，既关联学生的兴趣又具有挑战性，所以在很大程度上能够激发学生动脑想象和开口的动机。

四、思维品质的培养

《英语课程标准》（2017年版）把学习能力和思维品质作为英语学科核心素养的两个成组部分，在学科核心素养的四个构成要素中，它们属于并列的关系。华南师大吴颖民教授认为，学习能力的核心是思维能力。思维能力是减负增效的关键。思维能力包括逻辑思维能力、批判思维能力、想象力、创造力等。相比于知识，思维能力尤其是创造力更具价值。

《英语课标》指出，思维品质指思维在逻辑性、批判性、创新性等方面所表现出的能力和水平。思维品质的发展有助于提升学生分析问题和解决问题的能力，使他们能够从跨文化视角观察和认识世界，对事物做出正确的价值判断。

英语课堂教学深受低智能的诟病，英语课堂一直被贴上思维缺乏症的标签。随着课程改革的深入推进，英语课堂要从传统的低阶思维向高阶思维转化。低阶思维是德国学者赫尔巴特提出来的，低阶思维的特点是重视对知识的理解、记忆和应用等，而高阶思维则倡导分析、综合、评价（批判）、创造、想象。

在英语教学中，培养学生的思维能力有许多途径和方法：①通过问题驱动培养学生的思维能力；②借助各种各样的思维导图培养学生的思维能力；③设计能够调动学生思维的活动；④通过以解决问题为导向的项目驱动培养学生的思维能力；⑤挖掘教材中可以培养学生思维能力的内容；⑥给学生留足思维的空间和时间。

提问能够启迪学生的思维。通过不同层面的问题可以培养学生不同类型的思维能力，问题最好能激发学生高阶思维能力，如why和how引起的问题。另一个需要提醒的是，不是提问越多越好。有的教师在短短的40分钟内向学生提问上百次，平均起来，留给学生思考的时间平均只有2秒。也就是说，教师没有给学生留足思维的时间。那些不加思考就能回答的问题一般都是缺乏思维含量的，而具有较高思维含量的问题往往需要学生去分析、综合、创造，因此需要有足够的等待时间。

第六节　英语课程资源和教材

现在的英语课程资源有两多的特点：多渠道和多模态。以前的课程资源主要是教材，现在的课程资源还包括教材以外的各种学习资料和设施。课程资源既包括纸质资源，也包括其他媒介的资源，如电子教材。

在教育实践中，教材的重要性是不言而喻的。学生在学校80%以上的时间都用在学习教材上。教材论还处于起步的阶段，不同学者对教材的价值和地位有不同的看法。

人们对教材的定位历经了从知识载体到探索平台的转变。首先，教材被视为权威的知识载体。对教师来说，教材的知识体系是权威的，教材所指明或蕴含的教学规范也是必须遵从的，教学就是对教材的讲解。对学生来说，学习就是对教材的掌握，因此，有学者将这种教材观命名为"圣经式的教材观"。而教材作为一种特定的文本，教育性是其所要实现的首要目的。同时，教材还应是价值载体，即承载着社会所倡导的价值观念，但价值具有主观性，这种教材观屏蔽了其他观点和看问题的视角，对激发学习兴趣和培养人的创造性极为不利。郭晓明把教材定位为教师进行教学的材料和工具；石鸥、张学鹏将教材定位为教学资源；孙智昌则认为教科书的本质是教学性；杨启亮也将教材定位为教学使用的材料，是引起某种关系理解、智慧活动的辅助性材料。《课标》则暗示了教材服务于教学的新定位。高得胜认为，教材是学生探索生活世界和文化世界的平台。

教材是一种特殊的教学资源。教材编写要求编写者具有教学思维的技能，即能把内容变成可以有效实施的课程的能力。教材是教学的蓝本，而不是教学的根本。不少教师在使用教材时未能批判性地对待教材，他们过度信任教材和教师用书。教师使用教材进行教学可能会导致教师丧失技能或降低跟教学有关的那部分认知能力，原因是他们把教学看成是合理化和标准化的劳动过程，这里的合理化指教师不用质疑，只跟教材走就行；标准化指教师无需对教材进行个性化、个人化处理。如果教师失去一些必备技能，特别是失去处理教学材料所需的教学思维能力，那么教师的角色就会被弱化、边缘化，最终导致他们沦落为使用教材的技术员。如果让教材为教师做决定，而教师只是充当学生学习教材的管理者，那么这样的教学就是很肤浅的教学。

关于教师如何使用和处理教材，斯图多尔斯基提出：①教师不可以用教材中的话题，但可以用自己的材料来替换或补充教材中的材料；②教师可以采纳教师用书中的教学建议，但可以不用学生用书中的资料。教师可以用其他教材中的材料，或者用其他教材中的材料来作为补充。克拉申的窄式阅读理念在中小学英语课中的运用方法之一就是把主教材之外的其他教材中出现的同一主题的材料用来作为扩展学习，从而取得较好的教学效果。此外，教师还应挖掘教材留白，把留白处作为一个生成点来为学生创造语言语用或者情感体悟场景。

伍德沃德在回顾了教材使用的研究后得出如下结论：教材使用取决于两个因素，教师的经验和教学的主题。经验欠缺的教师使用教材多于经验丰富的教师；学科教师把教材当作学习内容，但不一定按照教材提出的步骤施教；阅读课则会严格地按照教材进行教学。

教材提供的原材料只有进入课堂才能活起来，因此，教材内容需要被加工成一个个的活动。著名的小学英语特级教师朱浦认为教材就像原材料，为了达到预定的教学目标，教师需要对教材进行合理的重构，使教材文本更加丰富，融入自己的想法。教材是"死"的，需要被教师用"活"，而只有10%的教师能把教材用"活"。教师要将作为范例的教材变成自己的教材。

教师和学生也可充当教学资源。在英语课堂上，教师常常利用自己的个人信息、经历等作为教学的出发点和课程资源。这样的资源能够引发学生的学习兴趣，因为学生一般比较关注跟自己老师有关的事物。另外，教师喜欢把跟学生有关的材料当作教学的资源，例如，学生的家庭信息、学生的喜好、学生的照片等都成了英语课堂的教学资源。教科书中出现的人物经常是虚构的李华、韩梅梅、李雷、Robin等，在学生看来，这些人物跟他们毫无关系，因此学起来了无趣味。在第十二届全国初中英语课堂教学展示活动中，东莞松山湖学校的韩松锦老师在Why Don't You Talk to Your Parents一课中使用了自己拍摄的学生与妈妈用英语对话的微视频，来呈现如何运用PFRP原则跟大人磋商事情，产生了很好的效果。

把学生的个人生活、体验、情感等当作教学的资源和内容是人本主义教育观的体现。这样的资源和材料有助于学生的个人发展，能引导学生接纳自己并被他人接纳，从而培养学生对自己和他人的积极情感。

在课堂教学中，虽然教师有完成大纲及教材中教学任务的压力，他们还是希望能够用上以生为本的鲜活的、跟师生密切相关的材料和资源，因为这样的材料和资源更能够激发学生的学习动机。比如，练习现在进行时的用法时，一般教师会去创设能够用上现在进行时的情境，但具有人本主义意识的教师可能会思考如何用上学生及其家人的信息作为课堂语法练习的资源。例如，教师可以这样设计现在进行时语法练习：

1. Ask the class to close their eyes and think about what their family members

are doing now. Ask them questions: What is your mother doing now? Your father? Your sisters? Your brothers? Your aunt? ...

2. Ask them to open their eyes and tell their partner what the different members of their family are probably doing at that time.

优质课的课程资源往往是由授课教师及其团队精心挑选或制作，它们的共同点是立足于教材而高于或超越教材，且大都体现了人本主义的精神，因而趣味盎然，能够激发学生的学习兴趣以及参与课堂活动的动机。

总的来说，教学水平高或者是教学经验丰富的教师能够批判地、灵活地处理教材，教学水平低或者教学经验欠缺的教师往往紧扣教材开展教学。如何对待教材反映了教师的课程资源观。

任务：

（1）观察一节课，讨论教师处理教材的方式。

（2）观察一节课，讨论该课课程资源的模态及来源。

（3）观察一节课，讨论该课课程资源的特点。

第七节　英语课堂活动

一、学习情境和语境

韦尔斯认为，在课堂学习中，教师的主要任务不仅仅是传授知识，更重要的是创造良好的学习环境，设计合适的学习活动，搭建符合学生认知水平的平台，以便鼓励学生敢于和肯于通过交流来探求和获取知识。

教师要有设计高效学习环境的能力。外语课堂里面的学习环境既包括物理环境、语言环境，也包括情感环境，即氛围和语言使用情景。威多森认为，课堂不但是物理空间，还是社会空间。课堂上的社会心理情境跟教师在课堂中所承担的角色有关。

　　语言的练习和运用要依托语境，因此，许多教师在语境创设上花费了很多的心思和时间，但仍然无法处理好教学内容和教学形式的关系。为此，孙媛提出可以基于教材语境本身，利用横着加，深里挖的方法，对教材语境的情感线索和逻辑发展进行丰富，并在经过丰富的语境中实现情感带动、语用体验、语言训练和思维的发展的共进。好的学习情境自然，能够串起课堂里的一切活动。

　　教师在课堂上应该为学生创设安全的课堂气氛。安全课堂气氛的建立基于学生之间的信任和自信。有了互信和自信的氛围，小组成员能够自信、大胆地参与小组活动，敢于表达自己。在外语课堂里，当学生学着去用所学语言时比较容易露拙或出洋相，因此营造一个安全、互信的氛围非常重要。学生之间要互相支持、鼓励和包容。缺乏安全感会导致糟糕的小组氛围，并形成恶性循环。如果学生弄不清楚别人对他的看法，他就不敢表现自己，害怕别人的批评和反对，担心当众出丑。而越不表现自己，就越弄不清楚别人对自己的看法。当班里有越来越多这样的学生时，小组活动就越难开展。另外，营造安全的学习氛围也需要教师的努力。教师本人要给予学生鼓励、支持和爱护，形成融洽的师生关系。不融洽的师生关系、生生关系会导致低质量的学习。

　　教师的三种品质有助于建立良好的学习氛围：真诚、尊重以及共情。如果在课堂上学生能够积极发言并享受"露拙"，那么这样的氛围就是安全的班级氛围。

　　从微观的角度来看，教师在课堂教学中要创设好的语境。好的语境激发学生表达自己、尝试运用语言与人互动的动机和愿望。王初明教授重视语境在语言学习中的作用。他提出的学伴用随理论就体现了语境的重要性。该理论强调，我们在学习外语时一定要把语言和它出现的语境一起学习，在使用语言时这个语境就能随语言一起出现，那么产出的语言才会地道，而不会一出口就是中式英语。

二、活动设置

　　教学设计在某种程度上是活动设计。《英语课程标准》（2017年版）指出，在英语课堂教学中教师要基于主题来设计综合性、关联性、实践性的学习活动。《课标》指出，主题为语言学习提供主题范围或主题语境。学生对主题意义的探究应是学生语言学习的最重要的内容，直接影响学生语篇理解的程度、思维发展的水平和语言学习的成效。英语课程的主题语境包含三大主题：

人与自我、人与社会和人与自然。在人与自我、人与社会、人与自然这三大主题中，人与自我涉及生活与学习、做人与做事两个主题群下的九项子主题；人与社会涉及社会服务于人际沟通、文学、艺术与体育、历史、社会与文化、科学与技术等几个主题群下的16项子主题；人与自然涉及自然生态、环境保护、灾害防范、宇宙探索四个主题群下的七项子主题。所有语境都应包含中外文化的范畴。

在许多外语课堂活动中，教师会请学生谈论他们自己的个人兴趣、喜好、生活方式、意见以及背景等。这种活动不但可以增加学生练习语言的机会，而且能够增强学生个人的学习动机和小组活力。但这些活动很大程度上涉及的是信息的转换，而不是培养学生运用交流中获取的信息去增进对彼此的理解。此外，我们发现，学生在就这些话题进行交谈时，他们更感兴趣的是说而不是听。一方面是因为他们把这些活动看作是练习口语的机会，殊不知听也是练习语言的很好的机会。另一方面是因为人类的天性总是认为自己的东西总是比别人好，需要拿出来跟别人分享。因此，我们在课堂教学中要培养学生共情的能力：设身处地，换位思维，从别人的角度来看问题。以课堂上的调查活动为例，可以让学生通过想象来填同学的个人信息：喜欢的颜色及原因、一天中最喜欢的时间段、担心的东西、喜欢什么类型的音乐、理想、喜欢什么样的人、人们为什么会喜欢我等信息。

如果教师经常让学生谈论班里学生的情况，那么学生就会越来越熟悉，这必然会带来另外一个问题：学生跟这些个人信息没有信息沟，他们分享信息的兴趣和学习动机会减弱。

如果一节课太闷的话，原因可能有如下几个：教材缺乏趣味；活动内容跟学生之间没有信息沟；学生任务太简单或太复杂。太简单的任务对学生来说缺乏挑战性，在英语课堂中，好的任务应该能够激发学生积极参与和思维的碰撞。

设计能够激发学生真实交际愿望或动机的活动。斯凯恩在他的班加罗尔语言教学实验项目中运用了三种能够激发学生参与的真实的交际活动，即信息差活动、推理差活动和意见差活动。

信息差也称信息沟。当交际者一方拥有另外一方所没有的信息时，他们之间有了信息的差距，即信息差，因此产生了进行信息交换的愿望和动机。信息差活动涉及信息的转移和转换，具体说来有三种情况：①把信息从交际的一方转给另一方；②把一种信息方式转换成另一种方式，例如把文字转换成图片；

③把信息从一个地方转换到另一地方。信息的转换涉及信息的解码和编码。信息差活动属于交际性活动，而交际性活动的目的是学生运用所学语言在真实和有意义的语境中进行互动。例如：

1. Giving instructions so that someone can use a robot sweeper.

2. Writing a bad comment on the hotel you stayed with your family last weekend.

例1和例2都涉及信息转换，所以都属于信息差活动，因此属于交际性活动。相反，重复、朗读、句型操练等就不属于交际性活动。

推理差活动涉及通过对文本信息的推断、演绎、思考以及对文本信息关系和模式的感知等方式获取新信息。例如，在班级课程表的基础上制作某一教师的课程表。

意见差活动涉及识别并说出一个人的偏好、情感或对某一特定情境的态度及反应。这种类型的活动可能涉及根据事实性信息形成论据来支撑自己的观点或意见，这种活动的结果没有对错之分，也不能期待每个人或每次活动的结果都一致。例如，利用学生对教师使用计算机辅助教学的不同态度，东莞邓宁霞老师设计了"Do you like CAI or dislike CAI？"的话题让全班学生分组进行辩论。在辩论的过程中，学生各抒己见，很快课堂参与到达高潮，这就是使用观点差而设计的活动。而在初中英语Smart or Harmful的阅读课中，教师也可以利用学生对智能手机的不同态度和立场，设计一场题为"Are smart phones smart or harmful？"的辩论活动，并写成一篇议论文。

在第九届全国小学英语课堂教学观摩中，周亚文老师在Say No to Bullying阅读课中设置了一个体现意见差的口语活动：So tell me，if you were Jerry，what would you want to do？学生纷纷发表自己的见解：

S1：I want to tell my teacher.

S2：I will call the government and I want the government help many children.

S3：Maybe I want to kill myself.

S4：I want to tell my friends.

S5：I want to cry because I am very sad.

意见差活动易于组织，只要设计的话题有趣并贴近学生生活，他们就有话可说，并能积极主动发表看法及见解。

吉尔·哈德菲尔德也提出可以利用差距设计讨论活动。他提出三种差活动：信息差、意见差以及价值差。问卷调查、排列活动、价值阐述任务等就是为了突显差异而设计的活动，它们能够激发讨论和争论。

斯克里温纳提出，在以语言的流利性为目的的口语活动中，教师要做到：不要太多打断学生的话语；提供有用的语言反馈；真正帮助说话者构建会话。为了使学生能够顺利完成交际任务，教师常常需要设计一些"手脚架"。提供"手脚架"，指语言能力高的会话者以鼓励和提供会话可能需要的元素的方式帮助语言能力不高的会话者进行交际。

教师在教学设计时对活动后做什么重视不足。教师通常采用现场询问现场解答的方式开展活动后的活动，例如，教师经常问"Do you have any problem？"并随后进行解答。

一直以来，人们倾向于把课堂活动或练习划分为机械操练、意义练习和交际性练习。有时我们可以从另外的角度来区分课堂活动类型，例如，可以把活动归为以下三类：认知类活动、情感类活动以及运动类活动。

三、活动方式

在英语课堂教学中，有以下几种活动方式：个人活动、全班活动、对子活动、小组活动等。

个人活动适用于读、写等不需要与人合作的语言学习活动，也可用于小组活动前对问题的思考或者对答案的梳理。它的优点是能够随时随地开展，不需要考虑是否有合作对象或者如何组织合作学习。

全班活动。全班活动可以分为两类，一类是全班一起活动，比如齐声朗读或者全班齐声回答教师问题。这样的活动有利于降低语言能力较低的学生的焦虑，保护他们参与活动的积极性，并且节省时间。缺点是不利于教师诊断个别学生存在的问题。

另一类全班混合活动。指的是全班学生站起来并在课室里走动来进行两两交谈，交谈对象不断轮换。这种活动在单位时间内能够给学生提供最多的互动机会。如采访活动，一位学生采访另一位学生后迅速转向下一位学生，到活动截止时每个学生都有很大的收获。这类活动教师设置的活动目标、活动规则以及教师指令语都要明确具体，比如活动结束时至少要采访多少同学、采访结束后要完成什么任务、学生在采访的过程中要填报或做记录、在多少时间内完成等。另外，这类活动需要学生有一定的自主性，能够负起监控自己、评估自己的责任。

混合式全班活动也可以用来做复习课的活动。教师可提前把要复习的内容写在纸条上，每张纸条上面的内容各不相同，学生带着纸条去跟不同的同学交谈。

对子活动。对子活动适合口语活动，因为口语活动需要有说话者和听话者的互动。其优点是易于组织。对子一般是同桌构成，这样可以节省时间；对子也可以是教师指定，或者学生自主选择，也可以是随机选择。开展对子活动时同伴可以是面对面，也可以是背靠背，还可以在课室里穿行。英语课堂里的典型对子活动是think—pair—share。这个模式是1985年由美国马里兰大学弗兰克莱曼教授及其同事提出的，在外语课堂中得到广泛的应用。它包含三个阶段的活动：独立思考、结对合作、相互交流。该模式可用于开展口语活动，有助于学生通过思考形成个人观点并与他人分享。

小组活动。小组活动的优点是可以在单位时间里增加学生的参与量，给更多的学生开口说的机会；能够用于开展较难或较大的任务，让每个学生都对任务的完成有所贡献，从而达到解决问题的目的。缺点是较难组织；小组活动容易被少数话霸控制，少数学生垄断了话语权；一些学生参与不积极；一些学生沉默不发言，不对小组活动做任何贡献。这些导致小组活动耗时低效。

对子活动是两个人的小组活动。对子活动和小组活动的人员构成是值得思考的问题。固定的小组成员会给小组活动带来一些弊端：成员固定不变的小组在使用语言时有局限，如经常使用相同的词汇或短语，不利于学生语言的发展。另外，这样的小组成员之间由于相互太了解而缺少信息沟，他们会彼此厌烦。

建立小组容易，但要维持小组并让它们良好运作并不是容易的事情。健康、有凝聚力的小组有赖于下面的这些措施：建立信任、维持积极的气氛、缩短文化差异和个性差异、所有组员保持联系、鼓励学生充分参与活动并能够互相倾听、培养合作和妥协的能力、鼓励学生具有同理心、给小组以清晰方向感、让小组产生成就感、培养小组的凝聚力和团结精神。

鉴于各种活动方式都有优缺点，我们在选用时应该基于我们的活动目标和活动特点，综合使用各种活动形式以优化我们的课堂教学效果。

四、课堂互动

社会文化理论认为，社会互动促进语言学习，社会互动催生语言习得。根据维果茨基提出的最近发展区学说，学习者通过社会互动和人内互动可以从现实水平达到更高的潜在的发展水平。离开互动则实现不了这种潜势。

互动是以交际为目的的语言教学的核心。互动是语言学习的机理；互动促进语言的习得。互动中的语言输入、反馈、注意以及输出等特征促进了语言的学习。通过互动，学生能够增加语言储备，运用学到的或偶然习得的语言知识于真实的交流当中。互动既是一个语言学习的过程，也是一个语言运用的过程。在互动中学生获得从话语中创造信息的体验，也获得创造话语去表达自己意图的经验。里韦尔斯认为，对语言的理解就是一个创造意义的过程，可以说，学好语言主要靠互动。

什么是互动？威尔斯认为，语言互动是一种合作活动；语言互动涉及了信息发出者、信息接收者以及语境之间的三角关系。在外语课堂中互动意味着学生接收真实的信息。互动是涉及信息交换的活动，是涉及真实信息交换的活动。它既涉及语言的表达，也涉及语言的理解，互动参与者在语境中理解和阐释话语的意义。外语课堂学习必须有这些要素：倾听、交谈、在共同的语境中磋商意义。

从教学的角度看，好的课堂不是教师唱独角戏，而是有师生互动、生生互动的课堂。师生在课堂互动中共同构建意义并达到相互理解；学生在互动的过程中学会意义磋商。

互动的质。互动使课堂充满生机和活力。什么样的互动有利于学生对语言的习得并促进学生的发展呢？含有意义磋商的师生互动和生生互动被认为是有利于语言学习的因素。当学习者和本族语者或语言水平比自己高的人互动时，有时会发生交际失败，而交际失败恰恰被认为是有利于语言学习的或者是语言学习过程的一部分，这是因为当交际失败发生时，会话者会运用一些会话策略去补救，即进行意义磋商。意义磋商的结果是增加了语言的输入。另外，在磋商时会话者会通过举例或者重构语言来澄清意义，从而也增加了语言输出的机会。此外，互动能够使学习者注意到自己语言的不妥之处和得到来自他方的反馈，因此获得语言发展的机会。

布朗认为，教师应该培养学生借助互动调整来清楚表达和理解意义的技能。意义磋商指互动过程中能够使语言变得更加可以理解和具有个人意义的手段。一般来说，意义磋商包括理解检查、确认检查、澄清请求以及重复等会话调整方式。而其中的重复是指说话者重复自己或对方话语以便修补失败的对话，例如：

A：She's on welfare.

B：I think she's working at the factory.

C：No，she lost her job. She's on welfare.

在这个会话片段中C重复了A的话语；C跟A取得了共识，实现了这个对话的目的：陈述"she"目前所处的状态。

在英语课堂中，当学生的互动出现意义表达和理解不畅时，学生能够用上这些互动调整手段，使自己表达的意思更清晰而能被对方所理解，以便最后能够顺利完成整个交际活动。含有意义磋商的互动最有可能出现在口语课、听说课或者讨论活动中。

成功的互动需要互动参与者掌握多种互动技能，包括如何开始一个话题、维持话题、转换话轮和话题、修补话语以及结束交谈等会话技能，也包括拥有多种互动言语风格。互动言语风格包括做好说的角色和听的角色；说话时直说和不直接说；既能愉快地参与平等、交互会话，也能参与不平等、非交互的会话。互动的多样性不仅涉及言语交际因素，也涉及音高、重读、语调、语速、频率等副语言因素，这些副语言因素也具有一定的意义。当然，互动技能包括使用身体语言，因为身体语言既可以单独使用也可以伴随言语表达意义。拥有多种互动风格的会话者能够适应不同风格的互动。在外语课堂教学中，教师在培养学生口语互动技能时，要注意培养学生的多元互动语言风格，比如在小组活动时，如果小组成员都比较沉默，会话者如何贡献自己的话轮；当小组里有话霸时，如何争取到自己的话轮，对小组活动做出应有的贡献。

沃尔什提出了课堂互动能力（简称CIC）的概念，他把课堂互动能力定义为教师和学生把互动当作调节学习和帮助学习的能力。从沃尔什的课堂互动能力的定义可以看出，课堂互动是师生用来调节学习和辅助学习的工具。课堂互动能力强的英语课具有下列的特征：①不单教师可以启动话题，学生也能开启话题。这样的课堂，学生的学习自主性高；②学生在回答问题或进行语言活动时能够自荐话轮，学生具有较高的学习积极性。这样的课堂效率高；③学生会自主管理和分配话轮，让大多数学生都有发言的机会。这样的课堂参与均匀。

活动的有效性是有经验的评课者的重要观察点和评价的内容。例如：

现在我想跟你交流一个问题，比如说活动是教学设计的中心，如果取得好的教学效果，那么活动要有效。关于活动的有效性，比如说你有两个产出活

123

动，第一，你要让学生进行接龙，通过mind-map的形式来描写、谈论Mickey Mouse，然后完了之后每个学生都说了想说的一句话。仔细观察了学生说的话，有重复的，比如讲到He's popular；He's smart。但我非常期待说出刚才陈老师提到的What do you want to，即通过这节课新学的东西，我们的学生没有说到。所以这个时候我这个活动是否说得有效，毕竟学生的输出，不是语篇的输出，而是碎片化的输出。第二，他们的输出没有坚持逻辑性。他们的输出是原来已经知道的，现在还是说我原来知道的。刚学到的没有派上用场。所以我建议这个活动可以放在读后中，前面可以搭建一些支架，除了你原来已知的，把我们新学的东西也把它说出来，或者这个课文当中没有提到的而你知道的也可以说出来。（根据课堂教学案例集转写）

第八节　教师的素质和教师角色

一、教师的思维品质

中小学教师资格证考试面试从八个方面来考查考生，职业认知、心理素质、仪表仪态、言语表达、思维品质所体现的教师基本素养和教学设计、教学实施和教学评价所体现的教学基本技能。教学资格整面试的考核内容反映了教师必备的基本素质。在评课中，我们不但会评教师的教学理念和教学技能，而且会评教师的基本素质。

我们经常说的一句话是"有什么样的教师就会有什么样的学生"，那么这句话也可以改为"要培养什么样的学生就要有什么样的教师"。要培养学生的学科核心素养，教师首先需要具备学科核心素养。正像一些专家所言，"要培养学生的素养，教师首先要素养起来"。

就思维品质而言，教师需要具有什么样的思维品质呢？表5-8是中小学教师资格证考试面试中关于教师思维品质"优"档的评定标准。

表5-3　思维品质"优"档评定标准

学段	测评要素	"优"等表现
小学教师思维品质	逻辑性	思维严密，条理清晰，逻辑性强
	准确性	能正确理解和分析问题，要点抓得准，反应敏捷
	创造性	创新意识比较强，解决问题的思路和方法具有一定的创新
中学教师思维品质	准确性	能迅速准确地理解和分析问题，综合分析能力强
	逻辑性	思维缜密，富有条理，看待问题全面，逻辑性强
	灵活性	思维灵活，应变能力强
	创新性	在解决问题的思路和方法上具有创新性

（改编自《教育部小学教师资格考试面试大纲》和《教育部中学教师资格考试面试大纲》）

我们怎样判断教师是否有或者有什么样的思维品质呢？我们可以通过教师设计的活动、教师提问、教师反馈、教师的课堂决策以及其他教师课堂教学行为来看教师拥有的思维品质和思维能力。

我们评价教师的思维品质是为了促进教师思维品质的发展，而教师思维品质的发展有助于提高他们实施英语课程的能力和提高学生的思维能力，并且最终能够促进学生的全人发展。一节好课总是能反映教师的优良的思维品质，或思维准确、敏捷；或思维有创新性；或思维有批判性。在很大程度上，因为教师有创新思维，所以能够进行有创意的教学设计；教师具有批判性思维能力，才能较好地引导学生去质疑、去探寻；因为教师思维敏捷，才能使课堂教学各环节衔接紧密，课堂节奏明快。很难想象一位思维不准确的教师能够培养出思维缜密的学生。可以说，教师优良的思维品质也造就了好课。例如，思维活跃的教师总是能带动学生去思考问题；具有创新思维的教师总是能够设计出新颖、有趣的活动，从而使学生能够投入学习并取得较好的学习效果，等等。

二、教师的直觉

教师素质也包括教师的直觉。斯克里温纳提出，教师进行教学时需要一种直觉。直觉是指教师本能地理解教学情境、超过常规的深思熟虑而进行决策的技能。直觉是能力，尽管直觉听起来很神奇，但却确确实实地存在于我们的教学工作中。直觉反应在教学中起着重要作用，因为课堂上的事情发生迅速，而且教师要关注的事情很多，没有太多思考的空间。因此，教师如果没有直觉就不能快速处理事情。

特级教师王崧舟老师说过，学音乐的人要有乐感，学美术要有美感，打球要有球感，学语文要有语感，教师上课要有课感。课感应该是教师教学的最高境界。课感就是你对教学现场的一种直觉，一种当下的把握，一种敏锐而别出心裁的驾驭。在教学过程中，有课感的教师对于那些突如其来的偶发事件能不假思索地、迅速地、果断地做出反应，而且这样反应是高效的，是巧妙的。

直觉是从哪里来的？直觉源于教师个人经验的积累。

直觉可学习可提高。根据在做中学，在学中用的理念，我们必须在教学中学教学，通过教学培养和提高我们的直觉。教师必须不断挑战自己，并且有意识地提升自己的直觉。学习成为一个更好教师的过程就是收集具体的反馈和信息的过程，通过这个过程，能够在课堂上有更迅捷、更准确的直觉。

课堂教学的流畅与否往往取决于教师能否快速认清课堂的情形并做出恰当的反应。

我们不常用直觉来评价教师，但笔者在某区的一次教研活动中听到一位教研员对另一位成绩卓著的教研员的评价。她说："××老师是一位很有天分的老师。"在这个评价语中，天分就是直觉、本能的意思。

三、教师的角色

对教师角色的定位和期待反映了一个人的教师观。威多森认为，教师是教学理论和实践的中介者；而把研究者定位为真理的生产者、把教师定位为真理的消费者是对教育事业莫大的损害。在外语教学的历史长河中，教师的角色和定位在不断地发展和变化，一直不变的是教师是课堂活动的组织者。在语法翻译法盛行的年代，教师在外语课堂中的典型角色是知识的传授者，课堂教学的权威。因此，课堂教学中师生的地位是不平等的，没有师生互动，只有教师的一言堂。到了直接法流行的时代，师生关系比较平等，教师和学生是合作者，具体体现在教师可以问学生问题，学生也可以问教师问题。最重要的是，教师角色是学生语言的样板和课堂的组织者。在听说法的课堂上，教师也充当学生的语言样板，是学生模仿跟读的对象。

作为提供便利者的教师，在交际法中扮演的角色是facilitator，为学生的学习提供便利，特别是在交际活动中为学生提供语言资源方面的支持。在2003年的广东省高中英语优质课比赛中，邓宁霞老师在学生写前环节设置了小组讨论环节，而在讨论中有一学生向邓老师求助。

片段1：

S：How to say "信息时代"？

T：You may say "time of information".

斯克里温纳提出，教师不要为学生提供过多的帮助，过多的帮助反而成为学生的障碍。当任务较难时，要给学生挑战自己的机会，不要急伸援手。

作为监察者的教师在课堂中充当监察学生语言行为和语言输出的角色。教师作为监察者的角色在学生小组活动时表现得最充分，比如，监察学生参与活动是否均匀；是否有学生总是保持沉默或者总是垄断话语权；学生完成任务的难易度如何；学生在小组讨论会是否会分配话轮；学生在遇到交际障碍时能否会调用交际策略等。

作为反馈者的教师在英语课堂教学中常常为学生提供针对他们语言行为的反馈，以便帮助他们改进和提高自己的语言能力。反馈包含评估和改正两个部分。当学生的语言符合要求或者答案正确时，教师的反馈只包含评估，如"You're right！"。换句话说，当学生的答案是正确时，教师反馈语模式是评估+零改正。而当学生的语言行为有偏误或者答案不正确时，教师的反馈就包含评估和改正，例如"I don't agree！Here we should say..."教师反馈是课堂教学的重要价值之一，是课堂教学区别于学生自学的一个重要特征。

作为教学资源及资源开发者的教师在课堂上常常作为课程资源的一部分。首先，教师语言和教材内容一样是语言输入，教师语言也是学生学习英语的样板。其次，教师的相关信息通常被教师用来作为导入、呈现及练习的材料。诸如此类的教师把自己当作课程资源的例子在中小学英语教学中不胜枚举。如在第七届全国小学英语课堂教学中，赵雪鹏老师就把自己的信息做成谜语让学生猜测而导入该课，取得很好的导入效果（详见下面片段）。

片段2：

T：So just now I know something about you and now let's play a guessing game about me，OK？

Ss：OK.

T：So the rule is if you think it is true，then you say "yeah，yeah，yeah".

Ss：Yeah，yeah，yeah.

T：If you think it's not true，you say"no，no，no"！

Ss：No，no，no！

深圳外国语学校的秦玲老师把自己带学生在美国游学的经历设置为语境来呈现和练习church、café、architect以及architecture等生词。

片段3：

T：...So I went to US three years ago...during my stay in America，I visited the city of Rochester. And I stayed there for three weeks. Every morning we had classes at a special place. Guess what it is?

Ss：Char—

T：What？Church.

Ss：Church.

T：That's a church. We called it a church.

作为思考者的教师思想统摄教师的行为，他们在教学中能够把教学工作和构成教学实践基础的思想和决策概念化。教师专业知识的获得被看成一个教师积极构建具有个人意义、切实可行的教学理论的过程。教师在教学中做的课堂决策是教师思考的结果。

总的来说，教师在课堂教学中扮演的角色取决于教师自身的教学思想和教学理念。在信息技术时代和弱人工智能时代，教学生态、教学环境、教学技术和手段都已改变，教师的传统角色还会继续发生改变。每一位老师都要做好转变角色的准备，教师角色以及教学行为是影响学生学习行为乃至教学效果的重要因素，因此，它们也是我们评课的着眼点。

四、课堂管理和课堂纪律管理能力

格布哈德认为，课堂管理的目的是为有意义的语言互动创设良好的气氛；理查兹认为，高效的课堂管理技能是高效教学的必不可少的要素；王蔷等认为，高效课堂管理必须满足下列六个条件：

（1）教师扮演恰当的角色。

（2）教师指示语清晰。

（3）学生分组合理，适合相应的教学活动。

（4）教师提问恰当。

（5）合理对待学生的偏误。

（6）课堂有序、和谐。

优质课很少呈现课堂纪律管理方面的技巧，这是因为优质课、公开课、展示课、观摩课具有特殊性。首先，全国或省级优质课例展示的学生常常来自学生素质较好的学校甚至名校，这种学校的学生学习自觉性强，在纪律方面无须教师花太多的心思和时间；普通公开课的学生也许来自普通学校，但在有听课教师在场的情况下一般都会比较帮衬授课教师，因此，在纪律方面也无须教师花费太多的心思。

然而，对于普通的学校来说，课堂管理是必须的。教师的教学的进度及有效性常常受课堂管理效果的影响。课堂管理和教学目标是相互联系的，教师在管理课堂的同时要最大限度地促进学生的学习。优秀的教师在适当的教学情景出现时自然而有意义地引出课堂规约和常规。而一般的教师一上课就花很多时间来建立规约和常规，这些规约和常规的建立大多时候是脱离情境的，没有将课堂规约和常规跟教学目标很好地整合起来。

不同的教师有不同的课堂管理风格，有的严厉，有的宽松。但不管风格如何，教师要让学生感觉到在课堂上参与活动是安全的，并因此而敢于冒险进行语言练习和语言运用。

教师要想取得课堂管理的成功，必须建立自己的威信。例如，前面说到要学生停止某一活动时可以直接、清楚地说出来：Stop now, please!，而不用遮遮掩掩或者拐弯抹角，例如：So if you don't mind, it would be very nice if you could just stop the activity if you feel that's OK。而一旦教师发出指令语，学生就必须执行。

第九节　教学媒体和教学信息技术

一、板书和简笔画

　　板书。语言教学在世界上千差万别，但语言课室相同的地方是，黑板（包括白板）是必不可少的配置。只有多媒体设备而没有黑板的课室不是常规的课室。黑板是一种教学资源，使用黑板是为了服务教学，而使用黑板的方式值得研究。

　　教师对黑板的使用可以划分为三类：系统的板书、随便的板书、介于系统和随便之间的板书。在英语课中，教师使用黑板有多种目的：教词汇，解释语法，画图等。黑板辅助教词汇又可细分为创设情境、引出词汇或者描述活动，等等。

　　在传统英语课堂上，教师对黑板的使用是用粉笔板书。而在现代课堂上，除了用粉笔或其他笔具板书，教师还用预制的词贴、句子贴等构图，以呈现教学的主题及主要内容或文本的结构等。张贴预制的词、句贴能够节省书写时间，还能带来整齐的视觉效果。但跟PPT一样，其生成性差，如果教师临时要在黑板上呈现知识给学生，还是要借助粉笔板书。

　　板书是每一位教师必备的教学技能。板书既需要授课教师的提前设计，也需要其根据教学的情境进行临时发挥。首先，教师需要对板书进行合理的布局，包括对黑板或白板区域的划分成两个版块，一边板课题和课程的重点，如重点语言结构、重要词汇、文本的篇章结构等；一边板补充性的东西，比如表达话题的一个课外词汇。

　　板什么，什么内容放在什么位置都跟教学的重点有关。首先，教师在备课时要筹划如何板书才能突出主题和教学重点，引起学生对重要内容的有意注意，帮助他们抓住知识脉络，并为最后的归纳、总结提供支架。其次，在突出主题和重难点的基础上，板书要层次分明，做到工整、美观和适量。板书不能太随意，想到什么板什么。我们在上课时不宜把太多的时间花在板书上，因为太多板书会使课堂烦闷。另外也不能完全依靠预制好的PPT来呈现知识或突出重点，只有适时适量的板书才能带来好的教学效果。图5-1是第七届全国小学英语课堂教学观摩课Baby Becky一课中李茵老师的板书。

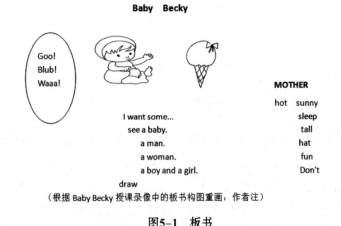

（根据 Baby Becky 授课录像中的板书构图重画，作者注）

图5-1 板书

（截自第七届全国小学英语教学观摩课Baby Becky课堂实录，2014）

在这节课中教师的板书至少有三个作用：①展示文本内容。文本讲述了发生于Baby Becky和她妈妈之间的故事，在语篇类型方面文本首先属于绘本故事，但故事展开的形式主要是通过Baby Becky和她妈妈之间的对话，因此，教师在板书时重点板出Baby Becky和她妈妈的话语中的关键词；②板书反映了教学的过程。教师按照故事发生的几个场景来呈现教学内容并组织语言训练；③在最后的复述环节教师要求学生借助板书对故事进行复述，因此，板书成了师生一起复述故事内容的工具或者支架。最后，教师在对故事进行升华前在上面这个板书的基础上加上了一些线条，使所有板书内容都置于一个心形图内，并指出每个母亲对孩子都有爱心。

好的板书还能凸显教师的教学风格。已故著名小英特级教师鲍当洪老师的教学风格是自然、朴实、本真，鲍老师的板书也自成风格。鲍老师在第14届现代与经典全国小学英语教学观摩研讨会上执教Festivals and Holidays一课时，是这样设计他的板书的：首先画一个心形，在心形里面板上节日名称，如 Mothers Day，Spring Festival，Teacher's Day，等等。在心形的外面板上谈论节日的活动的句型，如在右边，鲍老师板上Which festival did you like? When did they do at the Mid-Autumn Festival? 在左边，他板上Where did they have the party? Who did they have the part （with）? 见图5-2。

图5-2　板书

　　这个板书把谈论节日的词语和交际用语都呈现出来了，在某种程度上突出了本课的重点。另外，这个板书被用来当作复述任务的脚手架。

　　板书包括简笔画，漂亮的板书离不开简笔画。形象、直观、传神的简笔画有助于教师创设生动、直观的情景。简笔画技能是教师必备的教学技能之一。简笔画的便捷性是电脑画图所不能比拟的，掌握了简笔画技能，教师可以随时借助它来营造教学情境、呈现语言知识、组织语言练习活动等。教师不是专业的绘画人士，因此对教师简笔画在画技上不能有太高的要求，只要能够准确传递意义即可。

二、外语课堂教学中信息技术的使用

　　教育部在2018年4月发布了《教育信息化2.0行动计划》（下称《教育信息化2.0》）。《教育信息化2.0》落实到我们英语教学中的核心理念就是，促进信息技术与英语教学实践的深度融合。信息技术推动教学变革创新，构建教学新生态。信息技术在教育中的应用越来越广泛，但它的应用是有条件的，即要基于互联网、大数据和平台。人工智能、大数据等信息技术正在重塑着外语教育的生态，现代信息技术的蓬勃发展显著提高了外语教学的实用性和针对性。教育无法抗拒信息时代的到来，混合式学习、移动学习、游戏化学习是不可阻挡的趋势。

　　信息技术给外语教学带来了不少的益处。它的应用使学生练习量和质得到优化、作业批改智能化、评价数据化、教学智慧化。大数据可以帮助教师更精准地掌握学情，并能够更精准地实施教学。通过分析提取有效数据，比如，可以利用某个平台的大数据对某一阶段某班的学情进行分析。学情分析不但可以分析全班学生情况，甚至可以分析学生个人的情况。借助大数据，教师能够因材施教、根据学生的不同情况布置练习，因此提高了教学的效率。在学习后阶段，像翼课网之类的智能平台还能给学生提供适时的反馈，甚至可以指出学生改进的方向。

智慧课堂。智慧课堂源于智慧学习。智慧学习以学习者为中心，能够在任何时间（Anytime）、任何地点（Anyplace），以任何方式（Anyway）和任何步调（Anypace）（简称4A）进行轻松的（Easy Learning）、投入的（Engaged Learning）和有效的（Effective Learning）（简称3E）学习。对智慧课堂的分析和评价角度一般侧重于三个核心内容：课堂互动的程度、课堂反馈的情况以及对个性的体现。在高效的智慧课堂中，师生通过手写进行积极的互动；课堂的反馈基于大数据；学生都回答得好的问题无需进行讲解；学生的个体答题——呈现和适当的讲解是个性化的一个重要体现。

值得一提的是，在我们拥抱互联网+和《教育信息化2.0》时，不能让教师和学生成为信息技术的奴隶。2017年版《英语课标》指出，现代信息技术的使用不能替代师生课堂上真实而鲜活的人际互动、观点碰撞、情感交流的语言活动。教师要充分认识现代信息技术与英语课程融合的目的性、恰当性、合理性和有效性，在课堂教学中，使用信息技术要适度。如果无辅助教学能够取得好的教学效果，那么就没必要去使用信息技术，因为信息技术需要硬件的支持，而教师在使用硬件的过程中往往会产生一些障碍，白白地浪费了教学的宝贵时间。教育部出台的文件中规定，在平板课堂中使用Pad的时间不能超过15分钟，即不能超过整节课时长的30%。可见，信息技术于英语学习只是一种辅助手段。

任务：

（1）观察一节课的板书，看看教师板书是系统的板书、随意的板书，还是介于系统和随意之间的板书。

（2）举例说明简笔画的作用。

（3）观察一节整合信息技术的英语课，指出该课信息技术手段所起的作用。

（4）通过不断的课堂观摩，构建一套信息技术优化英语教学的评价指标。

第六章

英语评课的实践

第一节　小学英语评课案例

评课案例一　《It's Red》听说课

【课堂实录】

T：Hello，boys and girls！

Ss：Hello Kico.

T：Nice to meet you！

Ss：Nice to meet you，too！

T：Good！Boys，good morning！

Ss：Good morning！

T：Girls，hi！

Ss：Hi！

T：Hi，boy！I'm Kico. What's your name？

S：My name is Peter.

T：Hello，Peter. I like Peter. Hello，what's your name？

S：My name is Sarah.

T：Sarah. that's good name.

Leading–in

T：So today I have a friend for you. Ooh，look！（教师手里拿着一条变色龙）So many friends. I am a chameleon！Nice to meet you.

Ss：Nice to meet you too！

呈现新内容：What can a chameleon do？

　　T：A story for you.（播放PPT）Watch and find out what can a chameleon do in the story. OK?

Ss：OK.

Video（教师播放视频）

C：Good morning! I'm a chameleon! What's your name?

P：My name is Panpan. I'm a panda.

Ooh! It's red!

Now it's blue!

Now it's yellow!

Now it's green!

Now it's black！！

Now it's red，blue，green and yellow.

T：What can chameleon do in the story? A or B?

Ss：B！

T：Yes. Chameleon can change colors! Look，here's the chameleon! What color will it be? （教师拿出一个矿泉水瓶，上面贴着一条变色龙）It's green? Maybe! It's red? Maybe! Now，let's see，ooh! Ooh，the magic word：Chameleon. Chameleon，Chameleon，Chameleon，Chameleon，Chameleon，Chameleon! Woh，it's red! This is my hair. It's red?

Ss：No.

T：This is my pencil. It's red?

Ss：No.

T：The chameleon is red?

Ss：Yes!

T：Ooh! It's red!

Ss：Ooh! It's red!

T：Good! Ooh! It's red!

Ss：Ooh! It's red!

T：Very good! Now, group leaders, stand up, please! Ooh, it's red!

S：Ooh, it's red.

T：You, please!

S：Ooh, it's red.

T：Very good！（用手势邀请下一位group leader）

S：Ooh，it's red.

T：OK，so，now let's work together. Group leader，check and help，understand，understand？

Ss：Yes.

T：One，two，begin！

S：Ooh，it's red.（教师用手势示意一位小组长把话筒递给他的组员，并练习该句子，直至全组都有机会说出该句。有的学生red的/e/音发成/ai/，教师没纠正）

T：Very good！Sit down，please. Good job，group leader. And what color？（教师拿出红色变色龙）

Ss：Red！

T：Ooh，what color？

Ss：It's red.

T：Oh，it's red. Now，let's look at the chameleon on your desk. It's red，too？

Now，group leaders and partner，stand up！Hold them！（教师让他们把一个瓶子的水加到另一个瓶子里去）Everybody，magic word！Chameleon，chameleon，one two，go！

Ss：Chameleon，chameleon.

T：Ooh，what color？Ooh，it's blue.

S：Ooh，it's blue.

T：You're the teacher，please.（教师选一个学生作小老师，由他指定学生进行练习）

S：It's blue！（其他学生站起来读）Good！Boys，please！

Ss：It's blue.

S：You're very good！Girls，please.

Ss：It's blue.

S：You're very good！Group 1，please.

Ss：It's blue.

S：You're very good！Group 3，please. You're very good！

T：You're good teacher！Ooh，thank you . And what color？

S：It's yellow.

T：You're teacher，please！（组织学生练习It's yellow.）

S：It's yellow.

Ss：It's yellow.

T：Group 4.

S：Group 4，stand up，please. One by one.

S：It's yellow！

S：Ooh，it's yellow.

T：Clever boy！Group 2，one by one，or two by two？

S：Two by two！

Ss：Ooh，it's yellow.

T：Oh，you're Group 5. Together！Very good.

S：Well done！

T：Well done！Ooh，thank you. Sit down. Everybody！And what color？

Ss：It's yellow.

T：What color？

Ss：It's blue.

T：If we put blue and yellow together，what color？I don't know. I think you know.（培养学生的想象力）

S：It's green.

T：It's green. Are you sure？And you please.

S：It's green.

T：Really？You，please.

S：It's green.

T：Maybe. And now let's do it together. Everybody，magic word！Chameleon，chameleon，one two，go！Chameleon，chameleon，chameleon，chameleon，chameleon，chameleon.Put them together. Put them together. Chameleon，chameleon，one two，go！

Ss：Chameleon，chameleon！

T：Chameleon，chameleon，chameleon，chameleon，chameleon，chameleon. Chameleon，wow，now，sit down please. Everybody，sit down please.

Now，it's blue?

    Ss：It's green.

    T：It's green. Now，it's green. It's green?

    Ss：Yes.

    T：/iː/

    Ss：/iː/

    T：/iːn/

    Ss：/iːn/

    T：/iːn/

    Ss：/iːn/

    T：/griːn/

    Ss：/griːn/

    T：/griːn/

    Ss：/griːn/

    T：It's green. I like it.（教师指着自己绿色的上衣）

    Ss：It's green. I like it.

    Ss：It's green. I like it.（分组轮流重复该句）

    ...

    T：Oh，it's green. I like it（拿起一位学生贴在衣袖上的绿标）Let's find and say：It's green. I like it.（利用课室里的真实语境，练习含有green的句子）

    It's green. I like it. Who wants to try? This girl，please.

    S：It's green. I like it.

    T：Wow，thank you. You please.

    S：It's green. I like it.

    T：Another one.

    S：It's green. I like it.（学生指着教师的绿上衣）

    T：Green.

    S：It's green. I like it.

    T：Very good! And the last one，you please.

    S：It's green. I like it.（指着同学的袖标）

    T：I like it too. And what color?

Ss：It's green.

T：Now，let me guess. Let me guess.（教师把几种颜色的变色龙放在她的背后，然后快速抽出一个问学生，该练习主要是练习学生对表示颜色的词的再认，属于记忆类练习）It's green?

Ss：No.

T：What color?

Ss：It's red.

T：It's red. Red，/e/.

Ss：/e/.

T：red.

Ss：red.

T：It's green?

Ss：No，it's yellow.

T：Oh，it's yellow. It's green?

Ss：No，it's blue.

T：And it's green?

Ss：Yes.

T：Yes，is it green too?

Ss：No.

T：Oh，it's black. /æ/.

Ss：/æ/.

T：/æ/.

Ss：/æ/.

T：/æ/.

Ss：/æ/.

T：black.

Ss：black.

T：black.

Ss：black.

T：And what color? It's black.

Ss：It's black.

T：Um，what is black? Is this black? Oh，this is my hair. It's black.

Ss：It's black.

T：This is my pen. It's...

Ss：black.

T：Now，let's find and say. This is my...It's black.

OK，group leader，stand up! OK，one，two，go!（各组在小组长的带领下开展这个活动。利用现有真实的语境，在情境中寻找语言练习的资源）

S：This is my hair. It's black.

S：This is my clothes. It's black.

S：This is my eye. It is black.

...

T：Well，class，class!

Ss：Yes，yes!

T：You did a great job. Oh，where is my friend chameleon? Now，let's listen and think.（播放PPT）

What color is the chameleon? Why?

（教师播放有背景音乐的各种动物的声音：鸟鸣、牛羊叫、猫狗叫等）

T：Um，I think it's blue because the bird is blue. Maybe it's on the bird!（教师没有揭示变色龙靠近什么颜色的物体就变成该颜色的原理，导致学生把明显没有出现在录音里的事物也拉进来）So let's work in groups. Please try to be creative. Understand?

Ss：Yes.

T：Group leaders，stand up! One，two，go ahead!（学生分组活动，有的说云是白色的，天空是蓝色的，树是绿色的。这个环节的确能培养学生的想象力）OK，Let's stop here. Class，class.

Ss：Yes，yes.

T：Who wants to talk? You want to talk? What do you think?

S：I like yellow.

T：Oh you think it's yellow. Why?

S：My shirt is yellow.（学生没弄明白教师要他们做什么）

T：Oh，yellow. Good imagination!（教师没有做出恰当的评价，只是想给

学生以鼓励！）What do you think?

S：I think it's white.

T：Why?

S：Because rabbit is white.

T：The rabbit is white！Ooh！And anyone else?

S：I think green.

T：It's green. Why?

S：The teacher...

T：Coat?

S：The teacher's coat is green.

T：Oh，good imagination. And how about you?

S：I think it's brown.

T：Why?

S：Because it's on the cat.

T：Oh，very good. Everybody has good imagination. And now let's enjoy the story again.

This time let's listen and repeat the story.

Everybody please open your books. My finger！Show me your finger. Yes，good！Show me your finger. My finger. Point. Let's repeat.（教师再次播放该故事）

Ss：Good morning.

T：You can read like this：Good morning.（教师要学生模仿视频里的语音语调）

Ss：Good morning！

T：Very good.

Ss：I am a chameleon. What's your name？My name is Panpan. I am a panda. Ooh，it's red. Now it's blue. Now it's yellow.

T：Very good.

Ss：Now it's green. Now it's black. Now it's red，blue，green and yellow.

T：OK，look at the last sentence. Can you read like me. Now it's red↗，blue↗，green↗ and yellow↘. Show me your finger. "Now it's" one，two，go!

Ss：Now it's red↗，blue↗，green↗ and yellow↘.

T：Perfect. Now this time let's listen and repeat in groups. Group leaders，

143

stand up. Take out your reading pen，understand?

Ss：Yeah.

T：One two go！read together.（教师指导）Sentence by sentence！Group five，great！OK，class，class！

Ss：Yes，yes！

T：Now let's act out the story. Look，this is a chameleon. Let's act out like this.（教师示范：教师迈着舞步走向一位学生向全班做示范）Oh，hello，I'm Kico，what's your name?

S：I'm Joanna.

T：Oh，it's green.（指着自己的衣服）

S：Yes.

T：Oh，it's blue and black.

S：Yes

T：Goodbye！Now，do you understand?

Ss：Yes.

T：Here are some tips for you. No.1 push the snowball. No.2 speak loudly and correctly. No.3 act with gestures. No.4 be polite. Understand?

Ss：Yes.

T：Now let's begin the story. Ready？Go！（第一位学生开始表演故事）

S：Hello，my name is Joanna. What's your name?（这个活动的规则是活动的参加者由一位学生带动另一位学生——→两位学生带动两位学生——→四位学生带动四位学生以致全班学生都有表演的机会，由于有背景音乐，另外的学生在找人表演时迈着舞步，激发了他们参与的热情，学生们在表演时有成就感）

T：Class，class！

Ss：Yes，yes！

T：Um，my friend chameleon has some friends. Who are they？Let's find out and introduce them.Let's work out the jigsaw puzzle in 30 seconds and look at me. This is a jigsaw puzzle，and look at me，（教师演示如何拼图）this is the head, this is the body and this is the tail. Ooh，what's this?

Ss：It's a bird.

T：Oh, it's a bird. Oh, yes, it's Huahua. This is the mouth. It's green. This is it's body. It's yellow and black. This is the tail. It's blue. It is cute. I like it. Now，let's introduce it together.（学习朗读范例，该范例充当学生活动的脚手架）

T：Now，tips for you：1，2，3. One，two，begin！（教师给每组学生派发一个装有动物拼图的信封，每组的动物各不相同）

T：Introduce the elephant like that.

S：Look. This is an elephant.

T：Class，class！Who wants to introduce？And now let me choose—Group 5. Group 5，come here！Take your monkey. Good！May I help you？Come here，everyone，come here. Stand here. And you can introduce one by one！

S1：This is a monkey. It has red body.

S2：This is a monkey. It has yellow face.

S3：This is a monkey. It has a blue nose.

T：Blue nose.

S4：This is a monkey.It has a blue ear.

T：Blue ear.

S5：This is monkey. It has black hair.

T：Hair.

S5：Hair.

S6：It is monkey. It has black eyes.

T：Oh，thank you！Thank you. So do you like their introduction？Do you like their introduction？Yes，or no？

Ss：Yes.

T：So how many steps do you think？One or two？One or two？One？I think they are pretty good！I give them one and two. Thank you！Say thank you to everybody！（叫上来展示的学生对全班同学道谢！）Thank you！So today everybody did a good job. My friend Chameleon will give you a big Oooh to you. So it's time to say goodbye，everybody. And this is a little gift for you. You can play with it after class. Goodbye boys and girls.

SS：Goodbye！

T：Please say goodbye to all the teachers！Goodbye！

【背景介绍】

本课是第7届全国小学英语教学观摩中的一节听说课。课题名称是It's Red。授课教师是来自重庆巴蜀小学的甘翠竹老师。授课教师教学技巧娴熟，教师创设了多种形式的语言练习活动，在英语学科教学中融合了科学知识，课堂生动有趣，学生有大量的语言练习和语言体验的机会。

一、教学设计及教学过程

I. Greeting and lead—in

T：I have a friend—chameleon.

II. Presentation and practice

1. Presenting the story by video

2. Checking the answer to the question：What can a chameleon do?

3. Practice

（1）Group leaders act as small teacher to involve their group in practising the sentence pattern：It's red.

（2）Teacher mixes blue water with yellow water to produce green color and organizes the practice around it's green.

（3）Find and say：Teacher asks students to find something. That is green and practice in the following way：

It's green. I like it.

This is my... It's blue.

III. Fly your imagination：more practice

—What color is the chameleon now? Why?

—I think it's blue because the bird is blue.

IV. Listen and repeat the story

V. Let's act

VI. Let's talk：Introduce your friend

教师让学生拼图然后用所学表示颜色的句子即兴描述。

教师简单导入主题，然后，播放故事视频并提出一个问题What can a chameleon do? 接着，重点呈现句型It's red。之后，围绕着这个句型组织了小老师教读和评价活动；接着，教师做一个小实验，把两种不同颜色的水倒在一起并摇一摇使其变色，并继续组织学生练习It's…句型。接着，让学生找身边的颜色并用已学相关句型表达出来。此后，教师让学生根据听到的动物声音来想象变色龙的颜色以及这样想的原因，以此培养学生的想象力和创造性。此后教师再次播放故事视频，并要求学生把故事表演出来；在做这个活动前教师提供了表演所需语言的脚手架，并明确了表演的方式是滚雪球式的。最后教师让学生以合作学习的方式进行拼图并综合运用本课所学语言来描述自己的动物朋友。

二、该课的教学特色

在语境情境中呈现生词red，然后把red放在句子It's…中加以练习。练习的方式是教师对全班、教师对小组长、小组长对组员。让小组长当小老师，给他们以成就感，有利于激发他们的学习动机。教师对情境的利用有两种情况：一是教师自己的创设；二是教师把自己和学生当作教学的资源。

教师的活动指令语投在屏幕上，英文指令语后加上中文意思。因为是三年级的学生，教师指令语要做到清晰简单并且有效不容易，所以用中文加以说明可以帮助学生快速地明了教师要他们做什么。

体验式学习。教师设计情境让学生动手体验蓝加黄变成绿色，引起学生的学习兴趣，培养他们的动手能力和探究精神。在做中学，在学中做，例如动手拼图并用语言向全班介绍他们拼出来的动物身上各部位的颜色。

培养学生的想象力。教师在呈现和组织学生对新内容的练习后设计了放飞想象——奇思妙想的环节。教师在这个环节中播放各种动物的声音来想象变色龙的颜色。由于教师没有清楚地告诉学生变色龙的颜色和这些动物的关系，所以个别学生想象的依据并不是音频中出现的动物的颜色，而是教师的上衣的颜色。但瑕不掩瑜，学生在这个想象活动中表现积极，在讨论阶段，学生有较多的语言尝试，有的学生说变色龙是蓝色的，因为天是蓝的；变色龙是绿的，因为树是绿的。在检查阶段，学生能够大胆、踊跃地表达他们的猜想和依据，如：

S：I think it's white.

T：Why?

S：Because rabbit is white.

T：The rabbit is white！Ooh！And anyone else？

T：Oh，good imagination. And how about you？

S：I think it's brown.

T：Why?

S：Because it's on the cat.

跨学科知识的融合。这节课如果不融入跨学科知识，那么它就是一节典型的语言课，很难走高也很难挖深。

多处引入评价指标。帮助学生明确语言练习的要求，同时也让他们能够根据这些要求来评价自己的语言行为。

参与度较高。整节课能做到关注到大部分的学生，让每个学生都动口、动手。

三、该课的一些不足之处

（1）有时评价不到位。例如：

T：Who wants to talk? You want to talk? What do you think?

S：I like yellow.

T：Oh you think it's yellow. Why?

S：My shirt is yellow.

T：Oh，yellow. Good imagination! （实际上，学生没弄明白教师要他们做什么，因此产出的语言并不符合语境，但教师没有做出恰当的评价，给了学生正面的评价。这可能会误导后面发言的同伴）

S：I think green.

T：It's green. Why?

S：The teacher...

T：Coat?

S：The teacher's coat is green.

T：Oh，good imagination.

（2）对教材的处理技巧需要提高。本课的教材是一则对话，发生于变色龙和熊猫之间的对话：

C：Good morning! I'm a chameleon! What's your name?

P：My name is Panpan. I'm a panda.

Ooh! It's red!

Now it's blue!

Now it's yellow!

Now it's green!

Now it's black!

Now it's red，blue，green and yellow.

这则对话的主要内容是描述变色龙身上颜色的变化。主要词汇是表示颜色的词语：red，blue，yellow和green。句子结构是It's...教师拓展了一个句子：I like it. 虽然表示颜色的词语是本课的生词，但实际上不少学生已经会认读这些词汇了。因此，如果按照常规的教学设计，这节课很难让学生在认知和思维上有发展。鉴于此，教师可在教材的内容方面进行挖掘，立足教材的同时要敢于超越教材，跨学科知识整合就是一条路。如陈则航教授所言，可以就变色龙变色的原理进行拓展教学，比如，变色龙靠近什么颜色就会变成什么颜色。如果能走到这一步，那么教师设计的Fly your imagination部分可以做得更高效。在这个环节的检查阶段，有学生说I like green because our teacher's coat is green显然是不符合语境要求的。

没有考虑语用和活动设计的层次性。教师在教学设计时，需要从语用方面来考虑问题。It's red/yellow/green在什么情况下用，比如，用于猜测游戏时对事物颜色的描述。让学生清楚在什么情景之下使用，并能把It's red等迁移到真实的交际情境中。

这节课问题给我们带来一些思考：当教师未教学生就已掌握新知识时，教师怎么办？那么，我们可能需要拓宽或加深话题的情境，即像孙媛老师文中所述的——往横处加，往深里挖，这样才能满足不同层次学生的需求，以提高教学的效度。如果这节课最后一个活动设计成一个交际性活动，让学生用表示颜色的词语和描述事物颜色的句型进行交际运用，可能会达成更高的教学目标。

评课案例二 《Say No to Bullying》阅读课

【课堂实录】

T：Are you ready for class? So class begins!

Ss：Stand up!

T：Wow! Good morning, boys and girls!

Ss：Good morning, teacher!

T：What is my name?

Ss：Wendy.

T：Right, Wendy! Thank you! Please take a seat. OK, everybody, when you are speaking, face me. Right, like that? Um, so guys, look! Hey, look! Guys, look! Wow, so many teachers today! How do you feel? Remember to use microphone!

S：I feel very happy and afraid!

T：Feel happy and feel afraid!

S：I feel very surprised!

T：Very surprised! Why? Why? Why surprised? All right, guys, listen! You feel happy, afraid, surprised? As people, we all have feelings. And as people, our feelings can change very fast. Now I'm going to show you some photos. You, get to watch them and you have to tell me how do you feel, right? There you go! （教师播放视频）Now, how do you feel?

S：I feel very angry.

T：Why? What did you just see?

S：Um. because I see a... a student hurt her...

T：Because you saw the big hurting the small ones （recast the sentence）, good! Did you see one word? Did you see one word? One word. Yep?

S：Buying. （学生不会读bullying）

T：Buying.Um. Let's see. Sometimes when you see some people，they shout at you because they feel very good about themselves. And when some people pull your hair，hey，guys，girls，you have your long hair，right? And you see some people trip up，try "trip up".

Ss：Trip up.

T：Trip up.

Ss：Trip up.

T：Trip up because they're very big and very strong. All these kinds of behavior we call them—bullying. "bullying"，try!

Ss：Bullying.

T：Bullying.

Ss：Bullying.

T：And the people who are bullying are bullies，good. So try "bullies".

Ss：Bullies.

T：So bullies are bullying. Bullies bullying. Tell me，in your life at your school on the trip of others，do you see bullying happen? Yes or no? Oh，you're very lucky! Yes，what did you see? Who says yes? Tell me what happen!

S：Big students hurt smaller students.

T：Sit down! So bullying happened and bullying always happens to this little boy Jerry. We're gong to read about Jerry's story. But before the story do you have any question about Jerry? Do you have any question about this boy? （给学生开动脑筋的机会，使学生学会猜测、想象和思考）

S：Why his hair is losing?

T：Why does he lose his hair? I don't know.

S：Why he is sad?

T：Why is he sad? You see，you've got some questions，I'm not sure either. The only way is to find the answer in the story book because reading lesson is always about reading! （好的理念：阅读课就是要阅读/在阅读中培养阅读技能）For the 1st time of reading，I want you to read very fast and then try to understand what the story is about. Got it? Got it! Very good. So open your book and start reading.（教师播放音乐，学生阅读）All right，guys，when music stops ringing，time is up.

All right, can you tell me what happens in this story? Um, this is a big question, right? So, you know Miss Wendy always likes to give you a chance to work it out by yourselves. Now, for the first time, I want you to talk to your partner, use three or four sentences to tell what the story is about. If you think that is hard, maybe these words will help you. OK, you need to talk to your partner. Go! （学生进行对子活动，教师指导）All right, five four three two and one! The focus is right here! What happens? What about you?

S：Jerry is ill. And his hair...and he lose his hair.

T：He loses his hair.

S：The big boy is...

T：You mean the bullies bully...

S：Jerry. Jerry is very sad. And his classmates help him.

T：Wow! Listen to that! They bully Jerry. They help Jerry. Is she right? Now let's listen! This is main idea of the story. It is very important to have the main idea in your head, because when you are reading, this is the basic. OK? And now let's focus on the details. You say bullies bully Jerry, but how do they bully Jerry? What did they do? And how does Jerry feel? So a big question. Don't worry. Wendy is giving you another chance to work it out by yourselves, since I have got something for you. This is a little helper. Hey, right here. Listen and do it, all right? Listen. The yellow one is about what did they do. The blue one, the blue card is about how Jerry feel. You need to write and stick yellow to yellow, blue to blue. And then you ought to read and report in group like that, OK? OK, so work in group. Go! （教师播放音乐）Open your book. Find the key words. The key words are always in the book, is not in your head. It reminds you to use English, right? Use your pen, as you can.（教师巡堂指导）Hey, everybody! Let's read it. They trip up Jerry.

Ss：...

T：Come here, all of you. Come here, all of you. Hey guys! Now you're going to listen! ...Hey guys, listen! You're going to listen to your classmates because they are going to read and report. Here, together! Together! Together, the yellow one. OK, there you go! So what do they do to Jerry, can you report? Read it! Wait, wait wait! Why are you standing over there? Put it right here! Yellow page，right?

G1：...

T：They glue Jerry's book. They bald Jerry's hair. Oh, my God! Hey, are they right? Have a look! Are they right? Give them a big hand. Thank you very much for coming up here. It takes a lot of courage. Let's see they are on the same page. What do they do to Jerry? Trip up, you remember the pictures I show you so far! My God, they trip up Jerry. They shout— not bad! Bald, this is bald. Try "bald"!

Ss：Bald.

T：And...

Ss：...

T：I'll show you.（教师拿走贴在黑板上的人模的帽子，露出一个光光的头）Hey! Look at the him. He's bald! Hoo-hoo! He doesn't have any hair. Oh, how do you feel if you were Jerry?

S：I'm very angry and sick.

T：But you see this is what happens to Jerry. And then they glue— Jerry's books. What would happen? What would happen? Give him the microphone.

S：His book will（be）broken!

T：He can't read it, right! And then they—Puhh! Oh, my God, who would do that? So how does Jerry feel? Show your blue page, so you're going to report the blue page. That group, come up right here. Come on! Come on! All right. OK, there you go!

G2：Jerry runs away. He feels sad.

T：So one word：sad. Go!

G2：Jerry ... Jerry becomes afraid to go to school.

T：One word, one word.

S：Afraid.

T：Afraid. Go on.

G2：Jerry feels helpless but he tries no...

T：One word. Helpless. What is helpless? That means nobody to help him. Thank you, please go back. Jerry, Jerry, Jerry!（教师播放Jerry哭泣的视频）

Jerry is sad. Helpless and afraid! His life is always in the dark, dark in the black world. So tell me, if you were Jerry, what would you want to do?

S: I want to tell my teacher.

T: Trust me! Trust the teacher, good choice.

S: I will call the government and I want government help many many children.

T: Wow, that's a big word. So today government do everything, uh, government does everything .（教师修补自己的话语）Right.

S: Maybe I want to kill me.

T: You want to kill yourself. That is suicide. Try suicide. You know this word suicide. All right, what about you?

S: I want to tell my friend.

T: That's good! You know when you kill yourself, the bullies, how do you think? I think that is not very good. Now, please welcome.

S: I want to cry because, because I am very sad.

T: Tears are healthy! Have the tears out, your soul will be well. But you don't cry all the time! You always find the way. Good! Listen! Jerry doesn't ask for help. Let's have a look. OK, in the picture book, who helps Jerry?

S: Jerry's classmates.

T: Um, not his parents. Well, it's his classmates. But my question, very good! Thank you! Take a seat. But my question is: How do they help Jerry? What do they do? I believe the first time when you're doing the fast reading, you read about it. Do you still remember what do they do?

S: They cut their head. （学生发音不准）

T: They cut their hear.

S: Hear. （学生发音不准）

T: Hair. They cut their hair. Shake it out. This is cut their hair. OK, guys, listen! But why? Why? I don't understand why. Take your microphone. Why?

S: Because Jerry doesn't have any head.

T: Hair.

S: （Laughing）So he...so he（is）very sad. And the boys cut their hair. They like him.

T: So they are, look, same. So one says it. Very good! Thank you. Please have a seat. Every time you finish your answering, sit down, right? Oh, listen, it's a very good reading habit because you try to find the words from the story. It's like the story is talking to you. Remember, very good reading habit! Let's try. They cut their hair, so they look the same. Yes, that word. What about this one?

Ss: Just like Jerry.

T: Just like Jerry. Good. That's very good. Let's go on finding it.

Ss: ...

T: Right! They are the same.

Ss: ...

T: Not absurd. You try to find the word from the story. What word?

Ss: ...

T: Good try! Not alone. Try! Alone.

Ss: Alone.

T: Not only one. Not the only one. Look at his classmates. And look at the bullies. Same or different?

Ss: Different!

T: Very different, guys! Listen, now, I want you to follow me into the story. And let's see how different they are! And there you go! （播放视频）The bullies always bully Jerry. And how does Jerry feel? Luckily, his classmates, they stand up. They cut their hair. And they say—

Ss: You're not alone, Jerry.

T: You're not alone, Jerry. That's good! But that's not enough. Two of you. Let's go!

Ss: You're not alone, Jerry.

T: Remember, Jerry is your classmate. He is ill, doesn't have hair and very sad. Oh, you, this group, that group, stand up. Go!

Ss: You're not alone, Jerry.

T: Still not enough, （教师对学生的朗读不满意）but almost there.

Ss: You're not alone, Jerry. Now we are the same.

T: Thank you. Please take your seat. Now tell me: how do you feel now?

S：I feel happy and I feel safe.

T：You're happy and safe? Safe is a very good word. Actually it appears in the book.

S：I feel warm.

S：I feel the friends are friendly.

T：Very good. And you see? This is how his classmates——

Ss：Say no to bullying.

T：This is how his classmates say no to bullying. So this is what the story is about. And look! How does his teacher say no? Look at the picture. In the picture book, pictures are very helpful. Look at the picture! What does he do? What does he do, class?

S：He cuts his hair too.

T：Yes, yes! He just cuts his hair too. He cuts his hair and also he has a talk with the bullies. "Come to my office! ", right? So, look, they cut their hair and then the teacher has a talk with the bullies. This is what happens in the story. But when you're reading the story, always remember you need to think out of the story. If you were Jerry's classmates, how can you help Jerry? You want to cut your hair, because your hair makes you look like handsome and cool. So, what do you want to do? Use your microphone.

S：Tell this matter of police, policeman.

T：Uh, policeman, government. They do everything. From cutting the hair to telling the police. All right.

S：Tell teacher or call Jerry's parents.

T：Very good. So you want to tell Jerry's teacher.

S：I want to tell Jerry: Don't be sad. You're good.

T：Try to encourage Jerry.

S：I'll tell the boys they're fighting, they are bullying Jerry this is not good.

T：It doesn't work. This is not good. The last one.

S：I will tell boys bullying is wrong.

T：You want to tell the bullies bullying is wrong. All right, so guys, you see you have a lot of good ways, not only you want to tell. So I believe you're very clever and very creative. Maybe you can have different ways. I just want to show you one. Maybe. So if you've got any good idea after class, you can write it on the pink page, all right, anyway, anyhow they help Jerry. And look at Jerry. One, you see Jerry? Not very easy. But there we go. How does Jerry feel now? What about you?

S：I think maybe he feels warm and think they'll —

T：Warm, feels warm. This word is good enough. Look, Jerry doesn't only feel warm or happy, something more than happy. Can you find the word something better than happy? What is the word?

S：Safe.

T：Safe. Feeling safe is the best feeling for people like Jerry. So Jerry doesn't have a hat . That means Jerry feel safe. So guys, let's read this part together, right? "Jerry feels safe and happy." One and two and go!

Ss：Jerry feels safe and happy.

T：Decide...I see you have got some problems with this sentence. Don't worry. I'll tell you. He decides to help his classmates when the bullies bully them. Jerry, actually, in this picture book, Jerry experiences the different feelings. Just have a look.（播放视频）Before it ends, I believe Jerry must have some words to say. Look at this one：Oh, I am ill and the bullies, oh! I feel um!

My class is... my teacher... How do you see that word? Oh oh, great! Oh, like this! His feeling. I feel—

Ss：Happy.

T：What about your group? Let's choose one emotional state. You can either choose black, you can choose orange. And then you try to tell if you were Jerry. OK, there we go! Talk! All right, three two one! I am sorry I can't give you a lot of time to talk, so I'm going to choose. So you want to choose orange or black?

S：Orange.

T：So there you go!

S：My classmates, my classmates cut their hair and my teachers cut their hair too. Oh, I feel very happy and warm. I'll help somebody too.

T：I'll help my classmates. Wow, that's pretty good. Of course she's talking about orange. Let's talk about black one. What about you? Oh, your group, right!

S：Oh, oh my classmates! Oh, the bad guys, he puffs me. He pulls off my hair. They shout bad—

T：Bald.

S：Bald, funny. I don't like school. I want to go home.

T：Oooh, I'll give you a hug. Listen! I believe when you listen to this boy you may have different feelings. That's the same taste with reading the story with different feelings, like me. When I read Page 13, I feel very sorry, because Jerry tells his parents, but his parents never listen. I know that I should listen to my daughter. I have a daughter. I should listen to my daughter. What about you? Maybe there is one page that makes you feel. Now you've finish your book. Please go over, find it out, and I want you to share. Hey, guys, listen! All right, here we go! When I read, hey, guys, Page 16. Go!

S：My classmates help me, so in there, I feel very happy. I know friendship is important.

T：Friends are very important that we learn from the book. What about you?

S：When I read Page 20 and 21, I feel very warm, because the class—

T：Classmates.

S：Cut the classmates' hair. They cut the classmates' hair. I know that they're helpful.

T：Your classmates are always helpful. All right, listen, guys! You know you read a lot. Thank you. Today we not only talk about what do they do, how do they feel. Now we are talking about some serious question. We are talking about—

Ss：Jerry.

T：What is he doing? Verbal, physical, sometimes internet? And we're talking about—

Ss：...

T：Good conclusion. Very good. How bad is bullying! They're talking about the way to help others. I think as important as these three ones, there's something for you: how do we help ourselves? how do we protect ourselves? I'm going to show you the video. There're six ways. This is your homework. All right. And when you finish your homework, when you finish your homework, I have got a big page.

You're going to get these small pages, what do we have? Handbook. What is a handbook? What is a handbook? What does it say? Yes, what?

S：Say no to bullying.

T：That's good. And who says no in the story? Who says no in the story? Jerry? Tell me.

Ss：Jerry.

T：Not only Jerry. Very good. Every one of us says no to bullying. Everybody, stand up! Let's say no to bullying together. Also with music, right? Let's take a vow. Take a vow. I, Wendy.

Ss：I, Wendy.

T：You're not Wendy. I, Wendy, will not bully others! I will not let others bully me! I will help others when they are in trouble. Strongly, I say no to bullying! Say no to bullying! Say no to bullying! You say today. You'll do in the future. For today's homework, you can either read the story and also you can finish the pink and green page. As promise I'll show you a little bit video, which I'll put it in the box. You can.（教师播放视频）Anyway, because time is very limited, I put this into the e-mail box and when you finish your pink book, you can collect it. This is your empty handbook. In my school, my kids are doing a lot of handbook, so I hope this is not your last one. This is the first one of your handbooks. So I guess this is it. Goodbye boys and girls!

【背景介绍】

这是2018年在福建厦门举行的第九届全国小学英语课堂教学的一节观摩课。授课教师是来自南京外国语学校的周亚文老师。该课是一节阅读课，课题名称是Say No to Bullying，题材新颖并贴近学生的生活。教学内容容易引起学生的共鸣。因此，学生对该话题有一定的阅读动机，在讨论时有话可说。

一、教学设计及教学过程

I Pre-reading

Do you have any question about Jerry?

II While-reading

1. Read for the main idea of the story

What is the story about?

2. Read for details.

Read, fill in the cards and report in group about:

What did the bullies do? How do Jerry feel?

If you were Jerry, what would you want to do?

Who helps Jerry? How do they help Jerry? What do they do?

III Post-reading

1. How to protect ourselves?

2. The teacher and the students take vows to say no to bullying.

3. Homework.

二、该课的教学特色

1. 渗透教学理念并开展策略指导

教师在教学过程中渗透自己的教学理念，并开展策略指导教师的阅读理念如下：

（1）教师认为，阅读课就是要阅读；可以通过阅读来寻找我们需要的答案（The only way is to find the answer in the story book because reading lesson is always about reading! ）。

（2）教师认为，获取大意是一切阅读活动的基础（It is very important to have the main idea in your head, because when you are reading, this is the basic. ）。

（3）教师认为读取文本细节需要寻找关键词，即关键词是体现细节的地方，而关键词存在于文本之中，而不是在大脑里。教师传递的信息是，信息的获取要通过实实在在的阅读（And now let's focus on the details. Open your book. Find the key words.The key words are always in the book, not in your head. ）。

（4）从原文中找到关键词语是很好的阅读习惯（It's a very good reading habit because you try to find the words from the story. It's like the story is talking to you. ）。

（5）阅读是要解决现实中的问题，所以需要超出文本来思考问题（But when you're reading the story, always remember you need to think out of the story. ）。

教师不断根据自己的阅读理念对学生进行阅读策略指导。在学生读取文本细节前，教师指导他们如何获取细节：Open your book. Find the key words. 这样，教师帮助学生在细节和关键词之间建立关系，并经过联系形成自己的阅读策略。

2. 引发学生的共情，基于文本内容进行情感教育

教师根据教学内容适时将学生代入主人公 Jerry 和他班上同学的情境。例如，在读取 Jerry 遭受校园欺凌后，教师问 If you were Jerry，what would you want to do? 当学生读取同学们如何帮助 Jerry 渡过难关时，教师问：Now tell me：how do you feel now? 读完整个故事后，教师问：If you were Jerry's classmates，how can you help Jerry?

这节课的选材对小学生来说具有十分重要的意义，因为校园欺凌或多或少地出现在学生的学校生活中，而不少学生面对欺凌不知如何应对。教师通过设问不断引导学生和文本进行互动，成功地引导学生在学习文本的过程中不断地代入自己的情感体验。授课教师通过这个绘本阅读课为学生提供了读大意、读细节、读图片、走进文本、走出文本回归现实的一系列阅读体验，通过故事教学传递共情和友爱的积极人生观。总的来说，这是一节很有营养的小学英语阅读课。

评课案例三 《The Food Action》绘本阅读课

【课堂实录】

T：Hi，children，how are you today?

Ss：I'm fine. Thank you.

T：OK，I'm happy to see you. So I want to share a song with you. Can you stand up and sing with me?

Potato，spinach，salary...

OK，do you like the song? Are you ready for the class now?

T：Class begins! Good morning，boys and girls.

Ss：Good morning，Miss Fang.

T：Sit down please. Class，Just now we enjoyed a song about food. And today we're going to enjoy a story about food. Look here I have so much different food. If you do a good job, you can choose a food for your group. And now I want to put you into 3 groups. You're Group 1, you're Group 2, and you're Group 3. Clear?

Ss: Yes.

T: OK, and in the song we have three foods, they are potato, spinach and salary. Can you guess where they are? Can you guess where they are? Can you guess? Yes, you please.

Ss: There I think they are in the river.

T: Oh?

S: Maybe they (are) in a fridge.

T: In the fridge. Where is the fridge?

S: In the kitchen.

T: Yes, in the kitchen. Do you have other guesses? Let's see: where are they? Whole class. They're in the—in the kitchen. OK, follow me: in the kitchen.

Ss: In the kitchen.

T: In the kitchen.

Ss: In the kitchen.

T: And they are in the kitchen. Today we're going to enjoy a story *In the Kitchen*. And now let's see who is in the kitchen in this story. Who are they? Do you know them? Who can you see? Who can you see?

Ss: Egg.

T: Oh, you can see eggs. Where are the eggs? Where are the eggs? Come on. Very good. Eggs.

Ss: Eggs.

T: Good. What can you see? You please.

S: I can see a candy.

T: A candy, yes. Where is the candy? Show me the candy. OK, candy.

S: Candy.

T: Candy.

Ss: Candy.

T: Do you like eating candy?

Ss：Yes.

T：Yes，you like eating candy. What else？You please.

S：I can see a sweet potato.

T：Yes，a sweet potato. Where are the potatoes？OK，potato.

Ss：Potato.

T：Potato.

Ss：Potato.

T：Can you say potato？

Ss：Yes.

T：Potato.

S：Potato.

T：Good. Potato. And what else？What can you see？You please.

S：I can see a pineapple.

T：OK，pineapple. Where is the pineapple？OK，follow me：pineapple.

Ss：Pineapple.

T：Pineapple.

Ss：Pineapple.

T：Good，this is a big pineapple. And what else？You please.

Ss：I can see an eggplant.

T：Where is the eggplant？OK，follow me：eggplant.

Ss：Eggplant.

T：Eggplant.

Ss：Eggplant.

T：Good. Do you know what this is？What is this？OK，follow me：chips.

Ss：Chips.

T：Chips.

Ss：Chips.

T：And there is some pepper on the chips，pepper on the chips.

Ss：Pepper on the chips.

T：Good. There is lots of pepper. It's green pepper. Do you know what is pepper？Follow me：pepper.

Ss：Pepper.

T：Pepper.

Ss：Pepper.

T：Very good. And what is this？What is this？You please.

S：It's a sausage.

T：Oh，it's a sausage. Very good. It's sausage. Follow me：sausage.

Ss：Sausage.

T：Sausage.

Ss：Sausage.

T：Good！And they are a good family. They live happily in the kitchen.
（You）see it's a food family. At the beginning of the story，they are very—

Ss：Happy.

T：They are very happy. How do you know？

S：Because they are—

T：Smiling. Can you see they're smiling.（可以给学生更多思维的时间）

Ss：Yes.

T：Can you show me your happy face？Can you show me your happy face？
（体验式学习）OK，I love your smiling face. Very good！And one day，
everything is different！Oh，are they happy now？

Ss：No.

T：They are very—

Ss：Worried.

T：They're very worried. At the beginning，they are very happy. But now they
are very worried. Read after me：worried.

Ss：Worried.

T：Worried.

T：They are very worried. Can you guess why they are so worried？Why are
they so worried？Can you have a guess？OK，you please.

S：The rat come.

T：Oh，the rat comes. So you think the rat will eat them. Oh，good guessing.
Do you have other guessing？You please.

S：I think some dogs want to eat them.

T：Some dogs want to eat them. Yes，maybe，let's see. Wow，a big shadow. I'm so sacred. Look，the food，the food is very sacred. Do you know who the shadow is? And what is he doing? Now，the whole class，what is the shadow?

S：The rat.

T：Oh，it's the rat. It's the rat. And what is he doing?

Ss：He wants to eat the food.

T：Oh，he wants to eat the food. Now let's see.（播放视频）

Every night the rat steals food from the kitchen. All of the food is worried.

You're right. It's a rat. Follow me：a rat.

Ss：A rat.

T：A rat.

Ss：A rat.

T：A rat steals food.

Ss：A rat steals food.

T：Because the rat steals food from the kitchen，so all the food is worried. They say，"Don't eat me! Don't eat me!" The whole class，follow me：Every night.

Ss：Every night.

T：A rat steals food from the kitchen.

Ss：A rat steals food from the kitchen.

T：All of the food is worried.

Ss：All of the food is worried.

T：What do they say?

Ss：Don't eat me! Don't eat me!

T：OK，good! Now can you show a worried face，can you give a worried face? OK，all the food is so worried. They are thinking：What can we do? What can we do? So if you're the food，what can you do? I want you to work in pairs，work in pairs，OK? Talk about if you're the food，the rat wants to eat you，what can you do? Now，one，two，begin!（学生对子活动）OK，one，two，three!

Ss：A，B，C!

T：Good! Who has some good ideas? OK，you please.

S：We can run away.

T：Oh，you can run away. You're so afraid，so you will run away. Good！And what about you?

S：I can find a cat.

T：You can find a cat. What can a cat do? It can—

Ss：It can eat the food.

T：Oh，it can eat the food. What else? OK，you please.

S：We can use a knife and cut the rat.

T：OK，you can find a knife and find people to help you. Very good. Good guessing. This is your idea and let's see what do they do.（教师播放视频）Oh，a meeting，in the kitchen. What are they talking about? （教师继续播放视频） So do they run away? Do they run away?

Ss：No.

T：No，they are thinking about an idea. What's their idea? Let's see. What does the egg say?

Ss：We must do something.

T：OK，follow me：we must do something.

Ss：We must do something.

T：Good！And the potato says：Let's find a cat.

Ss：Let's find a cat！

T：And he can help us.

Ss：And he can help us.

T：Yes，and the sausage says：No，it eats rat.

Ss：No，it eats rat.

T：But it eats us too！

Ss：But it eats us too！

T：And the old corn says：I have a good idea.

Ss：I have a good idea.

T：Oh，It's an old corn. Says the old corn：I have a good idea.

Ss：I have a good idea.

T：Very good. Now I'll be the brave egg. And Group 1，you're the potato；

Group 2，you're the yummy sausage；Group 3，you're the old corn. We must do something.

G1：Let's find a cat. And he can help us.

T：Good!

G2：No，he eats rat，but he eats us too!

G3：Oh，I have a good idea!

T：OK，very good. And now I want to invite more students to come here. And who wants to be the egg?

S：Egg.

T：OK，you please. Who wants to be the potato? Who wants to be the potato? OK，you please. And I have the yummy sausage. OK，you please. We have all boys. And here is the girl，an egg.（角色朗读）

S1：We must do something.

T：OK，we must do something.

S2：Let's find a cat. And he can help us.

S3：No，he eats rat，but he eats us too!

S4：Oh，I have a good idea!

T：Can you be old? I have a good idea!（教师示范）

S：I have a good idea!

T：OK，very good! OK，let's give them a big hand，OK? Let's give them a big hand! Very good. Now the old corn says：I have a good idea! Can you have a guess：what is the good idea? Can you guess：what is the good idea? You please.

S：Run away.

T：Run away. You think running away is a good idea? Maybe! You please.

S：In the cup.

T：In the cup. Maybe you mean hiding in the cup. OK，what is the good idea? You please.

S：Find the cat and run away.（在前面方案的基础上产生新的解决办法）

T：Run away. Why?

S：Because the cat will eat them. Run away and the cat can't eat them.

T：Oh you mean you find a cat that can eat the rat and you can run away. OK， very good. And what about you?

S：We can sleep in the kitchen and when the rat goes into the kitchen，we jump on the rat and fight him.

T：Oh，you pretend you're sleeping and when the rat comes you 'll jump at it. OK，very good. You're so smart. Good idea！Let's see. What's their good idea？ OK，what can you see on the picture？What can you see on the picture？It's a big shadow. What is that？Oh，it's a rat. Look at his finger！What is he doing？He's eating food．He's eating food.

Ss：He's eating food.

T：And what can you see on this page？Oh，it's a cat.

Ss：It's a cat.

T：It's a cat. Where is the rat now？

Ss：The mouse is scared.

T：Oh，it's very scared.

Ss：It's very scared.

T：How do you know？Because it's mouth is very big，very big.

Ss：It's mouth is very big.

T：And he shouts "Ou！" Can you shout like a rat？Ou！

Ss：Ou！

T：It's so afraid！Then suddenly，he hears a sound：Miao！And what does the cat do？

Ss：Jumps.

T：Yes，jump at the rat. OK，he jumps at the rat. OK，now，children，I want you to take out your story book；you have your story book on the table. Please turn to Page 8，Page 8. And please read the story from Page 8 to 15. What can you see on the Page 8 and also what do they do to fight with the cat？Circle like me， OK，circle like me. From Page 8 to 15. Circle what they do. Use your pen to circle. Good.（学生阅读并完成老师布置的任务）

Finish？Are you ready？Have you finish reading the story？OK，now，please turn to Page 8. Listen to the story. Now let's listen to the story.（教师播放下一段视频）

T：So does the food family run away？

Ss：No.

T：They're thinking of a good idea about how to fight against the rat. They have a meeting. They want to fight against the rat，so they have a meeting. They have a food action. Follow me：the food action.

Ss：The food action.

T：The food action.

Ss：The food action.

T：They have a food action. And now let's see how do they fight with the rat in the food action. At night the rat comes again. He goes to the egg. And suddenly he hears a sound. What is the sound?

Ss：Miao.

T：Miao. And what does the cat do?

Ss：Jumps.

T：Yes，jumps at the rat. So follow me：Jump at.

Ss：Jump at.

T：Yes，the cat jumps at the rat.

Ss：The cat jumps at the rat.

T：OK，follow me：A cat jumps at the rat.

Ss：A cat jumps at the rat.

T：Very good！ A cat jumps at the rat. Here now I'm the rat，who wants to be the cat？ Who wants to be the cat？ The boy. Yes，the boy please.

At night the rat comes again. He goes to the eggs. But suddenly he hears a sound. Oh，Miao，the cat jumps at the rat. Very good！ Very good！ And let's see what happens next. What happens next？ What can you see on this picture？ What can you see？ You please. What can you see？ What's this？ Oh it's— Use the microphone. It's —

S：Butter.

T：Oh，it's the butter. But he's scared and he runs. He，he— What happens？ OK，you please.

S：He—

T：He slips. What happens next?

S：Butter.

T：He slips on the butter. So what words do you circle? What words do you circle? OK, you please.

S：Slips on.

T：OK, you circle "slips on". Very good! And here follow me：Slips on the butter.

Ss：Slips on the butter.

T：Slips on the butter.

Ss：Slips on the butter.

T：Very good. He slips on the butter. Now here, I have some butter. Who can come here and slip on the butter? Yes, you.（学生上来）Oh, slip on the butter. Good! And then let's see. What can you see?

Ss：Pineapple.

T：Oh, it's an pineapple. And is the rat happy now?

Ss：No!

T：He's very—

Ss：Worried.

T：Worried. Because it hurts, right? It hurts. What words do you circle?

Ss：Fall.

S：The rat falls on the pineapple.

T：Oh, the rat falls on the pineapple. Good! Falls on, follow me：Falls on.

Ss：Falls on.

T：Falls on the pineapple.

Ss：Falls on the pineapple.

T：Yes, the rat falls on the pineapple. And here what do I have? Oh, a big pineapple. Who can come here and fall on the pineapple? You please.

S：Ouch!

T：Ouch! He falls on the pineapple. Good! And here when he jumps up, what happens? Who are they? Are they the chips? You read the words. They are the chips. What do they do?

Ss：Pepper.

T：I put the pepper into his eyes. Follow me：Put pepper.

Ss：Put pepper.

T：Put pepper.

Ss：Put pepper.

T：Good！Put pepper into the rat's eyes. So here，I have pepper. Who wants to put pepper in his eyes? You please. OK，I put. Oh，the pepper is in my eyes. I can not see now. I can not see. And what can you see in this? What's that?

Ss：...

T：I cannot see the rat now. Where is the rat? Can you come here? Where is the rat? Oh，here is the rat！Who is pushing? Now can you see the—

Ss：Eyes.

T：Who are they?

Ss：Potato.

T：Who are they? They're potatoes. Good，potatoes. They're potatoes. And they say： "You need a shower！" Follow me：You need a shower！

Ss：You need a shower！

T：So the potatoes pour water.

Ss：The potatoes pour water.

T：The potatoes pour water.

Ss：The potatoes pour water.

T：Very good. The potatoes pour water. Here we have a glass of water. Who can come here and pour water on me? On me? OK，you please. Oh，I need a shower. Now，what happens in the end? What happens in this page? From this page what can you see? Yes，you please.

S：The rat runs away.

T：The rat runs away. Where can the rat run? OK，here right? Yes，the rat runs away. Who is the winner? Can you guess the rat is the winner or the food family?

Ss：The food family.

T：The food family is the winner. So they're very—.

Ss：Happy.

T：They're now very happy. And what about the rat，the poor rat? The rat—

Ss：Runs away.

T：The rat runs away. The rat finally runs away.

Ss：The rat finally runs away.

T：Now, the whole class, stand up and act out the story. Stand up and act out the story together.（教师播放视频，师生一边观看一边表演）This time the rat cries and run away! Thank you! I like your performance. Sit down please. Please take out your books. Let's read the story together. Read it aloud. Are you ready?

Ss：Yes!

T：OK. The Food Action.

Ss：The Food Action.

（教师播放视频，学生朗读故事）

T：OK, very good. And now I want you to take out your story books. Do you have your story books? It's time for us to read the story now. And here we have five questions：where, who, why, how, what. Now let's do the first two together. Where does the food family live? In the—in the—

Ss：Kitchen.

T：Right. Live in the kitchen. Very good. And who are in the food family? Who'll fight in the food action? We have the egg, we have the potatoes, we have, we have—who will fight in the food action.

Ss：Old corn.

T：Old corn, good! And what else?

S：Pineapple.

T：Pineapple, good!

S：Candy.

T：Oh, candy, maybe. And what else?

S：The chips.

T：The chips, yes.

S：The pepper.

T：The pepper, the pepper, good, the pepper. And so here they fight in the food action. Please work in groups. Work in groups. And finish the question Why, why are they so worried, how, how they fight in the food action and what happens in the end. Please talk, talk in groups and finish the story map. Talk in groups, one, two, begin!

Please talk, talk in groups, OK? （学生完成故事地图）OK, finished? Are you ready? Why are they afraid? Can you tell me why are they afraid? You please.

S: ...（inaudible）

T: Why are they so afraid? Can you help him? Can you help her? You please. Can you help?

S: The rat eats food in the kitchen.

T: OK, the rat eats food in the kitchen, yes. We can say the rat eats food or the rat steals food from the kitchen. And how do they do in the food action? How do they do? We have step 1: the cat, the cat...OK, you please.

S: The cat jumps on the rat.

T: Jumps on the rat. OK, good! Step 2, what do they do? And can you try?

S: ...（inaudible）

T: OK, very good. Can you help him? Can you help him? Use your microphone.

S: The rat slips on the butter.

T: Oh, the rat slips on the butter. Step 3: A pineapple—The rat—

S: The rat falls on the pineapple.

T: The rat falls on the pineapple, good! And step 4, you please.

S: The chips put pepper in the rat's eyes.

T: Eyes, very good. The chips put pepper in the rat's eyes. And what happens in the end? The whole class, tell me, what happens in the end? The rat cries and—

Ss: Runs away.

T: Runs away, good! And this is the whole story. Who can tell me what you can learn from this story? Uh, huh, you please.

S: We can find a cat to help us.

T: We can find a cat to help us. Yes, this is a good idea. And what can you learn from this story? Who can tell me what you can learn from this story? OK, you please?

S: We can find, we can find another good idea.

T: Uh, we can find another good idea. So the food family holds a meeting and have some good ideas. OK, now let's see. The food family wins in the food action, right? They win in the food action because they have a really big family. Then children, remember: a big family is always better than a single one. And now they win in the big action. But I heard the animal family has the same problem. The animal family is so worried. OK, so a big—

Ss: Tiger.

T: A big tiger wants to eat the animals. They are so worried. And I want to share this story with you. Now here is the homework: Enjoy this story. You have the story paper. You have the story paper. And today homework. 1. Read the story and finish the worksheet. We have five questions in this worksheet. Step 1: How many animals are there in this story? Step 2: Who are they? Step 3: Who are the animals so afraid of? Step 4: Why are they so afraid? Step 5: How do they fight against the tiger? Read the story and finish the worksheet. Now let's see who is the winner of today. Who is the winner? One, two, three, which group?

Ss: One.

T: Group 1. OK, so you have a big family and you fight with the... Now, class is over. Goodbye, boys and girls.

Ss: Goodbye, Ms. Fang.

【背景介绍】

本课也是在福田区教科院附小举行的三校联盟的一节绘本教学课，授课教师是来自福田教科院附小的方思颖老师。学生是福田教科院附小三年级学生。课题名称是Food Action。

一、教学设计及教学过程

I Lead-in

II Presentation and practice （1）

III Presentation and practice （2）

IV Presentation and practice （3）

V Practice

（1）Act out the whole story.

（2）Read aloud the whole story.

（3）Finish the story map: where, who, why, how, what.

VI Teaching moral

What have you learned from this story?

该课的教学过程是先分后总的课堂模式。教师分段呈现故事内容，分段练习生词及短语。

在呈现完整个故事后，教师组织学生进行各种形式的练习。先让全班学生跟着视频进行表演，然后再跟着视频朗读。接着，在回答where，who，why，how，what 问题的基础上小组完成故事地图。最后，教师引导学生构建故事的教益。

二、该课的教学特色

（1）声情并茂呈现故事，并提供机会让学生进行体验式学习。故事是用来讲的。

故事里面的情感表达需要外显的手段。教师能够通过声音呈现出食物对耗子的恐惧。当讲述到食物一家过着快乐的生活时，教师让学生Show me your happy face.当食物发现耗子在厨房偷吃东西时，它们感到害怕和忧虑，这时教师让学生Show me a worried face.在呈现了短语slip on the butter后，教师同样提供机会让学生体验slip on the butter的感觉，教师说：Now here，I have some butter. Who can come here and slip on the butter? 以帮助学生对该表达式进行理解甚至记忆。这种体验式学习会比教师对词语的解释产生更好的学习效果。此外，教师在呈现完整个故事后再次播放视频，让全班学生站起来一起表演故事，让每位学生通过朗读及动作参与到对故事的体验之中。

（2）注重培养学生解决问题的能力，启迪思维。

例如，教师设置了If you're the food，the rat wants to eat you，what can you do? 的问题让学生以对子的形式讨论解决问题的办法。提问时教师得到不同的方法：

——We can run away.

——I can find a cat.

——We can use a knife and cut the rat.

当故事中的老玉米说他有个好主意时，教师没有马上呈现这个好主意是什么，而是给学生设了问：What is the good idea? 以此来培养学生的猜测能力。

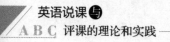

（3）课堂有生成，特别是来自学生的生成。

当教师让学生猜测老玉米有什么好主意时，一位学生在前面建议find a cat to eat the rat和the cat will eat us too的基础上提出了find a cat and run away的想法。教师问为什么要找一只猫并逃跑，学生回答：Because the cat will eat them. Run away and the cat can't eat them.这个互动片段说明学生有思考，并且有创造，是教师没有预设的答案。而另一个学生则说：We can sleep in the kitchen and when the rat goes into the kitchen，we jump on the rat and fight him.

该课的教学设计未能走得更高。教学设计侧重的是听故事以及有表情地读故事。如果教师能够设计能激发学生创造力的读后任务则更好，学生需要更具有挑战性任务的刺激。

评课案例四 《Guest Comments》读写课

【课堂实录】

T：Class begins！

Ss：Stand up！

T：Good morning，boys and girls.

Ss：Good morning！

T：Sit down please. Nice to see you again！Look，I have gifts for you. Some bookmarks. If you do a good job，you can get one. You can have it later，OK？And today we're going to make comments on something. Comments.

Ss：Comments.

T：Hm，do you know them？Do you know them？

Ss：Yes.

T：We often make comments on Taobao，on Didi，or on Meituan. We also make comments on cities. Which city is it？

Ss：Xiamen.

T：Yeah，your city Xiamen！You know I were here. I had a comment on

Xiamen. What is it? What's my comments on Xiamen? OK, I'll tell you later. First I want to know your comment on Xiamen. What's your comment? Can you? Please.

S：My comment is：It's a beautiful city. And food is very delicious. It's like a garden of the sea.

T：Wow, that's a good comment. I see and you have a beautiful sea view, delicious sea food and nice people, interesting opera, and the whole class are nice. So your comment is good! And what's my comment? Can you guess? What's my comment on Xiamen? You, please.

S：I think your comment is good.

T：Yeah! Good comment too. And I like the hotel too. I stay in Jiangwan Hotel these days. It's a wonderful stay. And the house keepers there are very helpful and nice. They help us clean the room and make the bed. What about this comment? What is the comment on? On Taobao? On a city? What's the comment on? Yes, you please.

S：It's a comment of a hotel.

T：Yeah, it's a comment on the hotel. And that's the housekeeper. She's Mrs. Broom. And how was the comment? Good or bad? How was the comment? Good, average or bad? Yes, OK, you, please.

S：I think maybe it's bad, because she is cry.

T：Oh, you mean Mrs. Broom was not so happy. She looked a little worried. Yeah! Because it's a bad comment, a bad stay. What's wrong? A bad stay. Yes, um, I think there must be some problems. Look, the guests took some photos of their rooms. Can you read the pictures and find out the problems from the pictures?

S：First, the bed, chairs and others are old and dirty.

T：Oh, everything is very old and dirty.

S：The second , the food is bad.

T：Maybe Picture 3.

S：The third, noisy music；the TV is broken.

T：Oh, the TV was broken. So many problems. In fact, the guests wrote some comments about that. Here are the comments. Who wrote the comments? Who wrote that? Can you find out? Who wrote the comments? You please.

S：Wu Yifan and his family.

T：Yes，Wu Yifan and his family wrote the comments.

Can you find all the problems in the comments? Can you? OK，you can have a try. Now，here are the comments. Can you read it and try to find out all the problems? OK，now，do it now! One minute! （学生阅读）OK，time is up! What are the problems? Can you tell me? What are the problems in the passage?

S：First，our room is big，but everything was very old.

T：First，everything was very old. That means old things and any other problem?

S：And the chair is broken，so our friend Robin deaned our room and fixed a broken chair.

T：Yeah，there was a broken chair.

S：And Wu Yifan wants to watch TV and the TV didn't work.

T：Oh，there was a broken TV. Any other problems? You.

S：And the noisy music.

T：Yeah! The people listened to loud music，noisy music. OK，you find any other problems? Thank you. Any other problems? Yes，you please.

S：My mum wants to read a book，but the lamp was too small.

T：Oh，a small lamp. Um hum.

S：And my dad got some hamburger from the hotel kitchen，but then was cold and tastes bad.

T：Oh you mean the cold hamburger from the hotel kitchen. Thank you. Yeah，so many problems. It's a good stay or a bad stay? Yes，of course，it was a bad stay. What a pity! And have you got all of them? OK，good job. If you have got all the problems，you can get one bookmark in the box，one bookmark from the box. Yes，you can get one bookmark in the box，one bookmark from the box. Yes，get one bookmark，everyone gets one bookmark from the box. And it was really a bad stay，so many problems. How did you think they feel? How did they feel，with so many problems? Were they happy? Of course not. You please.

S：They felt unhappy.

T：Uh，they were unhappy. It was a bad stay. Why? Why did they feel unhappy? Why? The chair was broken, so they...Bob, you please. You say: the chair was broken, so they couldn't sit. The chair was broken, so they couldn't sit. They were unhappy. What about the other problems? Why did these problems make them unhappy? Why? The chair was broken, so they couldn't sit. What about the other problems? Can you discuss in your group and share your ideas? OK, and do it now! Find out the problem. You can share your ideas in the group. Why did these problems make them unhappy and then tell me, OK? （教师巡堂指导）OK, now I am eager to know your idea! I heard some wonderful ideas. And who wants to share with us? OK, everyone, can you share the name card like this, so that I can see clearly? Thank you, so much. Richard!

S: My mother couldn't read the book because the lamp was too small.

T: Um hum, she couldn't read well because of the small lamp.

S: They missed the show because the TV was broken.

T: They couldn't watch TV and missed the show.

S: Wu Yifan didn't sleep all night.

T: Because of the noisy music, they didn't sleep well. Joana.

S: The hamburger is cold, so Wu Yifan's dad couldn't eat well.

T: The hamburger was cold. What about the old things? Why did the old things make them feel unhappy?

S: They couldn't use the old things so they are unhappy.

T: Unhappy. They didn't enjoy the hotel because of the old things. Wow, it was really bad for Wu's family. So Mrs. Broom did something. They must work on it. What did she do? What did the housekeeper do? Guess? What should she do? For example, the room was so dirty, so Mrs Broom—

S: She must clean the room.

T: Yeah, the housekeeper cleaned the room, but she couldn't solve all the problems. So she told someone else. Look, she wrote an e-mail to the manager, to the manager. Look, this is the e-mail. Dear manager. Oh, what should she write? Dear manager— Here are two choices for you. A. It's bad for me. B. I'm sorry to get a bad comment from our guest. What should she write? A or B, which one is? Jackie.

S: I think it's B.

T：B is better. Can you read it out?

S：I'm sorry to get a bad comment of our gods.

T：Guests.

S：Guests.

T：I'm sorry to get a bad comment from our guest. Yes，B is better. From this sentence we know that she is going to talk about the guest and the comment. So B is better. A is not. What is about No. 2，No. 3 and No. 4? What does she write here? Can you complete it now? Now，maybe，you can use your worksheet，now. Here are the comments. Can you read the comments carefully? And try to finish the e-mail here. OK，now，do it in your worksheet. Read the comments carefully and try to finish the e-mail. Hi，everybody，you can do it like this. Don't do it like this. Do it like this. Read the comments and then finish the e-mail. If you need some help，here are some tips for you，some tips.（学生完成worksheet，教师指导）OK，it seems that most of you have finished. OK，time is up. Now，No. 2，what is your idea? Lena.

S：There is a broken chair，so they have no chair to sit.

T：They have no chair to sit on or there was a broken chair?

S：There was.

T：Good. Different idea? Different sentence for No.2? There was a broken chair or... Rob，you!

S：The chairs were all broken.

T：All broken，oh! What a pity! So，there were all broken chairs . The chair was broken. Both are right! Different expressions，but they all make sense，right? Yes. What about No.3? Ada.

S：The lamp was too small. They can't read books.

T：The lamp was too small，good! Any other sentence? Eric.

S：The people in Room 301 listened to loud music，so they didn't sleep all night.

T：Sleep all night. Or you can say people in Room three o one or three zero one. Did they sleep? Oh，this is for No.4. And any different sentence for No.3? The mother couldn't read well or—? No.3.

S：So they couldn't fall asleep.

T：Oh，that's also for No.4. They couldn't fall asleep. They couldn't sleep well. And any different idea for No.3? Lena.

S: They couldn't enjoy the read.

T: They couldn't enjoy reading. Yeah! They couldn't enjoy reading. And No. 4. They couldn't sleep well, they couldn't fall asleep. They all make sense. Oh, it's awful for Wu's family. The manager did something for that. What did he do at the hotel? So many problems. He did something for that. What did he do? The TV was broken, what did he do for this? Reed!

S: They should fix the broken TV.

T: Oh, they fixed the broken TV and or they bought a new TV, a new TV, so, Reed, please try again.

S: So the Wu's family can enjoy the TV show.

T: Wow, of course. Thank you. And what else did he do? What else did he do? Joana.

S: The chair was broken so they buy a new chair.

T: Bought a new chair so the guests sit comfortably. Anything else? What did he do? Kevin.

S: The thing is old so they will buy a new thing.

T: Change the old things into new things so the people... Did they enjoy their stay? Yes, of course, they felt comfortable. They enjoyed their stay. Jason.

S: There is a small lamp.

T: The small lamp. What did they do with the small lamp?

S: They buy a big lamp.

T: They bought a big lamp and so—

S: So they could read well.

T: Of course they could read well. You please.

S: The hamburger was cold so they buy some delicious and fresh food.

T: They cooked delicious and fresh food. Well, they can eat and enjoy the food.

S: They tell people don't listen to noisy music so the people can sleep well.

T: Oh, they enjoy pleasant things. People can have good rest. If someone listens to loud music at night in the hotel, they should stop them politely, so they can have a good rest. So, in fact, they didn't lock the hotel. What was the hotel like? What did the manager do? He did many things. He offered free wifi. He did many other things. He bought a computer, and he offered freeone ; he offered some magazines; he offered some fresh food. Right? And the hotel has changed a lot. What is the hotel like? Look, uh, wonderful! Fresh and tasty food, a new bathroom, a swimming pool. What about the rooms? So beautiful! Everything is new! And do you still remember Wu Yifan's family? And the Wus' family was invited to the hotel again. They stayed there last weekend. They made some comments again. How was their comment this time? Can you guess? How was their comment ? Still bad? It was—

Ss: Good!

T: Yes, it was a good stay. And what was the comment? What did they write in the comments? What did they write in the comments? Kevin.

S: They maybe write: Our weekend at your hotel was very good. The room is big and very new. Everything was very new.

T: Oh, very good comments because it was a good stay! They were so happy with their stay. They wrote some good comments. What did they write? Now it's your turn to think and discuss in your groups and then share your idea with us, OK? Now, go! Share your ideas with your group. And everyone pays attention: Great teamwork should be like this. So try your best to get five stars. OK, and here are some tips for you. So think and make more comments. I think the group can help you now.（教师指导）OK, now, time is up. I heard many nice ideas, many good comments. Now, it's time to share your comments. Any volunteer? Group 1, 1 would have a try. Share your ideas here. Which group? Um, Ada, what about your group? Can your group share your ideas here? You please. The whole group. You'll share your ideas with us. Yeah, come, come to the blackboard. Yes, you can use your bookmark. OK, now can you share your idea one by one and sentence by sentence? OK, face the audience. Listen to them.

S1: We had a delicious breakfast and had a good sleep.

S2: We had a wonderful time.

S3: The room was bright, big and clean.

S4: We had a KTV room.

S5：The restaurant was very big and beautiful.

S6：We had a enjoyable stay.

T：Oh，you had an enjoyable stay. Wow，so many good comments. Thank you. And wait a minute. Hi，what's your comment on their comment？ Good or great？ Oh，great！ You did a good job！ So you can get five stars. Congratulations！ Thank you！ Go back to your seat and sit down. You know，comments can be good or bad. It could be an encouragement or improvement. People would like to get comments from other honestly. And do you know my comment on you today？ OK，good or——

Ss：Great！

T：Great！ Yeah！ My comment on you is great today. And you did a good job！ And I like your smiling and I like your English. I like your voice and all of you are so active，so polite in the English class. I think you must learn a lot. Right？ So I really enjoy having English class with you！ And hi，ladies and gentlemen，do you agree with me？ OK，big hands for our students，big hands for ourselves. And today's homework is：Write some comments on the hotel or things in the real life. Good comment or bad comment is OK，and write them in details. OK？ So much for today！ Class is over. Stand up please. Goodbye，boys and girls.

Ss：Goodbye，Ms. Zhong！

【背景介绍】

该课是2018年在厦门举行的全国小学英语课堂教学观摩活动的一节读写课，教学内容选自人教版PEP六年级（下）第二单元，课题名称为Guest Comments；执教教师是来自东莞莞城中心小学的钟秀清老师。该课的指导教师为东莞市教育研究院的张凝老师。整节课的教学设计高屋建瓴，从阅读文本表达"差评"的文本中提取信息和语言入手，到把获取的信息和语言运用到写e-mail中去，从而实现信息和语言的迁移，再到运用信息和语言创造一个新表达"好评"的文本。

一、教学设计和教学过程

I Pre-reading

1. Free talk：What's your comment on Xiamen？

2. Guess what my comment on Xiamen is.

3. Guess what happened by viewing the picture and find out the problems.

II While-reading

1. Read and underline.

Questions：Who wrote the e-mail? Can you find out all the problems in the comment?

2. Think，discuss and say：Why did they feel unhappy?

3. Read and complete Mrs. Broom's e-mail to the manager（worksheet）：

（1）What are the comments of the guests?

（2）What did the manager do?

（3）What was the hotel like this time?

III Post-reading

1. Discuss，think and share：How was Wu's family's comment this time?

2. Summary.

上课伊始，教师直接切入话题comment。然后让学生说说他们对厦门的评价，接着让学生猜测授课教师自己对厦门的评价，从而激活学生关于对事物进行评价的背景知识：评价语：good，average，bad。评价的事物：淘宝、宾馆等。接着教师引入文本中的人物——酒店客房管家Mrs. Bloom以及顾客Wu Yifan一家（下称吴家），让学生猜测Mrs. Bloom的心情以及造成其心情的原因——得到差评。教师让学生先看图片并对图片进行描述，为后面的阅读做好铺垫。

在读中阶段，教师先让学生阅读吴家给酒店管家写的e-mail，先找出谁写的e-mail，然后再找出吴家在e-mail中陈述的所有问题，并用鱼骨图把信息呈现出来。鱼骨头思维导图的鱼头是bad（stay），鱼骨的一边先放着酒店存在的各种问题；教师在学生用语言表达在问题时帮他们对语言进行了重构，以使这些语言足够简洁而可以放在鱼骨的一边。教师接着引导学生说出这些问题为什么会使吴家感到不快，并把这些原因放在鱼骨的另一边。鱼尾则放置了心情：unhappy。

在读后阶段教师设计了两个任务。一个是写的任务，即吴家向酒店管家投诉，管家写e-mail给酒店经理，向其转述吴家对酒店的差评。实际上这是一个把从阅读中提取的信息和获取的语言应用、迁移到写作中去的任务。酒店经理在接到管家的电邮后对酒店进行整改，然后又邀请吴家再次入住，这个时候酒店在硬件设施和软件服务上都有了很大的改进。所以，教师设计了另一个读后任务，小组讨论后给酒店写个好评，然后选取一个小组口头汇报他们讨论的结果；每个学生看着手上的书签（用来写好评的）都来说一句。第二个任务看似一个写作任务，但最后的表现形式是口语活动。第二个写作活动已不再是写差评，而是写好评，在信息和语言方面都跟前面写差评截然相反，因而可以看成是思想和语言上的创造。教师在授课接近结束时，学以致用，对学生在本课的表现进行了归纳总结并给了"好评"。最后，教师布置了分层次课后作业。

整节读写课的教学思路是输入——→模仿性输出——→创造性输出，对文本的处理也分别经过了文本结构——→文本重构——→文本创造三个阶段。在输入到输出的过程中，教师致力于培养学生的语言能力、学习能力、思维品质和文化品格。下面将从几个方面来阐述它的特色和亮点。

二、该课的教学特色

1. 语境的创设和贯通

吴家住酒店——给管家差评——管家写e-mail给经理——酒店整改——吴家给好评。整节课的猜、看、读、说、写等活动就在这个大语境中展开。从阅读comments输入到输出comments，都是围绕着吴家住酒店的感受和评价展开的。该课创设的情境脉络清晰，一气呵成，能够很好地体现语言课程中学习、发展和创造的需要。

2. 加入了view的元素

教师在导入了话题后，播放酒店管家Mrs. Broom的图片，让学生猜测她收到的评价是好、中、差。学生猜测"差"，因为通过看可以感知管家不说话，那么她收到的可能是差评。图片和动画是看的，文字是读的，尽管它们都需要用眼睛来吸入信息，但这两种信息感知模式还是有区别的。通过观看获取的信息可能不够准确、细致和深入，但因为它直观、快捷，因此可以用来培养学生的猜测能力和对事物的观察能力或者作为阅读活动的铺垫。

3. 教师擅长重构学生话语

在师生互动中每当学生语言有不妥之处时，教师都会重构正确的话语。这里的重构实际上是一种改错，即教师改错。这种改错方式的好处是不会使学生丢面子，学习动机强烈及注意力集中的学生能够从这样的重构话语中学习语言的正确的表达方法。但部分学生可能意会不到教师的意图及重构话语的作用。以此来作为反馈并给学生。

4. 教师在词汇教学方面采用的是隐性教学，如comment，stay等

教师在整节课中有15次teacher talk中使用了stay一词，说明stay是本课teacher talk的高频词；其中两次是作动词使用，其他13次用作名词。而stay作名词使用的情况是较少的，因此应该是学生比较陌生的。教师没有明确地告诉学生作为名词的stay的用法，而是经常反复地在语境中使用它。教师在stay前面加上不同的形容词或形容词性物主代词来表情达意，如wonderful/good/bad/their/enjoyable。

5. 教师使用鱼骨型思维导图帮助学生提取和归纳文本信息

在这节课中，一个明显的亮点是教师使用鱼骨图来帮助学生提取文本的主要信息。文本中的信息主要是因为宾馆的问题使顾客住得不开心，也就是说，导致他们给宾馆差评的是他们在那里住得不开心，而不开心是因为宾馆的设施和服务有问题。因此，教师首先带领学生提取宾馆服务方面的问题，如房间东西旧（old things）、椅子破（broken chair）、灯小（small lamp）、汉堡包冷（cold hamburger）、电视损坏（broken TV）、音乐吵人（noisy music）等一系列问题，然后问学生It's a good stay or bad stay？得到bad stay的答案后把bad词卡贴在鱼骨图的头部位置。接着，教师问学生：How did they feel？得到unhappy的答案后把它贴在鱼骨头的尾部。最后，要学生小组讨论导致Wu Yifan一家不开心的原因。东西旧玩得不开心（didn't enjoy）、椅子破不能坐（couldn't sit）、灯小不能读书（couldn't read well）、汉堡包冷不好吃（didn't feel well）、电视损坏错过节目（missed the show）、音乐吵人睡不好（couldn't sleep well）等。各种问题以及导致心情不好的原因分别置于鱼骨的两端，一一对应，让人一目了然，而bad（stay）和unhappy（feeling）在鱼骨线主线的头尾，是文章的主要脉络（见图6-1）。鱼骨图把文本的脉络和主要信息清晰地呈现出来。

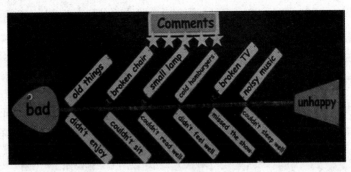

图6-1　鱼骨图

（截自钟秀清授课光盘：第九届小学英语课堂教学观摩课案例集，2018）

　　当酒店经理接到差评的信息后对酒店的各个方面进行了整改，并于整改后邀请吴家再次入住酒店。这次吴家住得舒服，感到开心，想给酒店写个好评。教师把原来表示差评的鱼骨图的卡片背面一一翻转过来，便构成了一个表达好评的鱼骨图（见图6–2），这是一个非常有创意的教学设计。

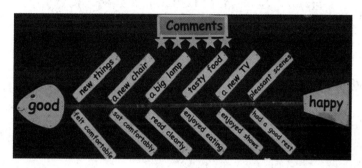

图6–2　鱼骨图

三、结束语

　　专家在评课时提了一个建议：用不同的颜色来给存在的问题分类，使学生在以后对事物进行评价时，能够对存在的问题进行分类，比如房间的问题、食物的问题、设施的问题等，因而可以更加有效地与人沟通。但总的来说，这是一节很有高度和深度的课，无论是对于教材的整合、重构和挖掘，还是细节设计方面的创意，都给观课的教师留下了深刻的印象。

第二节　初中英语评课案例

评课案例一　《Why Don't You Talk to Your Parents? 》 听说课

【课堂实录】

T：Hello，boys and girls！How are you today？

Ss：Fine，thank you！/I'm fine，thank you！

T：Great！I'm so happy too，because of all of you. Just now I heard a song *Merry Christmas*. Now I'd like to sing a song.

S：What？

T：Yeah！（学生鼓掌）"I heard that you settle down that you find a girl and married now." So do you like this song？

Ss：Yes.

T：OK. And in this class if you do a good job，I'll sing a song made by myself，OK？（情感协同）So are you ready for my class？

Ss：Yes.

T：Here we go！So today we're going to talk about how we can talk to our parents when we have problems. Tom，he has a problem. He is so sad. Do you know what happened to him？

Ss：No！

T：Is doesn't matter. Let me ask him.（引入自己制作的影视短片）Hey，Tom，why are you so sad？

Tom：Mary asked me to go to her birthday party but I can't go！

T：But why? Mary is your best friend!

Tom：Because I has an exam on Monday! So my mother doesn't allow me to go!

T：Oh, that's too bad!

Tom：Yeah, what can I do? What can I do?

T：So Tom's problem is... Who can tell me Tom's problem? Do you know?

S：Tom can't go to his friend's birthday party.

T：Very good! And she is the first student to answer my question! So everybody gives her big hand! OK, and mom's reason! OK, tell me mom's reason! Why? Why can't he go to the party? Because he...yeah, have a try. Have a try!

S：He has a exam.

T：He has an exam. Yes or no?

Ss：Yes.

T：You're right! He has an exam and this is a problem. And you know in our life we may have problems like Tom's. For example（在屏幕上打出情境）, I want to...but my parents... Who can tell me this problem? So，yeah.

S：My mother, oh no, I want to eat pizza but my mother doesn't like. My father also is.

T：Oh, a big problem. Yeah. You like pizza and I like it too.（情感趋同）Yeah! How about this one? I don't want to...but... yeah!

S：I don't want to, I don't want to get up, but my parents wake me up again and again.

T：Again and again. So your parents wake you up to...

S：Go to school.

T：Go to school, oooh, OK. That's a problem. OK, and besides these two problems，what problems do you have in your life? Can you tell me what other problems? OK, I'll show you some pictures. Here and let's see. What is he doing? He's washing the—

Ss：Plate.

T：Yeah. His problem is, his problem is he... Can you have a try? Yeah, his problem?

S：He doesn't want to wash dishes，but his parents force him.

T：Yes, you used a very good word "force". You know force? Yes, very good! And how about this one? The boy is crazy, hum! Yeah!

S：I don't want to take the after class, the after-school class, but my parents force me.

T：So how do you feel?

S：I feel very terrible.

T：OK, terrible. You feel so sad, right? Yes, so since we have problems, can you tell me what's the best way to solve these problems? What can we do? OK.

S：Maybe we should talk with our parents about his problems.

T：Do you agree with him? Yes, talk to parents. And now Tom is going to talk to his mom. We are going to watch a video and keep these two questions in mind.

1. Tom goes to the party.

2. What do you think of the talk?

Are you ready? Here we go! （教师播放视频）

（In the following T stands for Tom while M stands for mum.）

T：*Mum, may I talk with you a few seconds?*

M：*Yes, sure my dear boy! Come here!*

T：*Um, I feel so sad and I really need your help.*

M：*Oh, come on son. Just tell me what happen and I'll help you.*

T：*Um, you know. I want to go to Mary's birthday party but I'm afraid you don't agree.*

M：*Yes, but why is the party so important to you?*

T：*Because Mary is my best friend and she helps me a lot with my study.*

M：*I know that but I worry about your exam and it'll be dangerous if you come back late.*

T：*Mum, you don't have to worry about it because I promise I will study for the exam before I go to the party and I'll come back more early. With my friends it's quite safe on the street.*

M：*OK, I think I should trust you. Have a good time at the party.*

T：*Wow, mum, you're so great! I love you so much. Give me five.*

T：So could Tom go to the party?

Ss：Yes.

T：And what do you think of the talk? Yep，what do you think of it?

S：I think the talk is good and it's the way to solve the problem between Tom and his mom.

T：Give him big hand! Because he tells us why the talk is so good right? Very good. Do you think it's successful?

Ss：Yes.

T：Yes，it's so successful，right? And why is it so successful because Tom has powerful skills. And do you know what they are? Let's see. Wow，Tom you're so great! Can you tell us how you talk with your parents?

Tom：Well，that's easy! （影视短片增加互动性）When I was talking with my mother，I used so powerful skills：PFRP.

T：PFRP? What are they? Can you tell me?

Tom：OK，let me tell you. P means—

T：P means what? Uh，so do you know what is PFRP? The first powerful skill，do you know it? Don't worry. I think we can find it together! Let's go. First we should listen to their conversation again and try to find the answers，OK? Now students，take out this paper and we are going to read the material of Task 1 and try to predict the answer in 20 seconds，20 seconds. Go! Just guess the answers! So are you ready? Here we go! （教师再次播放对话视频）So when I walked around the classroom，I found a student in the class No.13，you are very good at handwriting. Your handwriting is so beautiful，yeah. And now I am expecting your answer. Who can tell me the answer? OK，the first one，Mum...（填空练习）

S：May I talk to you for a second?

T：Very good. Do you agree with her? May I... And how about this one? OK?

S：I feel so sad these days.

T：Yes or no?

Ss：Yes.

T：Yes，and how about this one? Because...OK，that girl，yeah.

S：Because...

T：Yes，go on，yeah!

S: Because Mary is my best friend. She has helped me a lot with my study.

T: Yes, you're right. I like your answer.

S: I'll study hard for the exam. I'll come back home early with my friends.

T: So is her answer right? Yes or no?

Ss: Yes.

T: Please give her a big hand. Very good because you can find the answer in a short time. And you know when Tom says "Mum, may I talk to you for a second?", we can say Tom is very... "May I..." yeah, Tom is very—polite, right? So polite. The first word is politeness, right? Wow, now you see P-F-R-P, do you remember that? They're four powerful—

Ss: Skills.

T: Yes, can you tell me what is F mean?

Ss: Feeling.

T: Feeling. Yes or no? Do you agree with him? And how about this one? Can you tell me? The boy, the most handsome boy.

S: Reason.

T: Reason. Yes or no? Because, right? Right. And how about the last one, P? Yes, speak loud. Tell your answer to all of us.

S: Promise.

T: Yes or no? Promise.

Ss: Yes.

T: Promise. So the four skills are politeness, feeling, reason and promise. And this one: May I talk to you for a second? We can also say—

Ss: Could I...

T: And Can I and Should I, I think this is OK. This one: I feel so sad and I can also say I feel...Yes, very good and... I feel... Yes, I like your answer. Tell us. Yes, use this microphone.

S: We can say upset.

T: Yes, do you know how to spell upset?

Ss: U-p-s-e-t.

T: Very good! And give me one more. Yeah, yes or no? OK, you're very good at this one. So when we are talking with our parents, we should remember the four skills. The first one is P. It means politeness. Can you help me to spell it?

Ss: P-o-l-i-t-e-n-e-s-s.

T: Yes, thank you. The next one is...So we should speak with politeness. The next one is...

Ss: Feeling.

T: Yes, it's feeling.

Ss: F-e-e-l-i-n-g.

T: Yes, boys and girls, I love you so much. So we tell our...

Ss: ...

T: No, F, F. Yes, our feeling, right? And how about the last one? No, the third one is R, right? So R means...

Ss: Reason.

T: Yes, reason. OK, and how about the last one. We should tell our reason, right? And the last one is...

Ss: Promise.

T: How to spell promise? Tell me.

Ss: P-r-o-m-i-s-e.

T: That means we should... just tell me. We should tell feeling, tell reason and have a try. We should, yeah, use the microphone.

S: Make a promise to our parents.

T: Very good, because she uses a sentences. Your answer is better than mine. So, now do you know how to talk to our parents now?

Ss: Yes.

T: OK, I believe in you. Now everybody, in your group, you have one envelop, right? Take out this envelop, everybody, every group takes out this envelop. First you open the envelop and find your task, OK? And discuss the questions, discuss the questions in your group, OK? And write down what answers on this piece of paper as many sentences as possible. And after that, one student in your group will come here to share your ideas. Understand? Here we go! (Use this pen, yeah! Wow, you have three sentences) OK, finished? Now let's welcome the group with the letter politeness. Come here. Politeness, with the microphone here. Good! And your task is to read out your task, yeah, your task is this one. Read it aloud.

S：Your mum is watching TV on the sofa. You need her help. How can you start the talk politely?

T：So your answer is...

S：Mum, could I have a talk with you? Or Mum, could you please give me some help? Or shall I talk with you?

T：Very good! She has three sentences, right? And I like your answers. Please put your answer here, OK? And this one is politeness, yes, put your answers here（展示后张贴）. Let me help you. OK, now let's welcome the group of feeling. Two group, come together. And I want one student to read out their task. Who can read this task for me for us? Who can help me to read their task? OK, yeah, do what you like.

S：Your dad asks you to take after-school classes but you didn't like it. How can you tell your feeling?

T：Lady first.

S：I feel very unpleasant or I feel so worried or I feel very angry.

T：Yeah, angry, I like this word. Boy!

S：I am in the bad mood. I feel so unhappy. I am sad because of this problem.

T：I like the sentence like "I am in the bad mood". OK, come here and put your answer here. And the other students give them big hands because they give us six sentences.（赏析教育）And then how about Reason Group? Two groups, right, come here! Yeah, the reason. And I want one student to read out their task. Who can help me? Yeah, the girl.

S：You don't want to take after-school classes. Please tell your dad the reason. Because I feel it's very boring. That is useless for me. I feel tired and I want to have more time to do something I like.

T：How many reasons? Any reason for you, right? That's your answers here. How about the boy?

S：Because all the teacher is ugly. I feel so tired. I want to have a rest. I want to play a computer game. I think it's wasting my time.

T：OK，waste your time. Here I have to say thank you because you come to my class. That means I'm not ugly，right?

Ss：Yeah!

T：OK，put your answers here. So now we have F and reason. Now let's welcome the last two groups. Come here. So I need one student again to tell me your task. OK，the boy，yeah!

S：Your parents worry about your study. What promise can you make?

T：OK，go on!

S：I promise I'll do my homework on time and I promise I'll read more books instead of playing computer game for a long time. I promise I'll do more exercise to keep healthy. I promise I'll go to bed early.

T：OK，boy!

S：If I always do badly in my study I will say：I promise I'll spend more time on stud（y）or I promise I'll take good grade at term. If I always play games I'll say I promise I'll reduce the time of playing.

T：Very good! I like all your answers. And please put your answers here. And here I have to say，I really appreciate the boys in our class because every time they answer the questions，the boy will let the girl answer the questions together，first. So let's give big hands to the boys in our class. You're a gentleman. And now you get really many answers，right? You've got rich achievement. You are using PFRP to talk to parents in a proper way just like Tom. Do you still remember Tom? （Tom是主线）He's coming（教师播放视频）.

T：Hey，Tom! Tom，Hey! Tom，where are you? Where you come back.

Tom：Yes，my problem is solved. But my friend Mary has a problem now.

T：So Mary，what happens to her?

Tom：Mary doesn't want to take after-school classes，but her parents ask her to go. I must go and help her now.

T：Well，I don't think you need to help her. The students in Zhaoqing can do this，right?

Ss：Yes.

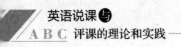

T：Because we have so many answers. Now let's come to the second part. Mary and her problem is...

Ss：...

T：What problem? Yeah.

S：She doesn't want to go to after-school classes.

T：Right? So in this task two students together one student will be mum or dad，and one will be Mary. （任务更复杂，后面的任务包含了前面的任务）Mary is trying to persuade her parents because she doesn't want to go to the after-school classes. And you need to first，don't forget PFRP. Second，act naturally. I think you are very good at it. And No.3，be creative. You're doing a good job on this part and humorous. OK? Now we have three minutes to prepare. Are you ready?

Ss：Yes.

T：Go! （学生开始准备）And if you need my help，I'll come to you. Which group will have a try? （时间不足3分钟）Put up your hands. OK，you two! OK，welcome them! And please bring your microphone. Two students，two microphone. Yeah! Who is Mary?

S1：I am Mary.

S2：I am her mum.

S1：May I have a talk with you?

S2：Of course.

S1：Mm，I want to go to a after-class class.

S2：Why?

S1：But I don't want to go! I want to do sports on weekend!

S2：Do sports on workday.

S1：I think it's very tired to do sports on weekday. I need more time to have a rest. And I want to get up late in the morning on the weekends.

S2：Getting up early is good for your health，you know!

S1：I promise I will study hard and get better marks. And I want to go to cinema or park with my friends on weekend.

S2：Listen! After-school classes can improve your study.

S1：But study is not the only thing in my life.

S2：OK, OK, I agree with you. But you should promise you keep a good mark.

S1：OK. Thank you!

T：So they tell us many reasons. Please remember one sentence she said, study is not the only thing in your life, right? OK, now let's welcome the next group. Two boys yep. Are you sure? Come here.

S3：Mary , come here.

S4：OK, Dad! What's wrong?

S3：Could you tell me why you failed in the exam again? Tell me why?

S4：I...

S3：I am very angry with you!

S4：OK.

S3：I am very worried about your study! I am worrying about your future!

S4：Fine, Dad!

S3：I think you must ...

S4：Oh, Dad! Calm down! Calm down! As you know our students must get up early in the morning. And we have too much homework because...so don't angry with me. Please!

S3：But I think you, you must go to the after-school class.

S4：So tired!

S3：This is...

S4：What can I say?

T：Reason! You need a reason.

S4：You know, as my classmates say, after-school classes not only is not the only thing in my life. You know, I promise you I'll get up early in the morning at first. And and I'll take my grades, I will take good grades in my next exam. I promise you, my dear Papa.

S3：Are you sure?

S4：Yes! I'm sure, OK!

T：So what do you think of their performance? What do you think of it? But I think Mary is doing a hard job because at first her father was very... yeah, hard for her to tell the reasons. And I think in this class all of you have done a very good job. Just give a big hand to yourselves！And I think you can get an Oscar Prize，right? And now for me，I don't want to have an Oscar Prize，I want to get a prize of Voice of China. This is a song made by myself. Someone like Tom，not someone like you. Here we go！"Never mind，I will find someone like you. Nothing but the best for you too." PFRP，you remember I say... Can we sing together? OK，everybody stands up！Let's have a try！OK！（师生一起唱）. Thank you，students！

【背景介绍】

这节课是2016年11月在广东肇庆举行的广东省初中英语课堂教学展示课之一，课型是听说课，授课教师是东莞市松山湖中学的韩松锦老师。该课授课教师具有较高的专业素养、教学机智及人格魅力，教学设计具有层次性，教学过程体现了对学生学科核心素养的培养，目标达成程度高，是一节具有较高感染力的优质课。

一、教学设计和教学过程

1. Lead in by singing a song.

2. Present Tom's problems.

3. Practice.

Listen to the dialogue and answer two questions.

Listen and fill in the blanks.

Analyze and sum up the four skills in talking to parents about the problem.

Analye one of the four skills to talk about problem to parents in group.

4. Production：Role play：Act as Mary and her parents to talk about Mary's problems using PFRP principles.

5. Sing a song to end the class.

二、该课的教学特色

1. 教师的教

（1）教学模式和教学设计。该课采用PPP（presentation，practice，production）教学模式来教授如何跟父母谈论问题的口语技能。教师在导入之后很快呈现一个包含学生Tom和他妈妈谈论他面临的问题及如何解决该问题的对话。然后组织学生围绕该对话进行练习，最后组织学生以角色扮演的形式进行口语输出。该教师模式结构简单易操作，特别适合教授某个具体的口语技能。

该课的教学设计具有一定的层次性，从小任务到大任务。教师在学生听前布置了两个思考题：听完填关键词——提取四个语用规则——分析应用四个语用原则——迁移四个语用原则。

（2）教师语言品质高。一方面教师指令语清晰、具体；另一方面教师反馈语以正面反馈语为主，重在突出反馈语对学生的鼓励作用。教师倾向使用提供信息型反馈语，即在肯定学生语言行为的同时，指出好的原因，强化学生正面的语言行为。此外，该教师的指令语呈现出机智、幽默的一面。

（3）课程资源的开发。在本课中，教师把学生视为课程资源。显然，该课是以学生Tom为主线来组织教学的。而视频是授课教师自己录制的，视频中出现的主角Tom是授课教师自己的学生。该生能够说流利的英语，并能够用得体的表情和语言把自己的烦恼生活化地表达出来。Tom和他妈妈交流他的问题时场面也比较真实。这样的材料对授课班级的学生来说有一定的真实性，是他们现实生活里面的场景。总的来说，这样的视频和对话对授课学生来说有真实性，会激发他们学习的愿望。

（4）思维品质和文化意识的培养。①通过问题培养学生不同层次的思维能力。如前所述，教师在听前布置了两个问题，第一个问题是事实性问题；第二个问题属于批判性问题；②不贴标签的文化教学重在为学生提供文化体验活动。

（5）教师具有较高的共情能力。共情是一种能力，它不只是单纯的感同身受，更是人际关系的滑润剂，是个人情商的表现。人类的共情能力源于模仿，没有模仿就没有共情。

2. 学生的学习

（1）学生参与度：学生的参与度在教师的引领和激发下逐步走高。

（2）学生的创造。该课有两个环节出现学生的创造。在第一个场景，学生说他不愿意去参加课后补习班是因为教师长得丑，反映了初中学生的喜恶。另外一个地方的学生创造为本课带来了课堂的高潮。在产出阶段，最后一组扮演Mary和她父亲的一对男同学。现实中的学生是一对男生，而他们要扮演的是一对父女，这就在某种程度上造成了认知冲突，所以学生一出场就引起了笑声并获得人们的关注。而学生在直接谈论课外补习班前扮演父亲的学生又制造了冲突：苛责Mary考试又不及格。请看下面生生互动片段：

片段：

S3：Mary，come here.

S4：OK，Dad！What's wrong?

S3：Could you tell me why you failed in the exam again？Tell me why?

S4：I—

S3：I am very angry with you!

S4：OK.

S3：I am very worried about your study！I am worrying about your future!

S4：Fine，Dad!

S3：I think you must...

S4：Oh，Dad！Calm down！Calm down！As you know our students must get up early in the morning. And we have too much homework，so don't angry with me. Please!

S3：But I think you，you must go to the after-school class.

S4：So tired!

S3：This is，this is...

S4：What can I say?

T：Reason！You need a reason.

S4：You know，as my classmates say，after-school class is not the only thing in my life. You know，I promise you I'll get up early in the morning at first. And and I will take good grades in my next exam. I promise you，my dear Papa.

该课值得商榷的地方：学生在角色扮演时有时会偏离礼貌性原则。那么教师有必要在活动结束时提醒学生在跟家长交谈时时刻记住礼貌性原则。

有的一线教师说，对初中生来说，图片已经激发不了他们的学习兴趣。因此教师必须另辟蹊径，而请学生录制与教学相关的视频作为学习的资源也是激发学生学习兴趣或维持他们学习动机的方法之一。教师既要做现成课程资源的使用者，也要做课程资源的开发者和丰实者。

评课案例二 《Smart or Harmful》阅读课

【课堂实录】

T：So boys and girls，good morning. I am glad to see you here. And I hope we'll have a great time together. All right? So before this class，I want to take a photo of you guys，because I want to remember your lovely faces. Shall we take a picture? OK? Now look at my phone. Let's say "One，two，cheers！" Everybody looks！Come in！Look！Let's make a pose. OK? One，two，cheers！All right，look！Happy faces，right? OK，I like to capture people for their happy moment with my phone. How about you? What would you like to do with your phone? How about you?

S1：I always use my phone to listen music for relaxing.

T：Yes，me too！I like to listen to music as well. How about you?

S2：I use my phone to watch some films.

T：Watch some films. How about you? Well，will you use your phone...?

S3：When I have some questions or problems I will check it on the phone.

T：OK，so you can check your answer on the phone，right? Well done，everyone！Now we can do a lot of things with our phone，right?

T：Now let's watch this！（教师播放有许多APP的视频）Oh，a lot of APPs. Do you have a lot of APPs on your phone? And this kind of phone is called smart phone. Do you guess why? Why is it called smart phone? Because it is very... why，can you guess?

S4：Because it is very smart and useful.

T：Yes，it's very smart and useful. And we all love to play with it，right? OK，let's think about the question. Does it sometimes bring some problems? Is it sometimes harmful for you? It means bad for you sometimes? Yes or no? Yes，OK，now，everyone，let's discuss in group and talk about why you think the phone is smart and why it is harmful, OK? And you can write down your answers around the circle. Got it? You can turn back and let's talk about why it is useful and why it is harmful. 〔You can talk and write in your paper. Anything will be OK. Think about the two sides.〕 OK, which group will have a try? How about this group? Which side do you want to say first? Smart or useful? Which one do you want to say?

S：We want to say the smart side.

T：Smart side, OK. So why is it?

S：Because we can get some information from the smart phone.

T：OK, you can get some information. So it's very helpful, right? The smart phone is very helpful. Anything else?

S：We can also listen to some music to relax.

T：Yes, it's very relaxing. That's right, relaxing. Anything else?

S：We can chat with our friends on the smart phone.

T：Yes, it's very easy and very useful. You can chat with your friends by using the smart phone, right?

S：Yes.

T：Very useful. OK, how about the harmful side?

S：The smart phone maybe is bad for our eyes and study.

T：That's right. The smart phone maybe is bad for your eyes, bad for your eyes and maybe bad for study. Anything else?

S：The smart phone maybe... is...

T：That's OK if you have got this one. OK. You can sit down. OK, sit down. Well-done! So now everyone, so we've got the two sides of using smart phone. OK? And we need to know that all things have two sides just like the smart phone. If we use it in a right way, it can be very smart. But if we use it in a wrong way, it can be harmful for us. OK? And today we're going to read a passage about using the smart phone. And the title of this passage is Smart or Harmful. OK, now, everyone, it's your time to read the passage and find out the two sides of using the smart phone in the passage, OK? You can underline some key words. But before that, let's look at the picture together. OK? This is a picture from the passage. What can you see from this picture? Anybody can tell me? What can you see?

S：The family member use their phones during the dinner.

T：Yes，they're playing their phones during the dinner. OK，do you think they play with their phones too much?

S：Yes.

T：Yes，why?

S：It's time for dinner and we can chat with family members. They spend too much time on their phones.

T：Yes.

S：Less and less love from their family.

T：Right，so they no eat no talk，right? This is called an addiction to phone. OK，so addiction means people can't stop doing something. All right，just like these people. They can't stop playing their phone. OK，they always love playing with their phones. So now please read after me：addiction!

Ss：Addiction，addiction.

T：Great! So if any other problem in the picture? Is there any other problem? Do they talk to each other? No! There is not face to face communication，right? It means they don't talk to each other face to face. Read after me：face to face communication.

Ss：Face to face communication.

T：All right. Now，everyone! It's your time to read the passage and let's find out the two sides. OK? You can underline some key phrases or key words about the harmful side and you can also circle some key phrases of the smart side. Got it? OK，now let's read and find.

（学生阅读）

T：OK，have you finished? OK，now，let's check together. First of all，tell me：Which side does the writer write first? Smart or harmful? Harmful，OK，tell me anything about the harmful side. Anybody? OK，have a try.

S：People cannot remember the telephone number.

T：OK，so people can't remember the telephone number. So do you think this is the bad thing?

S：Because when we go outside，we have no telephone and we don't know the telephone number, we couldn't, we can't call the parents.

T: Yes, we can't call anybody, right? We can't find them. That's right. And anything else about the harmful side?

S: The smart phone weak our skill of giving direction.

T: That's right. So we weaken our skill in giving direction. So that's the hard one. What's the meaning of this? What's the meaning of this?

S: We cannot tell the north and the south.

T: That's right. So where did you get the meaning? In the next sentence, right? So everyone, first of all, let's check. In the passage, the first harmful side is cannot remember. And the second one weaken our skill of giving direction. This is the hard one. But the next sentence explains the first sentence. Everyone, next time when you don't know the meaning, don't worry because you can guess the meaning from the sentence before or after it. Got it, OK? Anything else? Anything else about the harmful side?

S: Smart phone kills face to face communication.

T: That's right. Can you find the meaning of "kill face to face communication" in the passage?

S: People don't talk to each other even when they have meal together.

T: Yes, it's in the next sentence, right? Kill face to face communication. Right, let's check together. Here "kill face to face communication" means people even don't talk to each other. OK, anything else?

S: Smart phone does no good for study.

T: Does no good for studying! Yes, does no good for studying. That's right. So what does no good for studying? What does no good for studying?

S: Children who play more than four hours with their phone.

T: OK, does no good for studying, addiction, does no good for studying, right? And what you mention is an example from the research, right? So children who play more than four hours is called addiction which does no good for studying. All right, sit down, please. Now, let's go to the smart side. Anybody finds any smart side? OK, have a try? Use your microphone!

S: People can use their phones to search in the Internet and get news quickly.

T：All，right. Get news quickly，get news quickly. So can you give me an example? How does smart phone help people to get news quickly?

S：If we are away from our parents we can check on the Internet and we can..we can feel more close.

T：Yes，more close，you can chat with them but does not get news. Can you give me another example how to get news quickly? How about your partner? Can you help her?

S：We can use Baidu to get more information.

T：Excellent! You can use Baidu on your smart phone at any time anyway，for example，you can tape whether Mr. Yu Haiyang married is true or not. You can check on your phone，right? So that's right，get news quickly. Anything else? Anything else? How about this group? Please try! Use your microphone.

S：Smart phone opens people's eye，make life easy.

T：Yes，open people's eye，right. Here，open people's eye，what's the meaning of that? Does it mean open your eyes，close your eyes? No，then what's the meaning of that?

S：People can get more information.

T：Excellent! So people can get more information，open your eyes. Yes，information before...

S：Make life easier.

T：It's true. So can you give us an example? How does that make your life easier?

S：When we go shopping，we can use smart phone to pay what we buy.

T：OK，you can pay online，OK? You can shop online. You don't need to go outside，right? So now，everyone，let's check the smart side. First of all，get news quickly，open people's eyes and make our life easier. OK，so，now，we've got the two sides of using smart phone in the passage. And now let's see how does the writer organize or list these ideas in the passage，OK? First of all，tell me which paragraph talks about the harmful side. Which paragraph? Paragraph 2，3 and 4. Yes. So we have already know that Para. 2 is about the harmful side，right? From the words "can't remember" ，tell me. Is there an easy way or quick way to know that? Paras. 3 and 4 deal with the harmful side. Which word? OK，how about you?

S：Moreover.

T：Moreover and?

S：In addition.

T：In addition. Do you know the meaning of this?

S：It means— Let me tell you.

T：Yes，let me tell you more. Let me tell you more about the harmful side just like in Paragraph 2. So tell me which paragraph is the smart side? Para. 5，that's right. So from which word you can tell Para. 5 no longer talks about the harmful side? It changes to the other side. From which word？ "However" . All right，so "however" is like a turning point. Before "however" one side. After "however"，the other side. OK，so before "however" harmful. After "however"，smart. OK，Paras 2～5 is the body part of the passage，which has two sides. And we need to know that two things have two sides just like this. What's this?

Ss：A coin.

T：Yes，a coin. There' a saying：Each coin has two sides. So we need to two at things from two sides. OK，let's come back to the passage and now we still have a Para. 4. Let's see how does writer begin the passage. How does the writer begin the passage? By what? By asking—

S：By asking.

T：By asking questions，right? So Para. 1 is the beginning. And we still get Para. 6. which is the ending. OK，so now everyone，let's think about the question. In the passage，the writer writes about the two sides of using smart phone，but which side does the writer support? What's the writer's opinion? Does the writer believe the phone is smart or the phone is harmful? Now，let's read the last paragraph again. And there is a sentence in the last paragraph that shows the writer's opinion. Can you find it out? OK，which sentence? The phone is smart or harmful? The first one，right? Now，let's read first：It's true，one，two，begin!

Ss：It's true.

T：That is right. What's the writer's idea? The writer's opinion is that the phone is harmful? Smart. How do you know that? Which words? From which words?

S：But...

T：But，yes. And?

S：Best.

T：Best，yes，invention，right? So，OK，now everyone，let's look at the sentence together：It's true blog， but...OK? In this sentence there are two parts： In the first part it's true the writer agrees with the other side，for example in the passage， "it's true smart phone causes a problem." It means sometimes the smart phone is bad，is harmful. OK，it's harmful. From this part，the writer writes down his or her own opinion，OK? For example， "but it is one of the..." ，one of the what? Best invention which means it's very smart. All right，now let's think about those questions：You say that the phone is very smart. But why it still causes problems? Can you find out the answer in this paragraph? Why? Why is it smart but causing problems? Why?

S：Most people spend too much time on it.

T：Yes，because people just spend too much time on it. So what shall we need to do next?

S：We should...

T：We should?

S：Make a change.

T：Make a change. So it's very important for us to make a change. That is right，make a change.

So if you're the writer，what are you going to write next? If you're the writer，what are you going to write next? Maybe about—

S：Maybe I'll write about how to make a change.

T：How to make a change. That is right. So everybody，well-done，sit down please. Para.6 can also be a transition. So in a transition paragraph，it tells us something happens above，for example，two sides are true and they will also tell us what is the writer going to write now，for example，how to make a change. So can you guess the Chinese meaning of transition? What does a transition paragraph mean? Say loudly.

S：过渡段。

T：Yes，过渡段，that's right. Now everyone，it's your time to open up the color paper? OK? Tear off the part and let's read what the writer writes next. OK? Read this paragraph. And don't forget to answer the two questions on the screen: Who have helped to make such a change? How? How to make a change? You can underline your answers on your paper. Now, let's read and answer the questions. （学生阅读过渡段）

T: OK, are you ready? Let's check together. First of all, who have helped to make a change? How about this girl? Who have helped to make a change?

S: A new App named Forest.

T: Yes, an App Forest. OK, how does it help us?

S: Users come to plant trees and the trees will grow in the next 13 minutes. During the half hour users cannot use their phones or the tree will die.

T: Excellent! Maybe we can like this. And if we can't plant a tree like this, people can't play with their phone or the tree will die. And who else help us?

S: Uh restaurant in US.

T: A restaurant tries to help. How does it help us?

S: They give people a 5% discount if they don't check their phone during their meals.

T: Well-done! A restaurant gives people discount. What is the meaning of discount? Does it mean pay more or pay less?

S: Pay less.

T: All right, everyone. Now we know in the passage both an App and a restaurant help us to spend less time on phone. So to spend less time on phone is the right way to use your smart phone. Do you agree? Yes. Now let's think about ourselves. What can we do to make a change? For example, how to use the phone in a right way? OK, so now let's make a change of the harmful side, the harmful side in the passage and we can also change the harmful side you face at the beginning of the text. You can write something like this: One side but the other side. It's very important for us to make a change. OK, make a change of the harmful side and write for example, blog, blog, blog. Got it? And now let's turn back in a group of four. Let's make a change, OK? Let's discuss. You can write down on the paper. Turn back, turn back. Let's talk. Group of four. You can turn back. You four, you four, OK? （教师巡堂指导）How to make a change?

T：OK，everyone，are you ready? Now let's listen to your wonderful ideas. Which group wants to have a try? How about this group，OK?

S：It's true the smart phone is very smart but it kills face to face communication.

T：Yes，that is right.

S：It's very important for us to make a change，for example，if who uses their phone during dinner at the party as a result who will pay for the meal. It can also make us and our friends become more and more close.

T：Very good idea! It's helpful. I love your idea! How about this group? Have a try. What's your idea? How to make a change?

S：It's true smart phone is important in people's life but it's bad for our eyes.

T：OK，it's bad for our eyes，just like you mentioned before. So how to make a change?

S：It's very important for us to make a change. For example，we can invent some APPs like "Forest" to make us spend less time using the phone.

T：All right! You want to invent another APP just like "Forest"，right? OK，I hope you can make that...

S：It's also useful for us to let our parents to...let our parents control the time.

T：Oh，so you want to give your phone to your parents，right? And let them control your time. Right?

S：Yes.

T：Great idea! Yes，OK，well-done! I love all your ideas but because of the time，we can't share all of your ideas，OK? You can share your opinion after this class. And write a passage about how to use the smart phone in the right way. OK，now let's review，everyone! What have we learned today? First of all，we know that，all things have，all things have what? Two sides just like a smart phone. If we use it in a right way，it will be very smart. But if we use it in a wrong way，it can be，it can be harmful. OK，so after looking at the two sides of a thing，what are we going to do next? It's important for us to—

S：It's important for us to make a change.

T：Very great! It's important for us to make a change，make a change of the harmful side. Do you agree?

S：I agree.

T：That's OK，well-done！Sit down please！And now everybody，make a change today and hope for a better future tomorrow. Have you got it？So much for today's class. Thank you，everyone！

【背景介绍】

这是2017年在江苏镇江市举行的第12届全国初中英语课堂教学案例集中的一节阅读课。

授课教师是来自安徽合肥世界外国语学校的王冠博老师。该课教师具有较高的外语语言素养，对学生的阅读教学策略的培养较为充分，较好地处理了阅读课中提取信息的技能训练和语言点、文章篇章结构的学习的关系，是一节值得进行探讨的优质课。

一、教学设计

I Pre-reading

1.Lead-in：What do we use smart phone for？

2. Group discussion：Two sides of using smart phone：smart or harmful.

II While-reading

1. Teach vocabulary with the picture：No face to face communication.

2. Read and find the two sides：Underline and circle.

3. Check the reading：

Tell me anything about the harmful side.

T：Where can we find the answer？

Tell me anything about the smart side.

4.Text organization—how to organize the text：Moreover，in addition，however.

5. Read the last paragraph（silent reading）

Who have helped us to make a change？How to make a change？

III Post-reading

1. Discussion：What can we do to make a change？How to use in a right way？

2. Summing up what have been learned today.

二、该课的优点

（1）利用真实的情景。教师用自拍器和智能手机为全班拍照，并提问若干学生他们用手机做什么来导入本课主题。导入真实、有趣，与学生高度相关，能够很快把学生引入到即将学习的话题：智能手机有用还是有害？

（2）教师启发学生手机给人们的生活带来便利的同时也带来危害，然后通过小组讨论展示智能手机的两面性：smart or harmful。

（3）教师的语言质量高。教师的英语口语流利、地道。如评课专家所言，语言的颜值高。首先，教师的指令语非常清晰；其次，教师能较好地使用语音、语调来强调来表情达意，尤其是突出重要的词语，连读自然。

（4）教师在读中教生词。在读前教师利用图片处理了新词语face to face communication和addiction，但对更多词语的处理是放在读中阶段，即在检查阅读任务的完成情况时碰到生词教师会处理这些新词语的意义，她经常问的问题是What does it mean? What is the meaning of...? Do you know the meaning of this? What is the meaning of discount? 这属于在学生需要时教生词。教师在教词语时除了要学生说出那些词语的意义外，还不断让学生举例。通过让学生举例来确认学生是否真正理解词语的意义。

（5）突出对阅读策略的培养。教师经常要学生找出信息及指出信息所在的词和句子。阅读策略的培养是阅读课的重要目标之一。

（6）重视文本结构。教师在帮助学生获取信息后对文本的结构进行了分析：开头段、结尾段、中间段落、过渡段。分析文本结构是为了帮助学生从总体上把握信息的获取，也为学生以后的写作打下一定的基础。

（7）注意学法指导，特别是指导学生如何根据语境来确定词语的意义。例如：

T：So where did you get the meaning? In the next sentence，right? So everyone，first of all，let's check. In the passage，the first harmful side is cannot remember. And the second one weaken our skill of giving direction. This is the hard one. But the next sentence explains the first sentence. Everyone，next time when you don't know the meaning，do not worry because you can guess the meaning from the sentence before or after it.

（8）思维方式和价值观的培养。Every coin has two sides. We need to look at

things from two sides.理性看问题。教学能够联系学生的实际，在文本的信息内容和学生的实际生活之间建立联系，能引发学生的共鸣，引导学生学以致用。教师在帮助学生完成对文本信息的处理、语言点及篇章结构的学习后，用一个句子把学生从文本里的世界拉到了现实生活。玩手机上瘾是目前青少年中存在的普遍现象，中小学对学生的手机管理各出奇招，但那是从成人的视角出发来研究解决问题的方法和途径。在课堂上教师可以基于教材内容让学生发出自己的心声，提出自己的建议。这里，王老师问学生：How to make a change? 和How to use the phone in a right way? 。

三、本课的一些不足之处

（1）学生参与面不均匀，总是提问少数几个学生。好的活动有几个特征：①激发学生最大量的目的语输出；②均匀的参与；③高学习动机；④活动所需语言符合学生现在的语言水平。在这节课中，教师就小组讨论智能手机的利弊进行检查时，她跟同一位学生互动的时间太长了。应该指导学生如何向教师和全班汇报他们组讨论的结果：利有哪几点；弊有哪几点。而不是教师问一点学生答一点。虽然有师生互动，实际上这个环节并不高效，在很长的时间内都只是一位学生在跟教师互动，其他学生全部在作听众。教师花太多时间在"挤"答案上，而时间要给更多的学生，让更多的小组有发表观点和看法的机会。从话语分析的角度来看，在回答harmful side时，同一位学生的话轮偏多，话语量偏大，在某个时间段垄断话语权。

（2）教师指令语缺乏逻辑。例如，教师在读中先用指令语布置阅读任务，然后未开展阅读活动，就用一幅图片来教学新词语，教完后再来实施真正的阅读任务。

（3）教师在以流利性为目的的产出阶段总是打断学生的语流来做出反馈和评价。教师应该在学生完整表达自己后才进行反馈或评价。

对本课的一个思考：教师总是在学生回答完问题后再跟全班学生检查问题的答案。这个有必要吗？会不会产生重复而造成时间的浪费呢？总之，本课虽然有一些不足，但瑕不掩瑜，是一节比较成功的阅读课。

评课案例三 《Lost》写作课

【课堂实录】

T：Good morning, class!

Ss：Good morning, Ms. Zou!

T：OK, good memory! Some of you can remember my name. And this is a very big stage, right? So we're actually like having a concert here. So remember to use your microphone when you speak. Uh, so I'm very glad to be with you today and show my thanks to you, I prepare some chocolates for you, OK. I'll give these to you as a reward after class. To show my thanks, I'll give you the reward. Please say after me：reward!

Ss：Reward.

T：Reward.

Ss：Reward.

T：↗Reward, ↘reward.

Ss：↗Reward, ↘reward.

T：Good! Just now I've got to know something about you. OK, shall we play a game to know something about me? Look! What is my favorite movie? Cars and Utopia. Come on, raise your hand! Gao Qianyu, please!

S：B, boy!

T：B, Utopia, right? Sit down please. You're right! How did you know? Because I... yes, use your microphone, please! Just guess. Because of the flash I showed you? Right, thank you. Sit down please. Flash, flash, one hundred yard dash! And what is my favorite animal? Have a guess! Yes, please!

S：Rabbit.

T：Rabbit, how do you know? You're so clever! From the picture, OK, thank you! I thought it was because my teeth. And I visited a university this October.

Which university did I visit? Please read after me：university.

Ss：University.

T：University.

Ss：University.

T：So which university did I visit this October? Princeton or Oxford? Have a guess. Yes，please.

S：Choose A.

T：Princeton. Wow！ Thank you，sit down，please. That's right. Can you find the today three in a row？ I visited Princeton. Take a look. This is a photo of my students and me. And we had a wonderful time there. However，one of my students lost something. What did my student lose? （中速）（停顿，让学生思考）What was lost? What was lost? A phone or a wallet? Have a guess！ Yes，please，Wang Junyu.

S：A phone.

T：A phone. Thank you. Sit down please. Thank you for your answer. However，（用得好！）my student lost the wallet，OK，the wallet，with cash and bank cards inside. And we were so worried. What could we do? What could we do? He lost his wallet in the USA. Yes，please.

S：Maybe you can call 911.

T：Yes，you're right. We could call 911 to ask the police for help. Very good！ Yeah，any more? Any more ideas? Yes，please！ What do you want to say?

S：Ask the policeman for help.

T：Thank you，good idea. Any more? Any other ideas? How can we get more people to help us？ We decided to write a lost notice. We can ask more people to help us. But what can we write? What should we write on it? What do we tell people? Do we tell people we lost a phone? We first should tell people...yes.

S：We should first tell people the thing we lost.

T：So，what. Yes，the thing we lost. Lost what.（板书）Yes，thank you. Sit down，please. And anything else? That can help people to look for it?

S：Where do you lose?

T：Yes，where. Thank you. Any more? Any more? Where was it lost? Yes，this girl please.

S：...

T：Yes, very good. So what was lost and describe it. Good job! Yes, please.

S：When was the wallet lost.

T：Good! Where was it lost. Any more? If they find it, if someone find it, yes, please.

S：...

T：Yes, what's in the wallet. Inside description. Any more?

S：Reward.

T：Reward, OK. What's the reward, OK, what they can get. Any more? How can they ask you for help? Uh, Jiang Yudong, please.

S：Telephone number, their——

T：Very good! For telephone number. How to contact you, right? Your phone number, your QQ number, your Wechat, things like that. Please read after me：↗contact.

Ss：↗Contact.

T：↘Contact.

S：↘Contact.

T：Right. How to contact, number. Good guessing. So now let's have a look at an example if your guessing is right. Please take out the paper on your desk. Read this Lost Notice and answer the five questions below. Please finish it in three minutes.（学生阅读并做题）

T：One more minute. [Oh, you have finished. Good job! Can you use a complete sentence?]

Excuse me, time is up. So what was lost? Zhao Ruoshan, please! Microphone!

S：A brown leather is lost.

T：Good. A brown leather is lost. Please read after me：↗leather.

Ss：↗Leather.

T：↘Leather.

Ss：↘Leather.

T：This is a brown leather backpack. What are they? Yes, please.

S：Leather shoes.

T：Yes, they're leather shoes. Black leather shoes. And what was inside? What was inside? Wu Yi, please.

S：Two books.

T：What are the two books?

S：One is a maths textbook. The other is a history book.

T：Correct! Thank you. And where was it lost? Where was it lost? This girl, please. Use the microphone.

S：It lost at a bus stop.

T：Right, it <u>was</u> lost, thank you, at a bus stop near... George Town University. Thank you. Sit down, please. When was it lost? That boy, please, at the back. The microphone, please.

S：It is at Monday night.

T：Thank you! It was lost. Everybody pays attention to here：was lost.

Ss：Was lost.

T：Was lost.

Ss：Was lost.

T：OK, it was lost on Monday night, right? And how to contact the owner? What is the telephone number of the owner? Anyone? Yes, please.

S：At 5552121.

T：Right, <u>contact</u> the owner at, sit down please. Everybody, please read after me：contact.

Ss：Contact.

T：↗Contact.

Ss：↗Contact.

T：↘Contact.

Ss：↘Contact.

T：Right, contact the owner means we can call（慢速）the owner at this telephone number. And what is the reward? Gao Qianyu, please.

S：50 dollars.

T：Right. 50 dollars for reward. Thank you. Sit down please. That's just one example for a Lost Notice. Let's have a look at more. Now, you're going to do group work. Group leaders, please take out the envelopes on your desk, open it and take out four pieces of Lost Notice inside. Read as a group and compare them. Which one do you think is good writing? And why is that? And which one is not good? And why is that? Do you understand me? Finish it in five minutes. Read as a group, turn over! Turn back so you can read as a group.

（学生分小组阅读，并选择好的和差的Lost Notice）

T：OK, are you ready? So which one do you think is good writing? OK, group leaders, come on. Anybody? Gao Tianyu, please.

S：The fourth picture is the best.

T：Which one? One, two, three, four, the blue one.

S：Yes.

T：No. 4. Why?

S：Because we can know clearly about what was lost.

T：Thank you. So it has very clear arrangement, right? Thank you. And do you agree with him? What do you have? If you have the same idea, or you'll have different idea, it's OK. Zhao Ruoshan, microphone, please. Yes.

S：The first one has no reward.

T：Uh, OK, thank you. Do you agree? Is reward very important? Of course it can make people look for you, right? But still we have to think about it, can we afford it? And if this thing is very valuable, if it is important, maybe we'll offer a reward. If it is something not so important, maybe not. Right? So sometimes we have reward, sometimes we don't. That's OK, but thank you very much. Any other ideas? Which one do you think is really very good? How about this group, girls? What do you think? Wh—

S：I think, I think the blue one is—

T：Why?

S：Because there is a picture.

T：Oh, picture! How about the yellow one and the green one? Thank you, OK, anyway, we agree here we need pictures, right? Because it's very eye-catching. It tells people what we are looking for. Right? And what do you think?

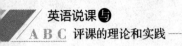

How about the pink one? Is it very good?

    Ss：...

    T：Why not? Why isn't the pink one good writing? Yes?

    S：Because we don't know where the—

    T：Wallet.

    S：Wallet was lost, when is the wallet lost.

    T：Exactly. Thank you. So make sure it is complete. We need when and where, right, helps people to look for us. Any other reasons why the pink one is not good writing? It just told you a wallet. Did it tell you what kind of wallet it is? Did it tell you? Wang Qingyu.

    S：No.

    T：It didn't, right. Thank you, sit down please. It didn't give a detailed description. We need detailed description to tell people. How do we describe a lost item? We can talk about white, yellow, blue, green, what's that?

    S：Color.

    T：Color, good! What else? Big, small ——→ size.

    Ss：Size.

    T：Round, square, triangle, shape. We can also talk about material. Can you name one material? This is wood, yes, leather, leather. And this is a bronze bag, and this is a nylon bag. You can talk about material. And you can also talk about brand, Star-barz Cup, this is a brand. This bag is Adidas. This is Nike. This is Lining. We can also talk about other features. If we have two books looking exactly the same, how can we tell which one is yours? We have the name, right, personal information. This one is Blake's. And also other features including clothes, or a hole in your socks can be the features. And when we take a look at all the lost notices, are they very long? No, no one wants to read the long lost notice. We make it to the point. Now you know how to write a lost notice. And most time a lost notice may be something we can see. However, can be something we can see. Who is a very good reader, good reader in this class? We talk about it just now, OK, Gao Tianyu, please help me read it to the whole class. I'll help you, OK? Ready? Go!

    S：Last.

T：Patience, patience.

S：Last patience, in Room 9 at our elementary school. It is our ability to students desperately do need their teachers' patience return. Huge reward of chocolate offered. If found, please contact 200139. Ms. Pacola.

T：Thank you very much for your reading. So what was lost here? Patience. Sometimes confidence is lost when you fail a maths test. Friendship will be lost when we have a big fight with your friends and other things. So think about it：In your life what was lost can be something you see or something you can't see? Now your turn to write the lost notice. Please take out this piece of paper with a lost example and turn back, turn over and you can write your lost notice on the back. You can also take a look at the good example, write your own lost notice. Please finish it in 8 minutes. And you can also use an E-dictionary on your desk to help. Of course you can raise your hand if you need my help. I'll be there for you.

（学生开始写作）

T：Excuse me, class. Are you ready to show, are you ready to show it? Uh, let's see. Um, Dou Jiacheng, could you please come up and show your lost notice to us? This is a very good one. Come on and do this! Come up to the front, please. Yes. Put them here. That's OK if you have a very good beginning. If you have not finished it, that's OK. You have very good beginning. Take a look. Could you please read to everyone, because it's kind of too small here? And let me see what I can do here. OK, that's better. That's better — here, here, like this. OK, good! Could you please read it for us?

S：Yesterday I lost my pet. It was an honest dog. It was six years old.

T：His fur?

S：His fur was black and it has bright eyes. I lost it in the area of the first street. If you find my pet, you can call at 13562728901, and you...

T：You'll get—

S：And you get my pet and you can get 100 yuan.

T：One hundred yuan reward. OK, thank you. A big warm applause for her, please! Good job, take a look at this one. Is it, does it have very detailed description, right, the fur, the color of the fur, right? Brief and complete, right? Maybe we can make it more eye-catching! A picture of the dog will help. And also we can highlight some parts to make it look better. Maybe we can highlight the title, right, OK, thank you very much. And who else would like to come here? Could you please? Come here, yes. I'm having trouble with this machine. Really. Could you please read it for us? Better. OK, this is better. Dai Jinshan, please.

S: I lost my friendship in Class C on Tuesday morning. I have different ideas with my friend and I shouted at him, and he didn't talk to me any more.

T: Contact.

S: Contact.

T: Dai Jinshan, that's your name, right?

S: Reward: forever friendship!

T: Oh, wow! That's a very nice reward, even better than money! Right? Do you agree? Let's give her a warm applause. Thank you very much, Dai Jinshan. Good job! So we cannot show more lost notices in class. But I think we can make that one more eye-catching if you have a picture. Maybe we can do this after class. So when we finish the lost notice, where can we put it? Where can we put it? Do we put it on the wall in our house? No, where shall we put it? Please.

S: We should put the lost notice around the place we lost the thing.

T: Excellent! Near the place where we lost it. Any more? We want more people to read it. And nowadays where do people look at all the time?

S: We can put it in a busy street.

T: Busy street. Very good! So more people can read it, right? Thank you. Sit down, please. Good idea. Yes, please.

S: We can put it on the Internet.

T: Very good idea. How can you know that? You can read my mind, Internet! Thank you! Any more? What do people look at nowadays, everyday? Is that QQ, a lot of people look at Wechat, right? So this is the homework for you today. Please remember to make your lost notice more eye-catching, OK? Please send it to my e-mail box: creativewriting@123.com and hope you'll love writing, creative writing. And may the good luck be with you! Don't lose everything here. But whatever you lose, don't lose hope. So much for today, goodbye, everyone!

【背景介绍】

这是全国第12届初中英语教学一节观摩课。授课教师是来自杭州外国语学校的邹潇霄老师，该课是一节写作课，教学设计背后的理念是从输入到输出，即通过阅读样板获取写作范例，包括文章内容、结构等。写作前有阅读，阅读前有头脑风暴。头脑风暴主要是解决写什么，阅读为如何写提供范例。学生真正的写作时间不超过整节课的1/4；在写后教师展示了两篇学生习作并做了评价，并进行适当的拓展和提升。

一、教学设计及教学过程

I. Pre-writing

（1）New words：reward.

（2）Brainstorming：What to write about in a lost notice.

（3）Reading an example of lost notice.

（4）Reading 4 more lost notices in group to work out which one is good or bad and why good and why not.

Ⅱ. While-writing：

Write a lost notice.

Ⅲ. Post-writing

（1）Two students showing their writing in class.

（2）Teacher evaluating the two lost notices.

（3）Education：Don't lose everything here. But whatever you lose，don't lose hope.

二、该课的教学特色

1. 教师英语语言质量高

① 语言非常漂亮、简洁；②语调的表意功能拿捏到位；③语速把握到位。重要的信息点教师用中慢速，并且会适当停顿，让学生有思考及领悟的时间。例如，在描述情境时，教师采用中慢速及重复来呈现本课活动植根于其中的大情境：This is a photo of my students and me. And we had a wonderful time there. However，one of my students lost something. What did my student lose? （中速+停顿，让学生思考）What was lost? What was lost? ；④教师措词准确，最精彩的

地方是学生猜邹老师的学生丢失的是手机，但实际上是钱包。这里邹老师在反馈时说的是：<u>However</u>，my student lost his wallet. 这里however教师用得自然、用得妙。很多教师在训练学生用它来表示转折，但在教师语言中很少听到他们自己用however来表情达意。

2. 教师指令语非常清晰

在本课中，教师指令语清晰高效，例如，当教师要学生阅读Lost Notice的样板时，教师说：So now let's have a look at an example if your guessing is right. Please take out the paper on your desk. Read this Lost Notice and answer the five questions below. Please finish it in three minutes.

在这条指令语中，教师用三个单句来告诉学生要做什么、完成什么任务、用多少时间等。语言清晰易懂，可操作性强。

当教师要学生以小组为单位拓展阅读更多的lost notice，选出写得好的和写得差的并说明原因时，教师用短句和慢速说：Group leaders，please take out the envelopes on your desk，open it and take out four pieces of Lost Notice inside. Read as a group and compare them. Which one do you think is good writing? And why is that? And which one is not good? And why is that? Do you understand me? Finish it in five minutes.这条教师指令语清晰地表达了做什么，如何用，用多少时间来做。

3. 在语境中教词汇，在需要时教词汇

教师在读前教词汇，在读后教词汇，在碰到时教词汇。reward是在设置大语境时教的，leather是写作前、阅读后教的读音及意义。这些都是根据需要进行教学的。词汇这么教主要可能是因为这是写作课，生词量不大；另外是因为写作课的主要目的是综合运用已学的语言手段及已储备的写作资源进行表达，不是放在学习新的语言点上。

4. 培养学生的思维能力

活动有助于培养学生的思维能力，特别是发散性思维能力、批判性思维以及创新思维的能力。例如，教师设置了阅读并选择和判断哪个失物启示写得好或不好并陈述原因的活动。学生不断进行判断，还要找依据。而这些答案都不是现成的，学生要经过分析、概括、综合、辨析等过程才能较好地完成任务。因此，在完成任务的过程中，学生的发散思维能力和审辨思维能力都得到了不同程度的发展。又如，学生写出一个遗失友谊的启示，请看下面片段：

S：I lost my friendship in Class C on Tuesday morning. I have different ideas with my friend and I shouted at him，and he didn't talk to me anymore.

T：Contact.

S：Contact.

T：Dai Jinshan，that's your name，right?

S：Reward：forever friendship!

5. 教师在输出阶段能够为学生提供信息型反馈

布罗菲和古德指出，信息型反馈是针对学生的能力和进步做出的反馈。琼斯指出，从动机的角度来看，信息型反馈应该是教师反馈的主要形式，因为它使学生明白他们跟目标之间的距离以及要保持或取得更大进步所需的努力。在本课中，教师采用了信息型反馈方式，例如，教师在评价第一位学生撰写的失物启示说：Good job，take a look at this one. Does it have very detailed description? Right，the fur，the color of the fur，right? Brief and complete，right? Maybe we can make it more eye-catching! A picture of the dog will help. And also we can highlight some parts to make it look better. 教师除了肯定学生的习作，指出它的优点：brief and complete，还指出了改进的方向：Maybe we can make it more eye-catching! A picture of the dog will help. And also we can highlight some parts to make it look better.

6. 个性化的评价语

个性化评价语往往带有教师的个人风格，富有教学机智并且区别于其他教师的评价语。例如，在本课中，当教师问学生失物启示可以放在哪里，并启发学生现在人们最经常看的东西是什么时，一位女生说：We can put it on the Internet. 教师的反馈语是 Very good idea. How can you know that? You can read my mind，Internet! 能够读懂老师的心是对学生的最高评价，是比肯定式评价语 excellent 等要好得多的个性化评价。

三、该课的一些不足之处

写前用了差不多23分钟，其中阅读四个lost notice、评判它们的好坏、挖出好的Lost Notice包含哪些信息点到布置写作任务，足足花了九分钟。换句话说，写前的准备做得非常充分，帮助学生扫除了写作的难点——写什么。在写中阶段，教师给了学生八分钟的时间来撰写一个lost notice。而写后阶段，课堂上只展示了两位学生的写作，而且只是教师在评价，学生没有充分参与进来。如果能让更多的学生展示写作成果或者主动参与评价则写作教学的效果会更好！

四、结束语

这是一节名副其实的优质课。课堂节奏明快、流畅，教学设计符合从输入到输出的语言教学理念，教师语言质量高，重视学生语言能力，评价语起到激励学生学习的作用，又能做到个性化，更能给学生指出改进学习的方向。课堂教学能够启迪学生的思维，也能关注学习能力的培养。

评课案例四 《Fun with English 8A Unit 2 Main Task：School》写作课

【课堂实录】

T：OK，today we have changed another place to have our lesson. Where are we?

Ss：Studio.

T：Studio，OK. Are you excited?

Ss：Yes.

T：Or probably a little nervous. OK，in this studio today we are going to learn a new thing. That is Fun with English 8A，Unit 2，Main Task. What is Unit 2 Main Task about？Don't worry！I can show you some pictures. And you may find the answer from these pictures. What is Unit 2 Main Task about？（教师播放一系列图片）Uh，I googled these pictures. As you can see，these are things we are going to learn. Yes，which word did I google to look for these pictures to find these pictures？Have any idea of what these pictures are about？Have a guess！Jim，do you want to have a try？

S：Life.

T：Life. Good guessing. Life. Um，but can you give more exaction？Life about what, what kind of life? Lucy, please!

S：It's...It is a set of landscape.

T：Landscape. Do you think it is landscape?

S：More.

T：You see landscape here? Are you sure? Flower.

S：Flowers.

T：Yes, flower. But flower is everywhere. In our school we have flowers. OK, good guessing. Very good. OK, Tony.

S：I think it is about a building.

T：Building, very close. But what kind of building? Where are the buildings? You, please.

S：It is pictures about our school.

T：Bingo! Very good! It's about school. I tapped "school" into Internet and I get pictures. This is what we are going to learn about school today.（板书）School, you must be familiar with school, OK. This picture is a baseball field.

Ss：Baseball field.

T：Follow me：baseball.

Ss：Baseball.

T：Baseball.

Ss：Baseball.

T：Baseball field.

Ss：Baseball field.

T：Baseball field.

Ss：Baseball field.

T：Do you play baseball?

Ss：No.

T：Do you want to play baseball?

Ss：Yes.

T：Yes, OK. You want to play baseball. But we don't have baseball field in our school. So you cannot play it. OK? And remember this one? It's a tennis court.

Ss：Tennis court.

T：Yeah，tennis.

Ss：Tennis.

T：Tennis.

Ss：Tennis.

T：Can you play tennis in our school?

Ss：No.

T：No！Do you want to?

Ss：Yes.

T：So no！We don't have tennis court. We cannot play tennis in our school. It's a pity. You want to play. Very good. Remember this one?

Ss：Table tennis.

T：Yes，table tennis is very good. Table tennis.

Ss：Table tennis.

T：Table tennis.

Ss：Table tennis.

T：Can you play table tennis in our school?

Ss：Yes.

T：Yes. Do we have this table in our school?

Ss：Yes.

T：Yes，so it is good. Having table tennis. Any other sports you want to play in our school? Any other sports you want to play in our school，possibly we don't have but you want to? Edith，you please.

S：I want swimming in our school.

T：You want swimming，OK? You want swimming in our school. But do we have a swimming pool?

Ss：No.

T：For Edith，she wants a swimming pool，but we don't have a swimming pool. Very good！Excellent！Any other idea? Any other sports you want to have? Hanna，please.

S：I want to go skating in our school.

T：Oh，my God，skating，very good idea，skating. Do we have the field to go skating?

Ss：No.

T：No. So Hanna is not happy about that，OK? Any other idea? Uh，would you please，Bob?

S：I want to go canoeing in our school.

T：Canoeing? Oh，cool! Canoeing，very good! OK，can you go canoeing in our school?

Ss：No.

T：No，Bob is not heavy. Probably Bob is going to build a river，OK，yeah，in our school. He can go canoeing. Very good. They are different kinds of sports（指着板书）. And go back to this table. We have so many tables here. Can we play table tennis there? Yes or no?

Ss：No.

T：No. Why not? There are so many tables there! Why not? What are these tables for? What are these tables used for? For what? OK，anybody? Hansa，please! Coco，sorry.

Ss：They are used for eating lunch.

T：Oh，they are used for eating lunch. Very good. So this is a place we can have lunch，right? It is called dining hall. Follow me：dining hall.

Ss：Dining hall.

T：Dining hall.

S：Dining hall.

T：So this is facilities（归类）of the school. Dining hall.

Ss：Dining hall.

T：Is the dining hall in our school as good as this one? No.

Ss：No.

T：Which one do you prefer?

Ss：This one.

T：Of course，this one. The dining hall in our school is not so good. OK，do you know any other facilities in our school? Any other facilities? Places，for example，do you know where it is? What place is this one?

Ss：Airport.

T：Airport? It's the school, remember? I tapped school. Airport and school, creative idea! Good. I'm sorry. It's not an airport.

S：Office.

T：Office, bingo! It's a school library. Is it amazing?

Ss：Yes.

T：Yeah! OK, library.

Ss：Library.

T：Library.

Ss：Library.

T：Is there a school library in our school?

Ss：Yes.

T：Which one do you prefer?

Ss：This one.

T：OK, you want this one. You are not happy about this school library in our own school. OK, it's pretty cool. It also has a crouch there, right? OK, this one, a classroom. Do you like this classroom?

Ss：Yes.

T：Yes, OK. Beautiful, new, big. Do you like your own classroom?

Ss：Yes.

T：Yes. So which one do you prefer, this one or your own ?

Ss：Own.

T：Your classroom. May I know why? Why do you like your own classroom? For me, I like this classroom because it is very beautiful, and very big. What is your reason? Um, Catherine, you please.

S：I think our classroom makes happy remembering.

T：Oh, so classroom has...

S：And my friend.

T：I see, happy memories, wow, good idea! Very good idea, OK! And Tony, please.

S：And I think this classroom has a enough space for us to write because we don't have desks.

　　T：Ooh, so it is not it's not big enough, probably. OK, very good! Any other ideas? Alice, please.

　　S：Oh, I think it brings a lot of things but there's no desk with us.

　　T：Oh, I see so you...

　　S：Prefer.

　　T：Prefer your own, prefer your own, yeah, OK, very good! Very good! And other school facilities you want to have in our school? Any other facilities, any other places or we have some facilities here, OK, some facilities here that you like very much. Julia.

　　S：I like, I like the laboratory in our school.

　　T：Uh laboratories, yes, that is the lab, um. Why?

　　S：Because, because we can do a lot of experiments.

　　T：So can you use the full sentence, please?

　　S：I like this lab very much because we can do experiments.

　　T：OK, very good! So you must be good at physics or chemistry, right? OK, or biology. Yeah, OK. There are chemistry, physics, biology , are school subjects.（板书）Very good! Subjects, very good! OK, subjects. And where can I see the whole subjects of yours?

　　Ss：Timetable.

　　T：Timetable. Very good! Timetable.

　　Ss：Timetable.

　　T：Timetable.

　　Ss：Timetable.

　　T：（板书）Timetable here, school subjects. So this is one timetable from one class from Junior 2. OK, are you happy about the subjects here? Do you have your favorite subject? What is your favorite subject here? Uh, would you please, Amy?

　　S：I think I like English and the music. But in this timetable, uh, I think there aren't any music course.

　　T：Uh, so music class. So you want music class?

　　S：Yes.

T：Why?

S：Among music, I like singing. I also like music. And I like listening to music.

T：You want to have more music class, but there's no music class here, right? OK. That's your opinion. There isn't any, OK, very good! Any other idea about this timetable. Hilary, how about you?

S：I think I like computer class but because uh, uh as we can know we don't have enough time to enjoy on the Internet. And in the computer class we can after we finish our homework, we can play, we can play on computer.

T：Yes! Surf on the Internet. Right, OK, good! Computer study you want to surf on the Internet, OK, very good. Any other ideas? Any other ideas? How about Annie?

S：I prefer politics class because I think in politics class we can talk about our own idea or views.

T：Personal opinion, alright, OK, very good! （板书）Politics, OK. So I like or you can use. So we can talk about our own opinion about politics, very good! And what subjects you don't like, you are not happy about, you want to take them away from this timetable. Any idea? Sam.

S：Uh...

T：Remember Sam's favorite?

Ss：Yeah/No.

S：I like, I don't like... maths and P.E. Lesson.

T：Don't like maths?

S：Because in junior 2 maths is more harder than junior 1.

T：Um.

S：And, for me I'm a little fat so I am not not good at P.E. Lesson. So I don't like P.E. Lesson.

T：I am sorry for you, OK, but even you are a little fat doing exercise is really good for your health, OK. Tony, please.

S：I don't have Chinese class.

T：Chinese class, OK.

S：Uh because sometimes I think this class contains many things too hard to me.

T：Too hard for you to study.

S：And I don't like to recite the same sentence we've learned every time.If I don't do it very well，maybe the teacher will be angry and let me copy them for many times.

T：Ha I see. So you hope there will be fewer Chinese classes，OK，well.（板书）I hope there will be fewer Chinese classes. OK，besides these subjects，did you see these clubs，OK？ Do you see the chess club？ What do people do in a chess club？

Ss：Play chess.

T：Play chess of course. Do you play chess？

Ss：Sometimes.

T：Sometimes. Can you play chess in the chess club in your school？ No，so there，is there a chess club in your school？

Ss：No.

T：No. And how about this one？ Drama club. Uh，what do people do in the drama club？

Ss：Role play.

T：Yes，of course，have a role play or play different roles，OK？ And the like these two girls（指着照片），a boy play a role of a—

Ss：Frog

T：Frog and maybe this frog. And he's famous for drama. It's a cartoon. But can you recognize who he is？ Williams Shakespeare.

Ss：Shakespeare.

T：OK，very good. Talking about drama you must mention about this man. Do you like drama clubs？

Ss：Yes.

T：Is there a drama club in your school？

Ss：Yes.

T：Yes，good，that's good！ （板书）Happy have a drama club in our school. And besides this one，you may see the different. OK，you may see the different clubs here. This club，everyone like it very much. And this one？ Film club. Is there any film club in your school？

Ss：Yes.

T：Yes，good！Do you like it?

Ss：Yes.

T：Yes，happy，happy. OK. Film club. And how about this club，art club? Is there an art club in your school?

Ss：Yes.

T：Yes. What can you do in the art club in your school?

Ss：Draw.

T：Anyone，can you raise your hand? OK，Hans，would you please?

S：I think we can draw some pictures and also can make some sculpture or...

T：Oh sculpture，so you like art club.（板书）Happy about art club. Art club is your favorite. They are all put after-school activities. After school activities.

Ss：After school activities.

T：After school activities.

Ss：After school activities.

T：However，you can only have these after school activities after 4 p.m. Do you know why? Do you know why you only have these after-school activities after 4 p.m.? Do you want to have a guess?

S：Because 4 p.m. is the time we are going to leave school.

T：Very good！Bingo！Excellent.（板书）It's the school time. The school finishes at 4 p.m. The school finishes at 4 p.m. So we can only have these after-school activities after 4 p.m. here. Do you like it? Is this your ideal time，4 p.m.? The school finishes.

Ss：No.

T：（板书）Ideal.

Ss：Ideal.

T：Ideal.

Ss：Ideal.

T：Is it your ideal time?

Ss：No.

T：No. So what is your ideal school time? When does the school finish?

Anything? Any idea? Lucy. When do you think of school finishes at?

S：I think that school finishes at 12 o'clock.

T：12 o'clock! Why?

S：Um after lunch at school, after students finish the lunch.

T：So the students can only have half the day at school. OK, the rest of the day you can enjoy yourself, well. That's your ideal school time. So when does your school start? May I know when is your school start?

Ss：7：30/7：40.

T：When does your school start? OK, Bob.

T：Our school start at 7：30.

T：Starts.

S：Starts.

T：Yeah. And is this your ideal school time?

S：No.

T：No. So what is your ideal school time?

S：For me, it's a little too early. I think 8 o'clock is quite OK.

T：It's quite OK. So do you think, I think the school...

S：I think the school may...

T：Can start.

S：Can start at 8 o'clock.

T：Yes, OK. Then there will be plenty of time for you to sleep a bit longer. OK, very good! So that is about the timetable here. We've talked about subjects, sports, facilities and timetable. And I have more questions for you. Would you please open your book and look at Unit 2 Main Task Page 35? We have more questions for you about your ideal school. What is your ideal school like? （幻灯片播放 Questionnaire No.7 to No. 13）Would you please work in pairs? Work in pairs! Ask each other these questions, Questions 7 to 13 and write down each other's answers. OK, three minutes is given to you. Now, would you please? （教师布置新任务，为写作做语言准备，学生进行对子活动）Any questions? Ask me. OK, as most of you have finished, I want to know what would your deskmate like about these questions. What are their answers? Now can you describe it for meal of them? All of them, together, from Question 7 to Question13? What's your deskmate's opinion about these questions? OK, Ashley, would you please?

S: My deskmate likes to wear school uniform because he thought that it is very comfortable.

T: Fit

S: Fit and very comfortable. He thinks, he thinks our school is a good one because we have, our homework is less than other school. And he also wants to go on school trip and he goes on a school trip every half a year. And he likes to go to school on foot.

T: Um hum. Every year, thank you very much. Excellent, very good! Well done. Tony, that's very good idea, OK? Anybody else wants to share your opinion? Julia, would you please?

S: My deskmate says she don't like to wear school uniform.

T: She doesn't like to.

S: She doesn't like because she thinks our own clothes are more comfortable than the school uniform and that she thinks our school is very good because our school have a lot of activities and our teacher is very kind and she likes to, she likes to go on school trip also once a term on a school trip. And she likes to go to the cinema for the school trip.

T: Oh, she likes to go to the cinema for the school trip. Very good idea, very special one! You think where we go on school trip, we should go to the landscape, beautiful landscape. Well, OK, excellent, very good. Anybody else wants to share your opinion? Cindy, you please.

S: Um Hilary, Hilary thinks that she likes to wear the school uniform because it saves time and wearing clothes everyone will be the same... compare.

T: Yeah. You are all very happy with the school uniform. Very good, go on!

S: And she thinks that our school is a good one because we have, we have a lot of activities to train us be more confident.

T: Um.

S: She likes to go on school trip. She goes on school trip twice a year. Um, she would like to go to movies.

T：Um，you like to go to movies and school trip. OK，excellent! Anybody else wants to share? OK，Linda，one more.

S：My deskmate Lucy likes to wear school uniform because she don't want to attend to clothes，and she also thinks our school is a good one because she says in the school we can learn more things and she likes to go to school canoeing trip and she always goes to school trip twice a term and she likes to go to climb mountain.

T：Um，I see you have ideas about your school that you're very happy about school uniform and our school is a very good one and also for school trip，you have a lot of ideas，but I also think that you are not happy about some parts of our school such as baseball field. There isn't any and there is no tennis court and there is no swimming pool as well，OK，and we can't...

Ss：Skating.

T：Skating in our school，OK，（板书）and we can't go canoeing，OK? And the we don't have a very big dining hall. Remember the library，the picture，OK? And are happy here，maths，P.E. And also remember Chinese? But some of them we are not very happy about（教师在黑板上写出相关方面）and here like class club you are happy about that. So，if we want to change these unhappy things about school into the happy faces here，then they will become an ideal school. That is your ideal school，OK. So Daniel，a student from another school，also writes his ideas about his ideal school here. Now would you please turn to page 36? This is his article about his ideal school. And go through it. Then tell me some choices here.（播放PPT）Go through the article first ad then make some choices for the different parts. How does he write his ideal school? So how many paragraphs are there in this article? There are five paragraphs. And I put these five paragraphs into three parts. Part.1 that is Para 1 and Para. 2. What does Daniel tell his friends about his school in Part 1? You can make a choice here?（有答案可供选择）What does it talk about in Part 1? Can you see it? What does it talk about in Part 1? Does it talk about ideal time?

Ss：Yes.

T：Yes，OK，yes，he talks about ideal school time. Anything else does he talk about in Part 1?

S：He also talks ideal things to do in the dining hall.

T：Yes, OK, excellent! Very good! He also talks about ideal things to do in the dining hall in Part 1. Part 2, Para. 3, what does Daniel talk about his ideal school about in Para. 3? Bob, please.

S：Daniel talks about his ideal subjects.

T：Yes, ideal subjects.

S：And the...

T：Anything else?

S：And the um maybe the ideal homework and school.

T：OK, you may have to think about it. Annie, would you please?

S：Ideal uniform and classes.

T：OK, yes, he talks about ideal uniform and classes also in Para. 3 Part 2. The last part Part 3, what does he talk about the ideal school in Part 3? Yeah, we may talk about it together. He talks about—

S：School activities and homework and school trips.

T：Yes, that is how Daniel describes his ideal school in the article. Now we are going to have a try to write an ideal school just like Daniel writes about his ideal school. OK, and you can choose to use the different parts like what Daniel does, and two paragraphs talk about these two and one paragraph talks about subjects, uniforms, classes, and the last part talks about places, after-school activities, homework and the school trips. I prepare three different color paper for you, and you are going to pick one piece of paper with one color like this one, I'll show you here. And then work in pairs, work in pairs, each pair is going to pick one piece of paper with one color. And if you pick the red one, you are going to write—

Ss：Ideal school time.

T：And the ideal things to do in the dining hall. If you pick up the green one, you are to talk about—

Ss：Ideal after-school activities.

T：Yeah. And if you pick up the red paper, you are going to write about—

Ss：Blue.

T：Oh, sorry, blue one you are going to talk about—

Ss：Homework and school trips

T：Are you clear? Work in pair, work together. Each pair can only pick up one color of paper, OK? Now, here you go! Yeah, pass to the next. Here you go! Here you go! （分发纸片）And three minutes is given to you. Work together, yeah! （教师巡堂指导）

OK, may we enjoy an ideal school from three different pairs about their ideal school here, OK? Let's first see this part. （教师用投影仪展示学生文段，如图6-3 所示）First part, remember?

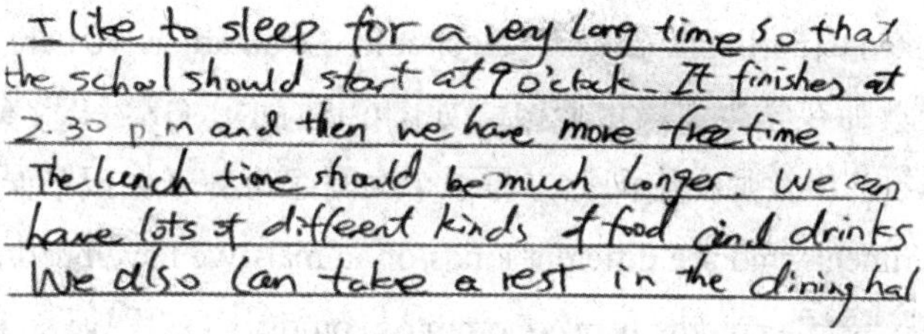

> I like to sleep for a very long time so that the school should start at 9 o'clock. It finishes at 2.30 p.m and then we have more free time. The lunch time should be much longer. We can have lots of different kinds of food and drinks We also can take a rest in the dining hall

图6-3　学生文段1

First part will talk about which part of your ideal school? Ideal school time.

Ss：School time.

T：And the ideal things to do in the dining hall. Very good.

Ss：Dining hall.

T：（教师读播放的学生文段以便进行修改）I like...in the dining hall. Um, very good idea! But the writing is a little poor. And this one "can" （圈出can）. Can you see "can" in this one? Pay attention to writing, OK? And then second part we talk about what? Ideal, ideal school subject.

Ss：School subjects.

T：And the school uniform.

Ss：School uniform.

T：And louder.

Ss：Class clubs.

T：Yes, class clubs. （教师读学生的第二文段，如图6-4所示）We have computer lessons... Also, you never use "also" here, OK? You'd better put "also" in the middle of the sentence. We also have, we also have biology everyday because we

237

can have interested experiments .（教师评价语）

图6-4　学生文段2

Ss：Interested experiments.

T：Interested experiments，yes. You should use an adjective here，interested，interested，（教师在学生文段上修改，如图6-5所示）OK？Pay attention. This is one of the words（教师在错词上方写了个大写字母W来标记错误类型），OK. Interested experiments and see different kinds of animals.We have hundreds of kinds of uniforms. Do we have a comma here? Comma，comma，OK? We so here we should capitalize.（此处教师误读了学生作文，学生是对的，这是一个定语从句）We can choose，we have hundreds of kinds of uniforms we can choose. Oh，this is a，sorry.（教师意识到自己的错误而涂去刚才加上去的逗号）It's an attributive clause here. And there are about 30 students in each class just like we have ，right. Very good.

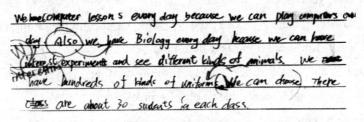

图6-5　学生文段3

And last part for the ideal school is what？Ideal—

Ss：Places and school activities.

T：And the...

Ss：School trips.

T：OK，let's see this group. OK，（教师读评第三段）there is a shopping center in our ideal school . Wow，shopping center in our ideal school. OK，never use this one（指school后面的圆点）, no, OK. And a very big cinema. Entertainment center have Karaokay, Karaokay is not this one, Karaokay, this one. We can play drama, dance. We can play drama, dance, sing popular songs, even play Tai Kwendao, OK, at after-school activities time, OK. And actually I think we we should use "and" here. And, remember? Conjunction, A, B, C and D. Yeah, pay attention, OK. Pay attention to the spelling at the after-school activities time. At time, or during. Very good! Pay attention to the preposition during. And then we often go to some places for far away, far away, especially go abroad at school trips. At school trip or on...

Ss：On...

T：On school trips, for example, London, Paris. Do we use example here?

Ss：Such as.

T：Such as, yeah. For example with a whole sentence, OK. And the most important thing when you do the writing here you need to pay attention to this checklist here, OK（打出checklist）. Spelling, we have some spelling mistakes. And WO, what is WO?

Ss：Word order.

T：Yes, word order. A mistake in word order we don't have just now. That's good. G means...

Ss：Grammar.

T：T means...

Ss：Tense.

T：Yes, it means wrong verb tense. So when you see teacher writes a T on your paper, it means you have mistake there. WW, what's that?

Ss：Wrong word.

T：Yes, P?

Ss：Pun—

T：For punctuation mistake, punctuation mistake. And for this one , it is something not necessary there, OK. And when you write down the article, you need to pay attention to this one. OK, here let's go back to the ideal school. Just write down the ideal school from different parts. This time we're going to write down your own ideal school here and you may write all things like the ideal food and snacks, other ideal facilities in the school, and also ideal places around the school, OK. Now you are going to take a piece of paper from me and write down your own ideal school. OK? And would you please pass（发白纸）? Own, your own ideal school. Tom, pass it here. For you. Pass it down. And I prepare a checklist for you. Make sure you don't make those mistakes. Everybody gets a piece of checklist. Make sure you don't. OK, since we don't have enough time, it becomes your homework. Go home and write down about your ideal school, OK. And finally I think our school is a very good school, so love your school and your teacher and classmates and enjoy your school everyday. The homework is after school you finish writing your own article about your ideal school. Would you please exchange article with classmates and correct mistakes according to the checklist you have. And if possible, you'd like to draw a picture about your ideal school, next to your writing. Class is over. Goodbye!

【背景介绍】

这是2011年《英语课程标准》颁布后拍摄的一节用以展示新课标理念下英语写作教学应该怎么教的示范课。授课教师是南京外国语学校的谢晓菁老师。该课的写前、写中、写后三个阶段任务分工明确，重点突出，教学目标达成度高。

一、教学设计及教学过程

1. Brainstorming about the school.

2. Reading text about ideal school.

3. Writing in pair according to the materials given by the teacher.（分解写作任务，减轻写作任务）

4. Making comments and correction paragraph by paragraph.

5. Providing a checklist for evaluating with symbols of mistakes together in class.

6. Assigning homework：Write about your own ideal school（communicative writing）.Exchange article with classmates and correct the mistakes. Draw a picture about the ideal school.

二、该课的教学特色

1. 该课是一节突出过程法的写作课

教师重视写前的准备，重视写作的过程，重视在堂上为学生的习作提供反馈。写作从对相关内容的激活、词句的铺垫、语篇的输入，到控制性写作到自由写作，虽然自由写作最后被教师布置为课后作业，它在某种程度上也反映了教师的写作教学理念：学习性的模仿写作和自由表达的交际性写作相结合；写作教学要遵循循序渐进的原则，即遵循从控制性写作到提示写作到自由写作的过程。

2. 在互动中教学

互动中教学"学校"这个话题之下的几类生词：sports，facilities，timetable，after-school activities等。在互动中谈论学生喜欢从事的运动，从而教学相关的词语baseball，tennis，table tennis，swimming，skating，canoeing及短语。接着，通过互动谈论与学校的各种设施与教学相关的词语，如dining hall等。教师在教学中能够联系学生的实际，例如，当呈现漂亮的课室时，教师问学生是否喜欢图片里的教室，是否喜欢自己的教室。联系学生的实际有利于激发学生开口说话的动机和真实的思想和情感的交流。例如，在谈论喜欢的科目时，一位女生说，I like politics class because I think in politics class we can talk about our own idea about a film. 教师围绕学校生活自然地引导学生进行相关话题的谈论，如学生什么时候上学、7：30是否理想的上学时间、学生想要什么样的上学时间、为什么等。这些都是很平常的话题，适当的利用或开发显得尤为必要。

3. 在互动中培养学生的批判性思维能力

写作教学要把写作和思维训练结合起来。在本课中，教师跟学生之间大量地互动，师生一起构建描述学校体育活动、设施、课外活动、课程表及喜欢的科目等内容。教师并没有停留在浅表的教学上，而是适当把学生引向深入，比如理性思考、对事物进行评价，或者探索喜欢或者不喜欢一个事物的原因等（见下面片段），以此来培养学生的批判性思维能力。

S：I don't like maths and P.E. Lesson.

T：Don't like maths?

S：Because in junior 2 maths is the more harder than junior 1.

T：Um.

S：And for me I'm a little fat so I am not not good at P.E. Lesson. So I don't like P.E. lesson.

T：I am sorry for you，OK，but even you are a little fat doing exercise is really good for your health.

4. 该课的作文评价采取了教师主导的全班评价的方式

作文评价有几种方式：全班评价、教师评价、同伴评价和学生自评。作文评价基于某些标准和内容进行。一般来说，如果要让学生进行同伴评价或者是自我评价，教师会提供评价表或者自我评价表，这些评价表通常包括评价的内容或者评价的标准，比如内容、语言、逻辑、篇章结构等。而对于自评，教师常常提供浅表性的评价要求，如检查拼写、语法等写作技术方面的要求，因为学生对像内容、逻辑等的不足常常不能自知或者无力修改。在以培养学生评价能力为中心的课堂，教师常常会先让学生进行自评和互评，最后才是全班的评价或是教师的评价。而在任务较多的课堂中，教师往往会选取一两篇学生的习作在堂上进行全班评价，这种评价方法既能评价学生习作的质量，又有示范评价的作用，既授人以鱼，也授人以渔。

三、结束语

这是一节很扎实的英语写作课。它是一节以过程教学法为主，辅以结果教学法的写作课。教师为学生所做的一切也是为了产出较好的写作成果；此外，教师在全班评价时也是偏向评价作文的语言质量。教师为了培养学生的写作能力，并适当降低写作任务的难度，先后为学生提供了包括词汇、句型、范文、写作检查表等各种层面的脚手架。当然，该课也有有待商榷的地方，如在写前教师花在为写作提供语言资源和写作内容的时间略长。可以把这部分的时间减少到10分钟以内，一方面为学生留下更多的思考空间；另一方面可以把更多的时间用于学生互评上，最后才是教师主导的全班评价。

评课案例五 《Welcome to Our School （Grammar：Personal Pronouns）》语法课

【课堂实录】

T：OK，class begins！

S：Stand up！

T：Good morning，ladies and gentleman！

Ss：Good morning，Mr. Zhao.

T：Sit down，please！How are you today？

Ss：I'm fine. Thank you. And you？

T：I am very happy to hear that and I'm also happy to be your new teacher today. I want to know something about your new school. So today your task is to introduce your new school to me. Is that OK？Yes，OK，now do you still remember in this unit Millie shows her mum around the new school，right？

Ss：Yes.

T：Here are three sentences about Millie's new school. Let's read them together. Billy's school looks beautiful. Millie's school has a playground. I am going to change them a little bit. Millie's school looks beautiful，one，two！

Ss：Millie's school looks beautiful. It has a playground. It has a modern library.

T：OK，the first and the second sentence，which one do you like better？Now you please. Would you please use the microphone？

S：I like the second one.

T：Why do you like the second one？

S：Because it is better.

T：Yes，the sentence is better and I think it is much—

S：Shorter.

T：Shorter. Which word makes it shorter？

S：It.

T：Excellent! "It" is one of the personal pronouns. It becomes shorter，sit down，please. It becomes shorter because when we use "it"，we needn't repeat. Who knows the Chinese meaning of "repeat"？You please.

S：重复。

T：Yes，excellent. 重复。Sit down please. Besides shorter，between these two sentences，which one is more fluent？OK，which one?

S：Also the second one.

T：Which word makes it more fluent?

S：It.

T：Also it. Sit down please. Thank you. So using pronouns is also an important way to link sentences together，clear? OK，if it's so great to use personal pronouns，why not use one more? Let's read them again.

Ss：It looks beautiful. It has a playground. It has a modern library.

T：This time we use another it. But do you know whose school we are talking about? We don't know. So I want to give you a tip：When we use personal nouns，we should use nouns first or just use the pronouns. You please. Use your microphone.

S：We should use nouns first.

T：Very good. Now Team 1 first. Thank you，sit down please. Let's give him a big hand. Good，good，very good. Now，in this unit，Millie is so excited about his new school，right? So he writes a letter to his friend about it. Would you please take out this piece of paper and try to read this letter by yourself? Try to find all the personal pronouns in this letter. When you find one，please circle around it，OK. Let's do it.

T：OK，have you finished? OK，I think most of you have finished! What kind of personal pronouns can you find in this letter? Put up your hands if you find one! Now，you please，the boy with blue glasses. Yeah!

S：I found that：I, you, I, it, I, it, I she, I, her. We, …, he, he, it, you.

T：OK，I think he has found all the personal pronouns. Very good! Sit down please. Let's give him a big hand. Good，good，very good! Excellent. Here are all the personal pronouns in this letter. And look at this sentence. I'll read this sentence for you: I have made a friend called Sandy. She's very hardworking and do well in all subjects. So I can learn a lot from her. This is from the letter, right? OK, in this letter, Millie tries to use "she" to talk about... Great! Louder please!

Ss: Sandy.

T: Sandy, right? And she also tries to use "her" to talk about Sandy, right? OK, now I have another sentence for you. Who will read this sentence for us? OK, would you please read this sentence for us?

S: Mr. Wu—

T: Would you please read this sentence "The man"?

S: He enjoys listening to music. It makes him happy.

T: Very good. Thank you so much. Sit down please. In this sentence, Millie uses "he" to talk about—

Ss: Mr. Wu.

T: Excellent! Mr. Wu And she also uses "him" to talk about—

Ss: Mr. Wu.

T: Mr. Wu. It means we can use different personal pronouns to talk about the same person or the same thing, right? So my question is: What is the difference between "she and her" "he and him"? Now, you please. Have a try.

S: One is a subject pronoun and the other is the object pronoun.

T: Which one is the subject pronoun?

S: "She" is the subject pronoun and "her" is a object pronoun.

T: Very good! Sit down please. Now the personal pronoun like "she" or "he" usually we put them at the beginning of the sentence, clear? And they are used as subject. So we call them subject pronouns. Can you guess the meaning of the subject pronoun? You, please.

S: 主格。

T: Excellent! Sit down please! And do we usually put "him" or "her" at the beginning? No, usually they are not at the beginning and they are used as an object. So we call them "object pronoun". What is the meaning of "object pronoun"? Together!

Ss: 宾格。

T: Excellent. Now, here are all the personal pronouns. Would you please take out this paper again? This time, please put all the personal pronouns in this table. OK? Now, let's do it!

...

T: Have you finished? Now, let's check the answer. What about the first one? What is the object of I? Who knows the answer? Put up your hand! Now, you please, have a try!

S: Me.

T: Me, right. OK. Very good! Read after me: I—me. Read after me: I—me.

Ss: I—me.

T: I—me.

Ss: I—me.

T: Very good! What about this one? You please.

S: You.

T: Excellent! Would you please spell you? How to spell you? What is the Chinese meaning of spell?

Ss: 拼写。

T: Excellent! Could you please spell it for us?

S: Y—o—u.

T: Excellent! Y—o—u. Sit down please. Very good! What are the object form of "you"? You please.

S: You.

T: Also you. Very good. Sit down please. You, you.

Ss: You, you.

T: OK, now let's come to the third person. What do you get here? You, please!

S: He.

T: He. What about the object form? If you've got "he" here, what about this one?

S: Um, him.

T: Him. Can you spell him?

S: H—i—m.

T：Excellent! H—i—m. Sit down please. We have "he", and we can also have "him". And next one is—

Ss："Her".

T："Her" is the object form. What about the subject form of "it"?

Ss："She".

T：Excellent! She and her. He, she, we can also have—What is the object form of "it"?

Ss："It".

T：Also "it". Read after me：It—it.

Ss：It—it.

T：It—it.

Ss：It—it.

T：Excellent! Let's come to the plural form. What about this one? You, please.

S：We.

T：We. What about the object form?

S："Us".

T：Very good! Sit down, please. Read after me：we—us.

Ss：We—us.

T：We—us.

Ss：We—us.

T：OK, next one. What about this one? You, please.

S：You.

T：You and—

S：You.

T：Excellent! You and you, what about the last one? The last chance goes to—, you please.

S：They.

T：They, very good! It's hard for someone to spell it. Can you spell it?

S：T—h—e—y.

T：OK, excellent! How about the last one?

S：Them.

T: Them. Can you spell "them"?

S: T—h—e—m.

T: Very good! Let's give her a big hand: Good, good, very good! Excellent! I think you are so familiar with this table, right? Would you please have a look at them again? Which one do you think is the most special one? Together!

Ss: "You".

T: Why do you think "you" is special? You, please.

S: Because the object pronoun is "you", and the subject pronoun is also "you".

T: Yes, OK, sit down please. How many "you" s can you find in this letter? Four. Very good!

Ss: Four.

T: It means it can be both a subject pronoun and an object pronoun. And it can also be both a singular and a plural pronoun. Who can try to translate this sentence into Chinese? Now, you please. Try to use Chinese to translate it for me.

S: you非常特殊，它可以在主格和宾格上都是you，单数和复数的主格和宾格也都是you。

T: Excellent! Give him a big hand: Good, good, very good! OK, in this table, there is another pronoun which can be both a subject and an object. Can you find it?

Ss: "It".

T: "It", very good! So I can say in this table "you" and "it" are two special ones. Do you agree?

Yes? OK, there is one more thing special about it. Usually we can use the rest of us to talk about people, right? But do we usually use it to talk about people?

Ss: No.

T: No, usually we use "it" to talk about a animal, an object or someone whose gender is not known. Is that clear? Yeah. OK, since it can be divided into subject pronoun and object pronoun, let's learn something about subject pronoun first. Here are some sentences from the letter. Would you please have a look at them? And here are all the verbs. According to them, can you tell me we usually use subject pronoun before or after verbs? Now, you please!

S：We usually use subject pronoun before verbs.

T：Excellent, before verbs. Sit down please. But is it always true? No! When is it not true? Now, you please have a try.

S：It is after the question.

T：If it is a question. OK, here look at this sentence, can you use one of the subject pronouns to help me finish this sentence? Now, you please, have a try.

S：I find an English book. Is it yours?

T：Yes, very good. Sit down please. In this sentence, we use "it" after the verb. Right? What's the difference between this sentence and the other sentences? Pay attention. I missed it. "Is it yours? " is a question. So except in a question. Right, very good, OK. Now besides the letter, Millie's mum wants to know more about Millie's school. So Millie is showing a picture of her friend to her mum. Would you please take out this piece of paper? Turn to Page 1. Can you use these subject pronouns to finish the dialogue. OK, now let's do it. OK, I think most of you have finished it, right? Can you check the answer? OK, yeah, what about the first one? Who knows the answer? Put up your hands. Now what about? Please, have a try!

S：He.

T：Would you please read the whole sentence, OK? Yes, it is. Right?

S：Yes, it is. Daniel is—

T：Clever.

S：Is clever and he is good at maths.

T：Very good! Sit down please. In this sentence we use "he" to talk about—

Ss：Daniel.

T：Daniel. Excellent! Who knows the answer? Please have a try. Yes.

S：Yes, mum, Simon is tall. He is in our school football team.

T：OK, sit down please. We use "he" again, but this time we use "he" to talk about, excellent, "Simon". Sit down please. Next one. Now, you please.

S：No, this is Amy. She has short hair.

T：Excellent. Next one.

S：That's Kitty. She has long hair.

T：Very good！Can you spell "she"？

S：...

T：Can you spell "she"？What's the Chinese meaning of "spell"？

Ss：...

T：Now，can you spell?

S：S—h—e.

T：Very good！Sit down please. Next one. It's a little hard. Now，you please. Use microphone.

S：Oh，yes，you are good friends，right?

T：Very good！Sit down please. He uses "you". Who has a different idea? Everybody use "you"？Now，you please. What have you got?

S：Oh，yes，they are good friends，right?

T：They are good friends. Why you use "they" here? She uses "you". You can use Chinese if you don't know. That's OK. OK，now sit down please. It's OK. Would you please，why do you use "you" here?

S：Because I think in this sentence "you" is about Millie and her classmates.

T：Excellent！Sit down please. Now，think if I am Millie's mum，if she's Millie，and if you're Millie's friend. I am saying：Hey，Millie，you're good friends！It means who are good friends? Millie's friend and Millie. If I am saying：Hey，Millie，they are good friends. It means who are good friends? Just Millie's friends，no Millie. Right，I think both of the sentences are right because they are used in different context. Right? Do you agree with me? Yes，so we should use the same or different personal pronouns according to different contexts. Maybe they are—

S：Different.

T：Different，very good！OK，what about the last one? Now，you please.

S：Yes，mum，they are all very nice. I love them.

T：Excellent！So I love them. Very good！These are all subject pronouns and you're really good at using them.（真正的运用不是填空）And "them" is one of the object pronouns. Look at these three sentences，and here are the verbs. This time we usually use object pronouns before or after verbs? Together.

Ss：After.

T：After，but do we only use it after verb? Look at these three more sentences. "in" "from" "to"，what are they?

S：介词。

T：How do we call that in English? Prepositions. We use before or after prepositions?

Ss：After.

T：Also after. It means we use object pronouns after both verbs and prepositions，right. Very good. Daniel is Millie's new classmate. He's also excited about Millie's new school just like Millie. So he calls his grandpa. Would you please turn to Page 2? This time try to use some object pronouns to finish the dialogue, OK? Let's do it. OK，finished? Yes，let's check the answers. The first one. Who likes to read the first sentence for us? OK，now，please. Have a try.

Ss：I'm at a new school. Let me tell you about it.

T：Good！Next one. What about Mr. Wu? Now，you please.

S：Mr. Wu is our English teacher. We all like him.

T：Right，sit down please. Next one. Now what about? You，please.

S：I have some new friends. I like to play with them after class.

T：Can you spell "them" for us?

S：T—h—e—m.

T：Excellent，t—h—e—m. Next one. Next one. You，please have a try.

S：I'm not good at English，sometime Millie helps me.

T：Very good！Millie is so helpful. OK，next one. You please.

S：His grandma is at home now. I want to say hello to her.

T：Excellent！What about the last one? The last one. How about the? You, please have a try.

S：Daniel，I can't hear you well on the telephone.

T：Excellent. You have got the right answer. Sit down，please. But I have a question her：According to the rule and according to this table，we have to use him to talk about Daniel，right? But why can we use "you" here? Now，you please have a try?

S：Because there are two people and they are talking.

T：Very good! Look at this picture. What are they doing, Daniel and his grandpa? They are talking on the phone. Very good. So next time when we use personal pronouns, we should use just according to the rule, or just the context or both of them? Together.

Ss：Both of them.（建构如何使用人称代词）

T：Both of them. Very good. Now, I'm going to give you today. Very good. Besides Mollie and Daniel, I also have a friend. His name is John. He's also a new school student. Here's a story of him. I think this story isn't fluent enough. Try to use personal pronouns to make it better. For example, let's read the first sentence together, OK? "John is an art student" one, two!

Ss：John is an art student...

T：Do you think it is fluent?

S：No/Yes.

T：Yes? Do you think it is fluent? John is another student and John. We say John twice. How can we make it better? You please.

T：OK, have you finished? Let's check the answer. Just now we have checked the first sentence. What about the second sentence? Who can make it better? Now, you, please.

S：May people think they understand more than other, but many teachers are not about anything.

T：Very good. He tries to use "they" to talk about many people there. Right, sit down please. I have a question. We've many people here, can we use "they" again like this?

Ss：No.

T：No, why not? Let's read this sentence together, OK? "They say that..." one, two!

Ss：They say that...

T：They say that they understand more than pictures. Pictures are not about anything. What's wrong? You please.

S：Who are they?

T：Because we don't know who they are.

S：They are.

T：They are. Sit down please. When we use personal pronouns，never forget what comes first: nouns first. Excellent. OK，now，next，next paragraph. You please. Have a try.

S：John's sister is only seven，but she often helps John something with the picture.

T：Excellent. She，then comes the preposition. "What's John doing？" John's sister asks John. You please.

S："What are you doing？" she asks.

T：She asks or John asks？Why can you use "what are you doing" here？

S：Because John's sister is talking to John.

T：Excellent. John's sister is talking to John. Let's give him a big hand: Good，good，very good！Excellent. Next one. John is hanging this picture. John is . Is that OK？Now，you please. Have a try.

S："I'm hanging this picture on the wall." John answers.

T：OK，just now you use "you" to talk about John. This time you use "I"，why？

S：Because it's John sister and John's talking.

T：Who is talking？Who else is talking？

S：Um，John is talking.

T：Yes. Very good，sit down please. OK，next sentence. This picture looks alright. But is this picture... How can you make it better？Now，in this sentence we can find two "Have a try".

S：This picture looks alright，but isn't it upside down？

T：OK，now，very good！Sit down please. Now today we've learned some personal pronouns and how to use them. Do you still remember the task for today's class？It is to introduce your school to me，right？As an example，I invited one of my students to introduce our school to you. Let's watch the short video to you. Hello，everyone！Today I'm going to introduce my school to you. I study at Xincheng Middle School，F Road Campus. It's not very big but beautiful. We have

24 classrooms and they're big and bright. We also have a library. It looks modern. I often read books in it. Our teachers are all very kind. My English teacher is Mr. Zhao. He's very helpful so everyone likes him. I have 36 class mates in my class. They are friendly to me and I love them very much. Welcome to my school.

T: Well, do you like my school? Maybe yes. When you introduce your school, I think first of all, you should tell me the name and different rooms, which school you study at. Now, you please.

S: I study at Zhenjiang Experimental School, Meilizhicheng Branch.

T: OK, I'll say experimental, right? OK, now, read after me: experimental.

S: Experimental.

T: Experimental.

Ss: Experimental.

T: OK, what do you think of it? What do you think of it? Now, would you please have a try?

S: My school is bright and modern.

T: Yes, I'll say: It is bright and modern, right?

S: Yes.

T: Now sit down please. What rooms do you have? Just now in my school we have library and different classrooms. What do you have? You, please.

S: Except the library and classrooms, we also have some music rooms, some computer rooms and—

T: And what other rooms, maybe? And what can you do there, usually?

S: I usually have class in them.

T: In them, excellent! Besides the school, I think you can tell me something about your teacher. Do you like your teachers?

S: Yes.

T: Why do you like your teachers? Now, you please.

S: Because they're very kind to us.

T: Very good. They're very kind to us. OK, besides your teachers, maybe your classmates are friends. According to this picture, what are they doing? Give me sentences. Who are running?

Ss：…

T：Very good. They're running. OK, do you like your classmates or friends? Maybe yes, maybe no. What can you do with them after class? Now, you please, have a try.

S：We can chat with each other after class.

T：Very good, sit down please. Now it's time for you to work in groups of four, introduce your new school?

Student A：Tell me the names of different rooms in your school.

Student B：Talk about your teachers.

Student C：Say something about your classmates and friends.

Student D：You're the reporter.

You have to come to the front and share it with us. Is that clear? Everybody, you should use at least two sentences or two personal pronouns. Is that OK? When you report, the reporter tries to give the opening line "Hello, everyone!" and the ending line "Welcome to our school." And try to use some linking words to link the sentences together, OK? Now, one minute, let's go.

T：（下课铃响）OK, I think time is limited. Who's ready? Would you please have a try? In such a short time, have a try. OK.

S：Hello, everyone! I study at Zhenjiang Experimental School Meilizhicheng Branch. Our school is big and modern. There are different kinds of rooms in our school. And we can do some activity in it. Our teachers are nice and I like all of them. They are very kind to me.

T：Maybe whose are friends?

S：I have many friends. They are friendly and helpful. I often chat with them after class.

T：［Welcome to our school］（教师提示）

S：Welcome to our school！！

T：OK, now let's give him a big hand：Good, good, very good! Excellent! Today we have learned how to use personal pronouns so your homework is to write a short paragraph of your new school life using at least 6 personal pronouns, is that OK? OK, now class is over. Thank you very much, bye-bye!

【背景介绍】

本课是第12届全国初中英语教学观摩课中的一节语法课，课题名称是 Personal Pronouns，授课教师是来自江苏南师附中新城初中黄山路分校的赵哲老师。教师口语流畅、身体语言规范简洁，语法教学突出在语境中教学、学以致用的理念；语法教学内容涵盖三个方面：形式、意义和用法。教师运用归纳法来进行语法教学，其中优点值得上语法课的教师借鉴。整节课有一定的感染力。

一、 教学设计及教学过程

1. Review 3 sentences about Millie's new school.

2. Work out the meaning of personal pronouns.

3. Read a letter and find out the personal pronouns in it.

4. Practise personal pronouns in several contexts.

（1）Mollie and her mum talk about the picture of her new school.

（2）Daniel talks about his school with his grandpa.

（3）John's story：Proofreading the story.

5. Introduce your school：Group discussion.

（1）Teacher shows a video to set an example of how to introduce one's school.

（2）Teacher shows students what aspects to introduce.

（3）Group discussion.

（4）Display the introduction of one's school.

6. Homework

Write a short paragraph of your new school life using at least 6 personal pronouns.

二、该课的教学特色

1. 基于语料培养学生的观察能力和归纳的能力

在本课中，教师采用综合法进行语法教学，具体整合了归纳法、有指导的发现法，借助典型的语料引导学生去发现、归纳和建构语法知识和规则，并在此过程中培养了学生的观察能力和归纳能力。例如，教师在确认学生知悉表格里的所有人称代词后，引导学生观察并找出其中最特别的词，经过观察和思考后回答的教学价值比教师直接告诉他们答案要高得多。

T：I think you are so familiar with this table，right？ Would you please have a look at them again？ Which one do you think is the most special one？

当学生归纳不充分时，教师会进行及时的补充，例如，当一位学生归纳you 的用法时，他只能说到you既能作主格，也能作宾格。这时，教师补充说you既 是单数也是复数（见下句）。说：

T：It means it can be both a subject pronoun and an object pronoun. And it can also be both a singular and a plural pronoun.

好的语法教学包含下列几个阶段：观察语言现象或语料，归纳及建构语法 点的形式、意义和规则，运用所学的语法点来表达和交际。

2. 在语境中对人称代词进行练习

语言的练习和运用离不开语境。教师在教学中创设了许多语境，例如，语 境1：Mollie的妈妈对Mollie的新学校很感兴趣，要Mollie在信里介绍她的新学 校，这个时候可以用来呈现代词。语境2：Mollie的妈妈看照片。Mollie跟她妈 妈谈论照片中的同学，这是一个使用第三人称代词的典型语境。语境3：Daniel 是Mollie的新同学，他对这所新学校感到很新鲜，给他爷爷打电话告诉他关于 这所学校的新鲜事，但打电话这个情境不自然，建议将其设计为Daniel跟爷爷 聊天。语境4：John's story。约翰的故事不太流畅，教师希望学生能够用人称代 词来改进这个故事的语言。完成此任务学生需要对故事进行阅读校对。

3. 有小组管理意识

精细的小组活动角色定位。很多老师让学生开展小组讨论时，只是布置了 讨论的任务，而没有给学生分配角色，结果在小组活动中学生的参与不均匀， 往往话轮掌握在个别学生手中，小组活动的目的不能很好地实现。在这个课例 中，当教师要学生以四人小组为单位准备介绍自己的学校时，他说：Now it's time for you to work in groups of four，introduce your new school？ Student A：You tell me the names of different rooms in your school； Student B：Talk about your teachers； Student C：Say something about your classmates and friends；Student D：You're the reporter. 这个例子说明授课教师有较好的小组管理意识，能够根 据任务给学生分配角色，使每个学生都负起自己的责任，每个学生都对小组有 所贡献，是值得借鉴的一个课堂管理策略。此外，教师的指令及任务要求非常 清晰，有利于小组合作学习有效展开，例如：

T：You have to come to the front and share it with us. Is that clear？ Everybody， you should use at least two sentences or two personal pronouns. Is that OK?

4. 教师重视学用结合

在语言输出阶段，教师要求学生用目标语言personal pronouns来介绍自己学校的各个方面。在布置课后作业时，教师要求他们写作的段落应该至少用上六个personal pronouns。在外语课堂中再真实的语言交际活动，都不是真正意义上的真实的交际活动，学生不可能真正享有选择说什么和怎样说的自由。因此，设计得好的语言活动，都需要学生用上本课学习的目标语言，以达到巩固或运用所学内容的目的。在一些优质课展示活动中，教师在设计任务时往往没有考虑设计出来的任务是否能够促使学生用上刚学的知识和技能。这里赵老师的任务及要求体现了学以致用的理念，是值得学习和借鉴的。

5. 语法教学的综合法

语法教学的综合法（synthesis approach）有几种方法：归纳法、演绎法、引导发现法等。在语法教学中，我们可以根据语法教学内容、含有目标语法的语料特点、学生的认知水平和学习风格等因素，灵活地将上述方法进行组合以进行语法教学，特别是语法的呈现，以优化教学效果。

三、该课的一些不足之处

（1）教师花了不少时间在课堂上带读人称代词，并且让学生口头拼写所学习的代词，这些都是低层次的学习活动，耗时低效，不能有效帮助学生对知识进行内化。例如：

片段 1

T：Read after me：it—it.

Ss：It—it.

T：It—it.

Ss：It—it.

片段 2

T：Him. How to spell him?

S：H—i—m

T：Excellent! H—i—m.

片段 3

S：That's Kitty. She has long hair.

T：Very good！Can you spell "she"？

这些人称代词在小学阶段就已学过。基于学生的已知，教师没有必要教人称代词读音。至于拼写，更无需用课堂的宝贵时间进行练习，而可以放在课后作业让学生去完成。对人称代词的学习重在它们在语境中的运用。

（2）教师经常用excellent对学生的语言行为进行肯定，不论任务的大小或难易（详见下例）。excellent是用来肯定或褒奖那些任务完成得非常漂亮的学生的，而不是这些无需多大努力或者根本不需要创造性劳动的语言行为。这里可谓是大词小用，久之久之会贬低excellent的使用价值，起不到激励学生的作用。

片段4：

T：Can you spell it？

S：T—h—e—y.

T：OK，excellent！How about the last one？

（3）教师请了一个又一个学生以句为单位来读Mollie写给她妈妈的信，然后又让一个又一个的学生以句为单位来读Daniel向他爷爷介绍他学校的电话内容，目的是检查学生人称代词的运用情况。这两个活动都可以优化，比如，每个活动只请一位学生以语篇为单位而不是以句为单位来展示他们完成练习的情况，可以节省从一个学生过渡到另一个学生的时间。个人认为并不是让更多的学生参与到展示答案的活动就是好的活动。好的学习活动应该符合语言学习和运用的规律。

（4）教师对学生引发过于细致，留给学生思考或思维的空间不大，也导致课堂节奏前松后紧。就整节课来说，教师说得多。在做最后一个活动时，教师在呈现了介绍关于自己学校的视频后，抛出了一个又一个的问题帮助学生学习如何介绍自己学校。这个过程有师生互动，但过于详细，耗时较多，不利于学生思考。实际上，他给学生小组讨论的时间只有一分钟。教师最好把更多的时间留给学生，让他们在小组内更充分地磋商介绍什么、如何介绍，以及后面的小组展示。由于前面节奏较拖沓，导致学生还没展示下课铃就响起来了。可见展示环节就不充分了。由于脚手架太详尽，学生在语言输出时缺乏创新，学生输出的内容几乎就是教师在启发时提供的内容。

总之，这是一节体现较新语法教学理念的好课。虽然存在一些不足，但教师的施教有不少可圈可点的地方。作为男性教师，可以在培养学生的审辨思维、创新思维等思维品质及加深课程深度等方面下功夫，以形成更鲜明的教学风格。此外，教师在提供脚手架时注意量的把握，以便给学生留下创造性劳动的空间。

第三节　高中英语评课案例

评课案例一　《A Few Simple Forms of English Poems》诗歌教学课

【课堂实录】

T：Good afternoon，ladies and gentlemen！

Ss：Good afternoon，teacher！

T：OK，sit down please. First，allow me to introduce myself. I am Wang Min，from Inner Mongolia. This is the third time for me to come to Xian. But this time，it's very cold. It reminds me a famous sentence（PPT投出雪莱的诗句）：If winter comes，can spring be far behind? Are you familiar with this one? Yeah，it comes from the poem Ode to the West Wind.（PPT投出雪莱的《西风颂》）This one is the last sentence. How many line does the poem have? One，two... fourteen. It is a kind of poem. We call it Sonnet，十四行诗. It is made up of fourteen lines. So today we'll enjoy and experience different kinds of poems. Now，please read the passage and try to find out the following two questions. The first one：What does the passage mainly talk about? By the way，I only give you one minute to finish the task. Do you need to read the passage word by word? No? Yes，of course. The second one：How many forms of poems are mentioned? What are they? Maybe you should pay attention to the key words of each paragraph. Clear? One minute！（学

生阅读）Excuse me，have you got the answer? Yeah? Oh，you can check the answer with your group members. OK，turn back! Yeah，your two! You two! Excuse me! Which group? It doesn't matter. Yes，the boy! Group 1，yes，please.

S：This passage mainly talks about a few simple forms of poems.

T：Do you agree with him? Yes，sit down please. Thank you. I think he also answers my question with the title. Yeah? OK. Next one. How many forms? OK，the girl please.

S：Nursery rhyme，list poem，cinquain and the Haiku，Tang poem.

T：Tang poems.

S：Um.

T：OK，sit down please. I think she answers my question with the key words. After we answer the questions，we can get two reading skills. If we want to know the main idea，we should know pay attention to the title，yeah? If we want to know some specific idea，maybe we should pay attention to the key words. Yeah? If we want to know some detailed information，please read our text once again carefully. Please look at the screen（投出第二个阅读任务）. After reading，please list the features of each kind of poem. Can you understand me? OK，let's go! （学生用约四分钟完成细节阅读任务）After reading，you can check the answers with your group members. You four，have you got the answer? Excuse me，The first one，let's look at them one by one. The features of each kind of poem. The first one：the nursery rhymes. OK，who can? OK，please，the girl.

S：The language is concrete but the imagination. They are easy to learn...

T：Right? Yes! OK，sit down please.（呈现参考答案）

Nursery Rhymes

1. children's poetry

2. concrete but imaginative

3. strong rhythm and a lot of repetition

Please look at the screen. We can use the key words or the short sentences. Next one，list poems. OK，which group? OK，the boy，please.

S：They have flexible line length and phrases. They have bot a pattern and a rhythm.

T：Right？ Right？ Yes！ Sit down please. No. 3， please look at the screen to check your answers.（教师呈现参考答案）.

List poems

1. a flexible line length

2. to repeat phrases

3. a pattern and rhythm

Next one， Cinquain. Uh， yeah， the boy.

S：It is made up of five lines. And it is written to convey a strong picture with a few words.

T：Yeah？ Yeah！ Great！ Well done. Sit down please. No. 4. Er， so many！ The boy.

S：It is a Japanese poetry that is made up of 17 syllables. It is written to give a clear picture and raise a special feeling.

T：Right？ OK， please look at the screen.（教师呈现参考答案）17 syllables. Do you know what it means？ What's its meaning？

Haiku

1. a Japanese form

2. 17 syllables

Syllables， syllables. 音节， yeah！ Tang poems. We're very familiar with this one because it's from China. I like this one very much. Today， we'll enjoy each kind of poems. Please look at the screen. I think the best way to enjoy the poem is to read them aloud. So let's read it together（师生一起朗读）"I saw"， one， two！

Ss：（Reading aloud.）

T：What about repetition？ I saw， I saw， I saw. Repetition. Clear？ OK， can you find something special at the end of each line？ The first two sentences. Fire， squire， /aiə/ clear？ The second group. Sky， high， /ai/， yeah？ How to pronounce this one？ Next one， lead， so the first one is. The second one：dead； the first one is lead； /e/， clear？ OK， next one， race， lace， /eis/， yeah？ /æ/， hat， cat. What about the last group? /uː/, so this is the rhyme, 韵, clear? But what kind of poem? List poems. Clear? OK, next one. If you know it, let's sing it together. What kind of poem? Nursery rhyme. We find it's very beautiful and easy to learn, right? What about this one? Do you know I use the red lines to underline the letters? Let's count them together. One, two, three, four, five, six, seven, eight, nine, ten, eleven, twelve, thirteen, fourteen, fifteen, sixteen, seventeen! How many? Seventeen syllables, yes, very good! What kind of poem it is?

Ss：Haiku.

图6-6　诗歌

（List poem，截自课例光盘 ）

T：Haiku. Remember it is a Japanese form. Yeah! OK? The meaning.（教师展示了中文翻译）. Do you know what kind of poem it is? Tang poem. We're very familiar with this one. What is the lady doing? Waiting for her husband. Do you know the name? Do you know the Chinese name? Yeah, great! 望夫石。What about her feeling? Sad or happy?

Ss：Sad.

T：Sad. So when we read it, please be slow and sad, clear? Now read it by yourselves. Then I want some of you to share the point. Read it by yourselves. Sad! Excuse me, who would like to have a try? OK, the girl, please.

S：Where she awaits her husband.（教师播放配乐）

T：OK, thank you! So sad! I think, after hearing you, your husband will come back soon. OK, this one! What kind of poem from the structure? Cinquian. Yes! Let's look at the structure. Please look at the screen. The first one. Brother—a noun, a person, yeah? Two adjectives to describe the person. Three doings to describe what my brother is doing. Four words. One word to conclude the poem. Now let's create the poem to describe one of your classmates. Who like to do me a favor? Yes, the girl, please. Yeah. Please come here. Excuse me. May I have your name?

S：Zhao Yulan.

T：Zhao Yulan, yeah! I'll create the cinquain.

Lan

hardworking, elegant

standing, smiling, studying

like a beautiful flower

great

Can you understand me? Yeah! Thank you, Lan. Now it's your turn to create a cinquain. Who can describe your teacher or classmates. Clear? Maybe Ms. Sun Hongli. Mr. Du Zunxue. Clear? Do it now! In your groups. (学生创作) Which group likes to share your cinquain? OK, the boy.

S：Teacher, handsome, humorous, teaching, laughing, writing, has a strong dream, friend

T：Um-hum, who's he? Who's he?

S：He's Du.

T：Mr. Du. Yeah! Are you writing him to our class? OK, and this? Another chant. Yes, another girl. Please.

S：Teacher, interesting, funny, shouting, running, waiting, enemy and friend.

T：Um-hum, who is it? Also—

S：Also Mr. Du.

T：He's very popular.

S：Mr. Zhu Haiguan.

T：Oh, yeah. Sit down please. And this! The boy, please.

S：Zhu, intelligent, brilliant, teaching, writing, laughing, lovely boy!

T：Yes, I know this lovely person. He's my friend. This one? Yeah! You're gifted. Maybe several years later, you will be famous poet. Let's enjoy more poems. Please try to translate it into beautiful Chinese.

It doesn't matter if you see me or not, I'm here.

I am standing right there, with no emotion.

It doesn't matter if you miss me or not.

The feeling is right there, and it isn't going anywhere.

It doesn't matter if you love me or not.

Love is right there, and it is not to change.

You can discuss with your group members. （学生尝试翻译并讨论）Excuse me! "It doesn't matter", who will have a try? Which group? The boy, please.

S：你看或者不看我，我就在那里。

T："It doesn't matter" please go on. The second sentence.

S：你想或者不想我，情就在那里，不离不弃。

T：Yes.

S：第三个就是：你爱或者不爱我，爱就在那里。

T：Yes, it's a little difficult. It doesn't matter. Have a seat please. Please look at the translation on the Internet. （教师呈现参考译文）

你见或者不见我，我就在那里，不悲不喜。

你念或者不念我，情就在那里，不来不去。

你爱或者不爱我，爱就在那里，不增不减。

So beautiful! I think because time is limited, I also learn a lot from you. Thank you, my dear boys and girls. OK, class is over.

S：Stand up!

Ss：Good bye, teacher.

【背景介绍】

这是一节高中英语阅读课，话题是诗歌，课题是A Few Simple Forms of Poems。授课教师是来内蒙古包头市北方重工第三中学的王敏老师。该课是2014年在西安举行的高中英语课堂教学的一节展示课。该课节奏明快，结构清晰，融文本解读、阅读技能培养诗歌鉴赏和创作于一体，是一节关于诗歌主题的优质展示课。

一、该课的教学设计和教学过程

（一）教学设计

I 诗歌导入

II 整体感知，把握主旨

Task：

Please read the passage quickly and finish the following two tasks.（ Think by yourselves. ）

1. What does the passage mainly talk about?

2. How many forms of poems are mentioned? What are they?

III 细读课文，挖掘细节

Task：

Please read the passage carefully and list the features of each kind of poem.（Do it by yourselves and check the answers in your groups. ）

IV 探索体验，感受诗歌

1. List poem：Understanding the form of a list poem； reading aloud the list poem with emotion

2. Nursery rhyme：Singing *Twinkle Twinkle Little Stars*

3. Haiku：Understanding the form of a Japanese Haiku

4. Tang Poem：Understanding and reading aloud the Tang poem《望夫石》with emotion

5. Cinquain：Understanding structure，teacher modeling a cinquain，creating cinquain

6. Translating a poem of《你见或者不见我》（作者为扎西拉姆•多多）

（二）教学过程

阅读。上课伊始，教师用雪莱著名的《西风颂》最后一句简单导入诗歌学习。然后教师让学生略读回答两个关于大意的问题；细读找出各种诗歌的特征。教师先提问，然后透出答案。

鉴赏和创作。在解读了文本关于诗歌种类及其特征后，每一种诗歌教师各展示一个例篇带领学生鉴赏。教师先解读了一首list poem，然后播放了儿歌

《twinkle twinkle little stars》。然后简单地解读了唐诗《望夫石》的英译和原文，让学生有感情地朗诵该诗的英译。接着解读了美国五行诗歌，并让学生进行诗歌模仿创造。教师以一位女生为描述对象创作了一首五行诗，然后要求全班学生选取一位教师作为描述的对象模仿创作一首五行诗，最后请了三位学生在班上诵读他们创作的五行诗。

在最后一个环节，教师给出一首英译的中国自由体诗《你见或者不见我》，让学生翻译成中文。

二、该课的优点

（1）教师的语言非常清晰，语速适中，能够在需要强调的信息前稍事停顿，并拉长强调部分词语的音长，以引起学生的注意。但本课中王老师的教师语言可以充当教师教育的教师语言技能训练的课程资源。授课教师首先把该课处理成一个阅读课，培养了学生两个阅读技能：找大意要读文章大标题；找细节要看关键词。

（2）在课堂管理方面，几乎每次学生完成任务时王老师总是让学生先在小组内讨论和分享答案，然后再在班上展示并评价。这个举措反映了以学生为中心的理念。学生在小范围内的分享和磋商既是一种互学，也有助于增强学生的自信心。

（3）为学生提供诗歌创作的体验。教师并不是把所有诗歌形式都拿来让学生模仿创作，而是选取了相对简单的美国五行诗cinquain来让学生现场创作诗歌。教师先请一位女生到讲台上来，询问她的名字，然后以她描述的对象即席作了一首五行诗作为示范，然后要求学生以他们的教师为描写对象创作五行诗，并邀请三位学生进行朗读展示。这个环节体现了典型的诗歌教学模式：解读——欣赏——模仿——创作。

三、 该课的一些不足之处

（1）宜把建构知识的机会让给学生，比如，教师在学生回答问题后自己总结阅读的两个策略，其实可以让学生来总结；如学生总结不到位或者不全面，这时候教师才进行补充会取得更好的教学效果。

（2）教学的深度有待加强。整节课给人的印象是课堂节奏明快，但对诗歌的解读大多只注意形式，没有结合它们的意义，所以学生很难有深刻的体会。

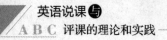
诗歌的感情的抒发、诗歌的意象等都没有很好地挖掘。整节课培养学生高阶思维的活动不多。在阅读阶段的问题基本是展示性问题，即可在文本中直接找到答案的问题。

（3）这节课教师讲得多。这可能是这节课显得过程流畅、节奏明快的原因之一。很多时候都是教师在讲解，学生活动较少，所以没有拖沓、停顿等现象。但从另外一个角度看，这些都是牺牲学生更多地参与和互动所得。比较典型的是教师对List Poems的分析，教师说是欣赏，但实际上是教师对该诗歌特点的解读：语言重复、韵脚押韵，但没有对内容进行解读，更加谈不上欣赏了。

评课案例二 《The Olympic Games》阅读课

【课堂实录】

T: Now let's begin our class. Just now I played the video. What did you see? Some sports items. You learned some new words for sports item. So what did you see, what sports items did you see in the video? Like swimming, like running, basketball, fencing, do you remember? Fencing. What is fencing?

Ss: 击剑。

T：And the-

Ss: Boxing.

T: Boxing. A lot of new words. And actually the passage we're going to learn is an interview. So what will normally take place in the interview? Normally there will be two people.And who will be in the interview? If I am interviewing you, I am the interviewer.

Ss: Reporter.

T: And you will be the interviewee. So the passage we'll read today is an interview. And now I would like you to find out who are the interviewer and who the interviewee. Please turn to Page 9. Read only the first paragraph. I'll give you 30 seconds. Read only the first paragraph and find out who is the interviewer and who is the interviewee. Finish this reading task, right?

Ss:（学生阅读）

T: OK, can you tell me who is the interviewer?

Ss：（Attempting to read aloud the name.）

T: What is the interviewer's name? It's a little difficult, right? Pausanias.

Ss: Pausanias.

T: Who is he? What does he do?

Ss: A writer.

T: He's a free writer. He is a free writer. Who is the interviewee?

Ss: Li Yan.

T: Li Yan. Who is she?

Ss: Volunteer.

T: She is a volunteer of Beijing Olympics, OK, sit down please, thank you. Good job! And you know that what people do when interviewing. So interviewing is about asking and answering questions. Now I'd like you to find out all the questions that the interviewer asks. OK, I'll give you example, this task is a bit difficult. You should first find out the questions and then and tell me tell us which aspect of Olympics. Do you know aspect? Aspect方面。So you should, after finding out the questions, tell me which aspect each question is about. I'll give you an example. Some questions are very easy to find out because they're directly asked but others are not so easy. So I'll give you an example. I find out the third question. You can look at your book, Line 25 on Page 10, Line 25, Page 10. This is not directly asked. And I combine several into one question, "Do all athletes come from the Greek world？", I find this question and then I find out this question is about one aspect of Olympics, that is about the athletes, the athletes. And you know how to finish that? the now. Please find the other questions. There are five questions. After you finish, fill in the table. Yes, you can write your answer on the student sheet. There's a table, there is a table.

Table: Aspects of the ancient Olympics and modern Olympics

表6-1　古代奥运会和现代奥运会的对比

Aspects	Ancient Olympics	Modern Olympics

Ss：（学生寻找问题并进行归类）

T：（教师巡堂指导）OK，who can share us the answer first? What about the first question?

S: How often do you hold your Games?

T: Yes, how often do you hold your Games? What aspect? It's about- ?

S: How often.

T: Yes, how often is a phrase. Please replace it with one word, one noun. How often is what? Anything that will-? Chinese?

Ss: 频率。

T: 频率, yes! Frequen- You've learned frequency! So the noun form of frequent.

Ss: Frequency.

T: Good! What about the second question?

S: How can the runners enjoy competing in winter?

T: Yes, how can the runners enjoy competing in winter? Which aspect?

Ss: Activity.

T: Activities, events, right? Events or sports. In ancient time there is only one set , but in modern there are two sets: summer and winter. What about No. 4?

S: Do you mean the Greek world?

T: Do you mean the Greek world? So we can change the sentence into "Where are all athletes from?" Yes. Which aspect of the Olympics?

S: Athletes.

T: Yes, athletes. No. 4! How are all the athletes housed? Which aspect?

Ss: Living.

T: Living, right? Living or use another word. Can you see in the sentence "house" is used as a......

Ss: Verb.

T: Verb. But here we need a noun. So actually we can change it into housing, housing, right? The last one?

S: Does anyone want to host the Olympic games?

T: Yes. Does anyone want to host the Olympic games?

Ss:（inaudible）

T: Yes, that's an honor, right? Host. The last one.

S: Do you compete for prize money?

T：Yes, do you compete for prize money? Which aspect? Prizes, good! OK, Sit down please. Now, are these all the aspects that Pausanias wants to know about the Olympic games?

S: Spirit or sports spirit.

T: Yes, spirit or sports spirit. Yes, I agree with your answers. Your answers are better than mine. Thank you. So let's move to another task. We've found out all the aspects Pausanias wants to know about the Olympic games. And now I'd like you to find out more detailed information about these questions. You should finish the table on the handout. Am I clear? And also with this.

Ss：（学生找信息完成填表练习）

T：（教师巡堂指导）OK, some of you have finished. So please tell me something about the frequency, some detailed information about frequency. What about the frequency it is held? It will be held-

Ss: Every four years.

T: Yes, every four years. It's not clearly said in the text, but we can use the knowledge we know. You can use, anything. What about the events?

Ss:（inaudible）

T: In ancient time there was only one set. In modern games there are two sets. How about you? Athletes.

S: In ancient times only the Greek cities. But in modern times people all over the world.

T: Yes, who can take part in the Olympic games? Yes, men, men around the world. In ancient games, yes, only the men in the Greek world and women do not take

part in. What about this, housing?

S: 奥运村。

T: Yes, you're right. Yes, they build a special village called "Olympic village". What about the host?

S:（inaudible）

T: So, Greek cities, because as you know, the Olympic games only take place in Greek world. Any country wants to host the Olympic games. And what about you, the last one? This what as a prize for the winner? What kind of...Olive wreath, right? Compete for what? Olive wreath signaling for peace, right. While modern Olympic games.....

S：They want to compete for a medal.

T: Yes, for medals. You did a great job.

T: For olive wreath. Yes, olive wreath for peace. Sit down please. And now, come to my next part. We can see that during these years many great changes have taken place. For example, for example, in ancient games, there is only one set. And in modern games we have two sets. So we have winter games and summer games. With more sets we have more sports events or items. For example, in ancient times people only have one or two sports. But now we have so many various kinds of sports items. So we can say that modern Olympic pay more attention to or put more stress on, put more stress on means pay more attention to. Pay more attention to what? Compare the situation above, we have fairly more sports items. We can say that modern Olympic pay more attention to what? You see-

Ss: Variety.

T: Variety. So we can say that modern Olympic pay more attention to the variety of sports item.

Ss: the variety

T: So my task now is I want you to find out more and you can use the sentence pattern "Compared with ancient games, modern Olympic games put more stress on..." Can you find more? You see the detailed information find something about

Ss:（学生合作讨论古代奥运和现代奥运之间发生的变化并尝试用教师提供的结构进行表达）

T：You have you finished, my class. So give me some ideas.

S: Have more freedom in democracy.

T: Yes. There is change in democracy or how to say that? How to say democracy?

S: The athletes from all over the world.

T: The athletes come from all over the world. That's a kind of justice or fairness. Yeah, you have in the listening exercise. Democracy. Yeah! Any more?

S: Great comfort.

T: Comfort for what?

S: For the athletes.

T: For the athletes, yes. Any more?

S: Glory.

T: Glory or honor for the modern Olympic nations, right? Yes, any more?

S: Gender.

T: Gender, right. Any more?

S: （inaudible）

T: Sit down please. And you didn't take this. Any more ideas? You know in the ancient times, only Greek men, no slaves, no women to take part in. But now everyone, including women, can take part. That means what change has taken place? The Olympic games put more stress on what?

S: There is more stress of democracy.

T: Yes, more stress on democracy. Why do you say that? How do you say democracy?

S: The athletes are from all over the world.

T: Athletes are from all over the world, that's kind of justice or freedom, right. You have that from the listening, democracy. Any more?

S: There is more comfort.

T: Comfort for what, for whom?

S: For the athletes.

T: For the athletes, yes. Any more?

S: Glory.

T: Glory or honor for er- modern Olympic nations, right? Any more?

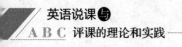

S: Fairness.

T: Yes, fairness. Any more, no? Thank you. And you know. Any more ideas? You all know that in the ancient times only the Greek men, no slaves, no women take part in. But now everyone in the world, including women can take part in. That means that means what kind of change? The Olympic games put more emphasis on what? What kind of equality?

S: Equality.

T: On equality. What kind of equality? Men and women are equal. So that's kind of.

S: 性别

T：性别。How to say that?

Ss: Gender.

T: Sex or gender. And at that time there were slaves, but now there are not slaves, So that's what kind of equality?阶级or who? Race, racial, racial equality. Racial equality. So you have so many brilliant ideas. And I know that many of you have got different answers. So we can do a conclusion that Olympics are very great because of the great changes. Do you think so?

Ss: Yes.

T: Do you agree that the Olympics are great?

Ss: Yes.

T: You have your own reasons. Now please complete the questions, complete the sentence: Olympics are great because......Make your own sentences.

Ss:（学生完成句子）

T：OK，most of you have finished. Now let's check. Show me your sentence, the first one.

S1: The Olympics are great because it helps people all over to become more healthy.

T: The Olympics are great because it helps people all over to become more healthy,right?

S2: The Olympics are great because it raise up people's spirit.

T: Yes, because it raise up people's spirit.

S3: The Olympics are great because......（inaudible）

T: Yes. Because they give more.

S4: The Olympics are great because they make people like sports.

T: Yes, because they make people like sports.

S5: ... because they make the world becomes one.

T: Yes, they make the world becomes one. So I like all your answers and you have really found out the- you've really understand the greatness of the Olympic games. Do you want to know my sentence?

Ss: Yes.

T: I think that the Olympics are great because each and every small athlete plays his/her own part. Do you agree?

Ss: Yes.

T: So there are so many of athletes, thousands of athletes, in the Olympic games, it's just because each one plays their own part and makes the Olympics great. So pay attention, there is a paragraph which is about "Small can be great". When speak of small, which word can you take over

Ss: Tiny.

T: Tiny, yes, tiny. Tiny, small. Are there any relation?

Ss:（inaudible）

T: So small means tiny,; small means , but small can be great!

Ss: Yes!

T: Each one plays his own part, and then the Olympic becomes great! Everyone feels so , but feel so all the time. And I am going to show you some people to show great is small.（教师播放一段说明Small Is Great的视频并要求学生在相关段落上填空）

Ss：（学生视、听并填空）

T：Have you got the answer?（师生一起完成该段的填空） A small animal can be-

Ss: Powerful.

T：So are you touched by the video?

Ss: Yes!

T: because I want to be small. I know even a teacher as small as me, I can be

great. Do you feel small sometimes?

Ss: Yes.

T: Very often，right? So my last question for you is: Do you feel small sometimes?

Ss: Always.

T: How do you deal with that? How do you encourage you? How do you? You can discuss in group：

What impresses you most in the video?

Ss:（学生讨论）

T:（教师请一位学生分享他的想法）

S: ...

T:（教师总结并宣布下课）.....That's all. Class is over.

【背景介绍】

这节课是一节校际同课异构课。授课教师是来自广州外国语学校的叶静老师。授课内容是人教版高中英语教材第二模块的第二单元的第二个课时阅读课。该单元的话题是Olympic Games。教学设计有新意，没有走传统阅读课的模式，而是从文本类型入手，以提取信息、处理信息、运用信息的活动为载体，层层开展教学。教学环节环环相扣，步步走高。整节课令人有耳目一新之感。

一、教学设计及教学过程

I Warming up & Pre-reading

1. Play the 2016 Rio Olympic advertising video.

2. Work out the type of the text：interview.

3. Ask the students to predict the main idea of the text.

II While-reading

1. Ask students to find out the questions asked by Pausanias.

2. Ask students to think about which aspect of Olympics each question concerns.

3. Ask the students to list the features of ancient and modern Olympics according to the aspects and draw a mind-map（group work）.

4. Ask the students to summarize what the changes stand for.

III Post-reading

1. Show the students the slogans of different Olympic Games and ask them to complete the sentence "Olympics are great, because/and/ but_____" based on the text and the slogans（group work）.

2. Show the students the video "the greatness of small" and ask them to discuss what impresses them most in the video（group work）.

IV Assignment：Writing—Life is like the Olympic Games.Ask students to write a passage starting with "Life is like the Olympic Games, and I'm a marathon athlete. There are times when I feel small. For example, ..."

二、该课的教学特色

1. 教师从文本类型入手开展教学

教师指出该课的体裁是interview，而interview是interviewer和interviewee之间的对话；interview的典型特征是interviewer问问题，而interviewee回答问题。因此，教师迅速布置，让学生找出该文本中的问题及答案。因此，整个文本的信息被快速地分成问题和答案，为后面对信息的进一步处理做了铺垫。

2. 对信息的提取和处理

阅读课信息的提取关系到如何表现提取出来的信息，即表现信息的工具。很多教师用表格、思维导图等方式。这里教师采用的是表格。选用什么信息转换工具是由教师的总体设计思路决定的。教师设计了细节阅读活动，该阅读活动的任务有两个：①学生把古代奥运会和现代奥运会的各个方面的特征做成表格；②学生基于表格总结出古代奥运和现代奥运的变化，并将信息绘成思维导图。师生通过表格和思维导图梳理出本文的信息结构图和结构化知识图。

3. 对学生归纳、概括能力的培养

本课教师在让学生找出采访者提出的问题和被采访者的回答后引导学生对这些问题进行分类，如问题是关于古代奥运会举行的频率的、包括什么赛事的、有什么奖赏、住宿情况怎么样、谁是主办方，等等。这样的归类能够培养学生处理信息的能力以及归类和概括等方面的思维能力。

4. 教学的深度

该课的板书主要是一个中心词为change的思维概念图，概念图的内容是奥林匹克比赛已经发生的变化，如变得民主、公平、赛事种类的增加、没有种族歧视、没有性别歧视、运动员的物质条件更舒适等。这不是对文本内容的原生

呈现，而是对文本内容进行深层次加工的产物。它体现了教师教学是有深度的教学，而不是停留在对文本浅表信息的读取上。

板书设计：

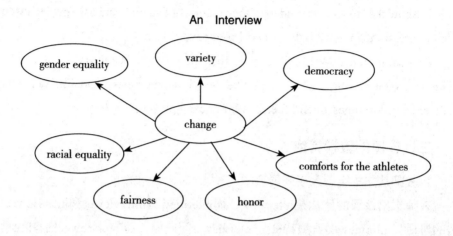

（此图系根据叶静授课板书重绘）

5. 教学的高度

该课的教学基于文本却又高于文本。教师除了引导学生读取文本信息和用表格、思维导图等处理文本信息，还对主题内容进行扩展和延伸。比如，她通过播放录像引导学生感悟到奥运会之所以伟大是因为参与其中的每一位运动员的努力拼搏；而渺小的人物也可能成为伟大的人物。教师在播放录像后让学生进行讨论：What impresses you most in the video? 这个活动渗透着文化意识和价值观的教育，体现了教学内容和教学活动立德树人的价值取向。

三、该课的一些不足之处

教师要求学生找出单个问题后马上将其归类，对学生来说这种训练是比较仓促的，学生没有很多的时间来进行充分的思考。建议还是让学生把所有问题都找出来后再进行分类。

总之，这是一节有深度、有高度的高中英语阅读课。它给我们展示了活动观下的英语阅读课学习活动如何体现综合性、关联性和实践性。

参 考 文 献

[1] Ambrose S. A. et al. How Learning Works: Seven research-based Principles for Smart Teaching [M] . Jossey- Bass, 2010.

[2] Behney J. & S. Gass, Interaction and the Noun Phrase Accessibility Hierarchy in J. H. Schwieter, Innovative Research and Practices in Second Language Acquisition and Bilingualism [M] . John Benjamins Publishing Company, 2013.

[3] Bransford J. D. et al. How People Learn: Brain, Mind, Experience, and School (expanded ed.) [M] . Washington: National Academy Press, 2000.

[4] Dörnyei Z. Teaching and Researching Motivation [M] . Beijing: Foreign Language Teaching and Research Press, 2005.

[5] Dörnyei Z, P. D. MacIntyre, A. Henry.Motivational Dynamics in Language Learning [M] . Shanghai: Shanghai Foreign Language Education Press, 2016.

[6] Ellis, R. Understanding Second Language Acquisition [M] . Shanghai: Shanghai Foreign Language Education Press, 1999.

[7] Fotos, S. Cognitive Approaches to Grammar Instruction in Celce-Murcia M, Teaching English as a Second or Foreign Language [M] . Beijing: Foreign Language Teaching and Research Press, 2006.

[8] Hadfield J. Classroom Dynamics [M] . Oxford University Press, 2009.

[9] Nation, P. Teaching and Learning Vocabulary [M] . Beijing: Foreign Language Teaching and Research Press. （时间不详）

[10] Nunan, D, K. M. Bailey. Exploring Second Language Classroom Research: A Comprehensive Guide [M] . Beijing: Foreign Language Teaching and Research Press, 2010.

［11］Ortega，L. Understanding Second Language Acquisition［M］. London：Routledge，2013.

［12］Richards，J.C. Beyond Training［M］.Beijing：Foreign Language Teaching and Research Press，2001.

［13］Rivers W. M. Interactive Language Teaching［M］. Beijing：People Education Press，2000.

［14］Saifer，S.HOT Skills：Developing Higher-Order Thinking in Young Learners［D］.Redleaf Press，2018.

［15］Scrivener J. Learning Teaching——The Essential Guide to English Language Teaching（2nd Edition）［M］.London：MACMILLAN，2005.

［16］Shrum J. L.，E. W. Glisan.Teacher's Handbook：Contextualized Language Instruction［M］. Beijing：Foreign Language Teaching and Research Press，2004.

［17］Tarone E.，G. Yule.Focus on the Language Learner［M］. Shanghai：Shanghai Foreign Language Education Press，2000.

［18］Troike，M. S. Introducing Second Language Acquisition［M］. Beijing：Foreign Language Teaching and Research Press，2010：111-112.

［19］Ur P. A Course in Language Teaching：Practice and Theory［M］. Beijing：Foreign Language Teaching and Research Press，2011：230.

［20］Van Manen，M. The Tact of Teaching：The Teaching of Pedagogical Thoughtfulness［M］.李树英，译.北京：教育科学出版社，1992.

［21］Wajnryb，R. Classroom Observation Tasks：A resource book for language teachers and trainers［M］. Beijing：Foreign Language Teaching and Research Press，2011.

［22］Walsh，S. Classroom Discourse and Teacher Development［M］. Shanghai：Shanghai Foreign Language Education Press，2016.

［23］Wells，G. Dialogic Inquiry：Toward a Sociocultural Practice and Theory of Education［M］. Beijing：Foreign Language Teaching and Research Press，2010.

［24］Widdowson，H.G. Aspects of Language Teaching［M］.Shanghai：Shanghai Foreign Language Education Press，1999.

［25］Wood，D. et al. The Role of Tutoring in Problem Solving［J］. Child Psychol，1976，Vol. 17：89–100.

［26］Wright，T. Roles of Teachers and Learners［M］. Oxford：Oxford University Press，1987.

［27］曾用强. 谈信息技术对基础外语教学变革的促进［J］. 英语学习（教师版），2018（11）.

［28］徐碧美. 追求卓越——教师专业发展案例研究［M］. 陈静，李忠如，译. 北京：北京人民教育出版社，2003.

［29］陈力. 外语教学法的"后方法"时代［J］. 基础外语教育，2009，11（3）：3–8.

［30］方海光，王红云，黄荣怀. 移动学习的系统环境路线图［J］. 现代教育技术，2011（1）.

［31］方直金太阳. 第七届全国小学英语教学观摩课案例集［CD］. 深圳万方数据电子出版社，2014.

［32］方直金太阳. 第八届全国小学英语教学观摩课案例集［CD］. 深圳万方数据电子出版社，2017.

［33］方直金太阳. 第九届小学英语课堂教学观摩课案例集［CD］. 深圳万方数据电子出版社，2018.

［34］方直金太阳. 第十二届初中英语课堂教学观摩培训案例集［CD］. 深圳万方数据电子出版社，2017.

［35］方直金太阳. 第十一届全国初中英语教学观摩课案例集［CD］. 深圳万方数据电子出版社，2015.

［36］方直金太阳. 第三届广东省高中英语教学观摩课案例集［CD］. 深圳万方数据电子出版社，2018.

［37］中国教育学会外专会. 高中英语课堂教学观摩课案例集［CD］. 江苏凤凰电子音像出版社，2014.

［38］傅瑞屏. 小学英语优质课例分析与评价［M］. 广州：世界图书出版公司，2017.

［39］傅瑞屏. 英语课程与教学论［M］. 广州：广东高等教育出版社，2014.

［40］傅瑞屏. 英语优质课例分析与评价［M］. 广州：世界图书出版公司，2010.

［41］傅小平.小学英语教学论［M］.长沙：湖南人民出版社，2007.

［42］高德胜."文化母乳"：基础教育教材的功能定位［J］.全球教育展望，2019（4）：92–104.

［43］戈向红.英语课堂教学现状及改革新趋势展望［J］.小学英语教与学，2018（2）：6–7，10.

［44］马克斯·范梅南.教学机智——教育智慧的意蕴［M］.李树英，译.北京：教育科学出版社，2014.

［45］刘晓斌.英语教师语言能力提升的网络新路径［J］.英语学习（教师版），2018（7）：5–8.

［46］罗晓杰，牟金江.如何说英语课——方法与艺术［M］.上海：华东师范大学出版社，2012.

［47］孙媛.基于教材语境设计教学，实现语言和思维发展的共进——以外研版小学《英语》（新标准）为例的教学设计探索［J］.英语学习，2018（7）：44–48.

［48］Thomas L. Good，Jere E Br.透视课堂［M］，陶志琼，译.北京：中国轻工业出版社，2001.

［49］王蔷.英语教学法教程［M］.2版.北京：北京师范大学出版社，2006.

［50］肖惜，李恒平.英语教师职业技能训练简明教程［M］.2版.北京：高等教育出版社，2016.

［51］张秋会，王蔷.浅析文本解读的五个维度［J］.中小学外语教学，2016（11）：11–16.

［52］周勇，赵宪宇.新课程说课、听课与评课［M］.北京：教育科学出版社，2004.

［53］朱超华.教师核心能力论［M］.广州：广东高等教育出版社，2007.

［54］朱浦.如何成为一名出色的"教练"［J］.英语学习，2018（9）：37–41.

［55］邹为诚.中学英语课程与教学［M］.上海：华东师范大学出版社，2015.